THE COMPLETE
CARIBBEAN
COOKBOOK

THE COMPLETE
CARIBBEAN
COOKBOOK

PAMELA LALBACHAN

Photography by Michelle Garrett
Food and Styling by Liz Trigg

Charles E. Tuttle Co., Inc.
Boston • Rutland, Vermont • Tokyo

For my Mother and my Grandmother.
Without their wealth of knowledge and
life-long training I would never have been able
to write this book.

For my Grandfather, who taught me so much
about Guyana when it was still an imaginary place in
my head during my growing years.

First published in the United States in 1994 by
Charles E. Tuttle Company, Inc. of Rutland, Vermont, and Tokyo, Japan,
with editorial offices at 153 Milk Street, Boston, Massachusetts 02109.

Published in conjunction with Lansdowne Publishing Pty Ltd
Level 5, 70 George Street, Sydney, NSW 2000, Australia

ISBN 0-8048-3038-X
Library of Congress Catalog Number 94–60894

Additional photographs: Caribbean Tourism Organization
(pp. 3, 107, 139, 207), Pamela Lalbachan (pp. 15, 39, 187, 247, 267),
Phillip Sandberg (p. 63)

Designer: Kathie Baxter Smith
Set in Stempel Schneidler on QuarkXpress
Printed in Singapore by Kyodo Printing Co (S'pore) Pte Ltd

Page 2: Stuffed Crab Backs, p. 37

CONTENTS

INTRODUCTION

*A Quick Tour Around the Caribbean • A Short History of the Caribbean
• A Culinary History • Caribbean Culture and Traditions
• The Caribbean Today*

APPETIZERS 14

SOUPS 38

MEAT AND POULTRY 62

FISH AND SEAFOOD 106

VEGETABLES, SALADS, AND SIDE DISHES 138

BREADS, BUNS, AND CAKES 186

DESSERTS AND SWEET TREATS 206

BEVERAGES 246
Non-alcoholic • Alcoholic

SAUCES, SEASONINGS, AND CONDIMENTS 266

GLOSSARY 290
Herbs and Spices • Equivalents and Substitutes

INDEX 300

INTRODUCTION

If you're not sure exactly what Caribbean cooking is here's your chance to discover an adventurous and varied cuisine. With this book, you can travel around the Caribbean without leaving home. But before we begin the journey, we should clarify the two terms "Caribbean" and "West Indian" as they are now used interchangeably.

The West Indies was the term used by the Spanish in the fifteenth century to describe those islands and parts of the mainland which they "discovered" and to differentiate them from the Portuguese "discoveries" in Asia which were named the East Indies. The British later used the term which included their possessions in the Caribbean Sea. It is still frequently used.

A quick tour around the Caribbean

What then is the Caribbean? Let's start with a quick tour.

The region is divided into two groups: The Greater Antilles and The Lesser Antilles. The Greater Antilles—consisting of Cuba, Jamaica, Hispaniola, and Puerto Rico—were once a continuous land mass extending from Cuba to the Virgin Islands. The Lesser Antilles stretch from the eastern Caribbean islands, down south to Trinidad, and include the islands off the Venezuelan coast as far west as Aruba. The Lesser Antilles are further divided into the Leeward Islands and the Windward Islands. The Leeward Islands arc from the Virgin Islands in the north to Dominica, while the Windward Islands begin with Martinique and arc southward ending with Grenada.

Also included in the Caribbean are the South American countries of Guyana, Suriname, and French Guiana, all of which border the north of Brazil. Although geographically part of mainland South America, economically and culturally they are part of the Caribbean or West Indies. Likewise the Central American country of Belize, and the Mexican centers of Cancún and Cozumel are also part of the Caribbean while being part of the Central American coast.

Now, let's have a look around! First stop is the British Crown Colony of Bermuda, somewhat isolated in the Atlantic, but still included. Due south are the Bahamas, made up of 700 islands and endowed with some 2000 cays and picturesque white beaches. A little south-west we hit perhaps the least known Caribbean islands, the Turks and Caicos, whose natural salt deposits were exploited by Europeans in the eighteenth century. Continuing south we come across Cuba and the beautiful coastal city of Havana, where the harbor protects stretches of Spanish colonial architecture and plazas.

A quick look at Belize will reveal the grand and impressive ruins of the Mayans. To the east lie the Cayman Islands, a haven for the turtle lover and tax exile alike. Then it's on to Jamaica's Montego Bay where the infamous music event Reggae Sunsplash is held. From there we head to St Ann's Bay, home of one of Jamaica's prominent freedom fighters, Marcus Garvey. Progressing to the capital, Kingston, we pass through the lush Blue Mountains, sampling Jamaica's fine coffee on the way. A quick look at Bob Marley's house reminds us of the inspiration his songs provided for working people all over Jamaica in the seventies.

Looking east, we can see the island of Hispanola on the horizon. Site of the region's first European settlement, it is now divided into two countries, Haiti and the Dominican Republic. Haiti, once a French colony, produced the world's first black republic, the result of slave rebellions inspired by the 1789 French Revolution. The Spanish-speaking Dominican Republic boasts the highest peak in the Caribbean with its Cordillera Central mountain ranges.

Like the Dominican Republic, Puerto Rico was once a Spanish colony but is now an autonomous commonwealth associated with the United States. A stroll through Old San Juan's cobbled streets followed by a taste of the infamous piña coladas is the perfect way to spend the afternoon.

Traveling south through the Lesser Antilles you cannot fail to admire the aqua-colored waters surrounding the Virgin Islands nor the serenity and natural beauty of some of the smaller islands such as Anguilla, Antigua, Saba, St Eustatius, and Barbuda. Nor, indeed, the diversity of language, food, and music found on the island of St Martin, itself divided into French and Dutch departments.

As we continue south toward the twin island of St Kitts and Nevis, to Montserrat and then as far as Martinique, St Lucia, Grenada, and the Grenadines, we are struck by the majesty of this mountainous landscape. Volcanic activity can be witnessed on the exquisite island of Dominica with its boiling lake, the largest of its kind in the world. From here, it's only a short trip to Barbados. This was the only country in the Caribbean to be settled by colonists from just one European country, England, which explains the English influence in the capital, Bridgetown.

Trinidad & Tobago—said once to have been part of the South American continent—is the home of political leader and historian, Eric Williams. It is also home to the largest carnival in the West Indies, known simply as Trinidad Carnival. A time for out-and-out fun, when people dance, eat, and drink for days.

Before visiting the South American countries of the Caribbean, let's drop by the Dutch Antilles. First, Aruba for a walk in the capital, Oranjestad, where eighteenth-century Dutch architecture blends with gorgeous Caribbean pastels. Next, Bonaire, surrounded by stunning coral reefs and beaches. Getting hungry?

We'll take a trip to Curaçao's floating markets where the merchants have just sailed in from Colombia, the Dominican Republic, and Venezuela. You can choose from the huge array of tropical fruit, vegetables, and spices freshly grown for the markets. Now, over to South America where we arrive in Guyana, where much of the natural beauty remains untouched. A trip to the interior will reveal the Kaieteur Falls with a drop of 741 feet (226 m)—it makes Niagara Falls look like a mere trickle!

A short history of the Caribbean

It is believed that the south west peninsula of Hispaniola and western Cuba were settled as early as 500BC by a people, known as the Ciboney, from Florida and Yucatan on the mainland. Later, around 600AD, came the Arawaks from the coastal regions of the South American continent, in particular the region between the Amazon and Orinoco Rivers. The Arawaks (the Tainos and the Lucayans) travelled as far north as Jamaica (Tainos) and the Bahamas (Lucayans). Later, they were followed by the Caribs, a warrior people from the north of South America from whom the region gets its name.

When Christopher Columbus and his crew encountered the Caribs and the Arawaks, they found the Caribs to be the most fearsome and tenacious in holding onto their land and better fighters than the Arawaks, who were virtually wiped out in just under 70 years of Spanish settlement. The Caribs, however, put up a long and arduous fight. They thwarted many attempts by European colonists to annihilate them. In Grenada, which the British had tried to settle in 1609, the colonists were crushed by the Caribs; later, in 1638, the French tried the

same thing, but they too were defeated. Today there are a handful of Caribs living in Dominica and St Vincent. Sadly, most of the Caribbean's indigenous population were wiped out either by war, slavery, European diseases, or group suicides (as was the fate of the Lucayans in the Bahamas).

Columbus, on behalf of the Spanish Crown, was the first European to arrive in the Caribbean where he first settled Hispaniola. It wasn't long before a Spanish settlement took hold in what is known today as Santo Domingo, capital of the Dominican Republic. The city's expansion saw it become the administrative center for the Spanish Indies, servicing Jamaica, Puerto Rico, and Cuba. Today, only the Dominican Republic, Puerto Rico, and Cuba have retained the Spanish language and culture.

It was in that early colonial period that the Spanish introduced the sugar industry, the premier industry in the Caribbean until its slow decline in recent decades. And so began the history of slavery in the West Indies.

Once the indigenous population died out, the colonists turned to Africa for slaves. When the British, French, Dutch, and to a lesser extent the Danish began to settle the West Indies in the seventeenth century, they brought millions of slaves between them.

Although at the time the West Indies did not offer those spices most sought after in the Orient, it had plenty to offer European slave owners, plunderers, and traders. Allspice was native to Jamaica, although Columbus had overlooked it. Sugar, salt, and tobacco were just some of the goods that could either be grown or exploited for profit to supply European demand.

The British, French, and Dutch fought over the Caribbean territories. Many of the islands passed through the hands of alternating

European powers over the course of a century. Testament to this are St Lucia and Dominica which experienced both British and French rule over a fifty year period. Today, evidence of that history can be heard in the language— a type of patois that resembles a mix of French and English.

In the seventeenth century the Dutch took over the islands of Aruba, Bonaire, Curaçao, St Eustatius, Saba, and St Martin which they possess today. During the same period, the Danish began their takeover of St Thomas, St Croix, and St John—an area known today as the U.S. Virgin Islands which was sold to the U.S. in 1917 for US$25,000,000.

It wasn't until the nineteenth century that abolition effectively brought freedom to the millions of slaves in the Caribbean. Unfortunately, it meant virtually another kind of slavery for the thousands of East Indians and Chinese who were brought to work the land under a contract of indentured labor. Laborers also came from the Yucatan Peninsula, Indonesia, and French Indo-China to a lesser extent. They were the next best thing to slaves—cheap labor! Although these workers believed they would be staying in the Caribbean for just the contracted amount of time, most never made it back home. The largest East Indian and Chinese populations today are found in Trinidad, Guyana, and Suriname (which also has a sizeable Javanese population), but there are smaller such communities around the West Indies.

This century's history has been one of independence struggles and revolutionary upheaval in countries such as Cuba and Grenada. More recently, the United States has had a greater influence on the Caribbean. Its relations with Cuba, Puerto Rico, Grenada, and Haiti reflect its desire to influence the destiny of the region.

The history of the Caribbean is the story of exploration, exploitation, and integration. Its many different people, whether by force or force of will, have each added and adapted to the region to make it unique. All brought with them their own cultural and culinary identities to produce a rich and diverse cuisine. Today that cultural diversity continues...

A culinary history

Each country in the Caribbean shares a similar historical pattern: European domination, slavery, and indentured labor, followed perhaps by independence. However, the unfolding of that history is unique to each nation and reveals how the local cuisine has evolved.

Although the Spanish sighted most of the West Indies before other Europeans, their influence today is more apparent in some countries than others. For example, Jamaica and Puerto Rico were settled around the same time yet Puerto Rico has retained the Spanish language and influence, while Jamaica was successfully taken over by the British, which added to its already evolving cuisine.

That said, the history of the region's cuisine began well before the Europeans arrived. The earliest records date back to the days of the Amerindians. The staple food of the Arawaks was agouti (a rodent), fish and shellfish, cassava (used to make breads, cakes, and cassareep), sweet potatoes, maize, yams, arrowroot, peanuts, beans, cocoa, guavas, and hot chili peppers. They also cultivated tobacco and cotton (used to make clothing and hammocks)—something the Europeans picked up on in a big way!

The Caribs' diet was protein based. It included iguana, game and small birds, shellfish and fish, papaya, pineapple, and turtle meat (still eaten today, especially in the

Cayman Islands where green turtles are farmed commercially). They used hot chili peppers and spices in their food, both to flavor and preserve it.

When the Spanish arrived, they imported many of their foodstuffs in an effort to bring Spain to the West Indies. They cultivated lemons, oranges, and bananas from the Canary Islands with varying degrees of success, and contributed such items as oregano, Seville oranges, and cumin which are today integral to their cooking.

The British, French, Dutch, Portuguese, and Danish colonists further added to this rich melting-pot with a range of continental foodstuffs. The British, for example, contributed fruit buns and tea cakes which gave rise to Jamaica's spiced bun. They also brought breadfruit to the region, which Captain Bligh (of mutiny on The Bounty fame) transported from Tahiti. The Dutch, via their trade with Indonesia, brought the fragrant spices nutmeg, mace, cinnamon, and cloves, and also introduced remnants of Indonesian cuisine through Suriname.

Many of those brought to the region to work the plantations added further to the cuisine. The African slaves, with their plantains, cornmeal, peas and beans, okra and ackee, tried to reproduce dishes from home either with the ingredients they were given or ones they could grow. The results were new and unique dishes now eaten by all in the Caribbean.

The East Indians brought their rotis, curries, chutneys, and snacks such as phulourie, while the Chinese brought their stir fries, soups, and chow meins—just some of the foods that helped sustain the workers through their hard lives.

Although these influences had great impact in the evolution of the cuisine, it did not end there. Since colonization, waves of immigration have brought people from all over the world who, to varying degrees, have contributed to the Caribbean's ever-developing culinary identity.

But, one thing that hasn't changed is the availability and choice of fruit and vegetables. In the West Indies you can enjoy fresh fruit and vegetables the whole year round and that's simply because each season brings a different wonderful crop. It is truly a garden of paradise!

Caribbean culture and traditions

Caribbean society is the result of a mixture of different cultures. These have mingled over the centuries to produce loud, lively, and colorful annual festivals and carnivals. Everybody in the West Indies, young and old, comes out at Carnival time to enjoy the food, music, people, costumes, and drinks. And, of course, there are regular celebrations when the West Indies cricket team scores a win!

Many of the carnivals, such as the celebration of Independence Day, have historical importance and so have been celebrated for many years. The importance of the labor of the land is reflected in the traditional Bajan festival known as Cropover which celebrates the completion of the sugar-cane harvest. It is also evident in Dominica which holds one of the most widely celebrated feasts known as the Fête de La St Pierre. It is celebrated in one of the many fishing villages with a feast of fish presented by the host village.

Religion plays a very important role in the lives of West Indians. Although historically dominated by European Catholicism and Protestantism, this is sometimes mixed with African religions, as is the case with Haiti's Voodoo. The cult Santería has its origins in a

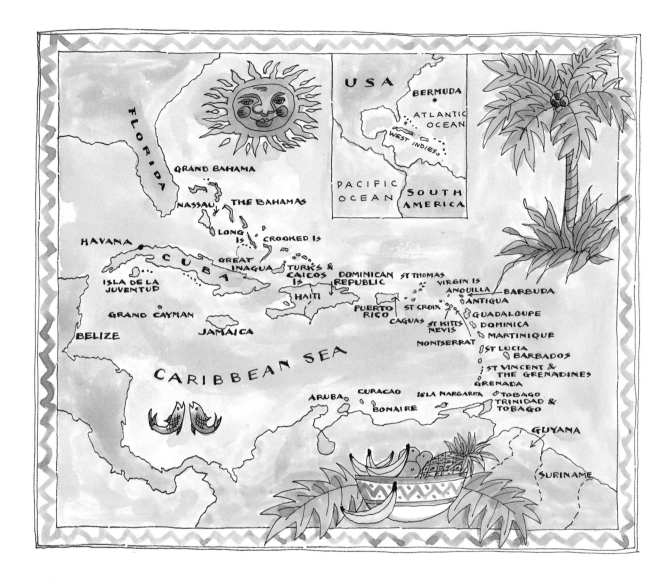

mixture of African religions (the result of prolonged slavery in Cuba), yet is dominated by the religion of the Yoruba peoples, and has evolved to encompass popular Catholicism. Santería has a stronger hold today than Catholicism and is a significant part of Cuban society. Similarly, Rastafarianism in Jamaica is a New World religion and began as a voice against oppression that looked to the Motherland, Africa.

The newer recruits to the region, the East Indians and the Chinese, held their religion close to their hearts. This can be seen in the festival of Phagwa celebrating the Hindu New Year and the Muslim festival of Hosein.

Music plays a central role in West Indian life. Not the commodity it is in other parts of the world, Caribbean music isn't separate from people's everyday lives. Wherever there is music in the West Indies, there are people singing, clapping, and, above all, dancing.

Tracing the development of music in the region is virtually the same as the history of the cuisine and results similarly in a unique mixture of styles. Anyone who equates Caribbean music solely with Bob

Marley's reggae is missing out on the rhythms and textures of styles such as the Cuban Salsa, Puerto Rico's Bomba and Plena music, the Merengue of the Dominican Republic, the Zouk and Beguine musics of Martinique and Guadeloupe, the Calypsos and Chutney Socas of Trinidad, and the Kawina of Suriname. As with the cuisine, the music of the Caribbean is a spicy mixture of European, African, and Asian influences.

The Caribbean today

Today in the Caribbean, like elsewhere, many women work in the general workforce as well as in the home. Not untypically, women have traditionally been the cooks of the household (although, like elsewhere, men occupy professional chef positions in major restaurants, hotels, and resorts). There is, therefore, a need for quicker and simpler things to prepare for the family and faster methods of preparation.

Another major influence is the establishment of fast food outlets. Hamburgers, hot dogs (especially in Trinidad which does a great hot dog), pizzas, and the like, are finding their way into the busy lives of people in the Caribbean. That's not to say that a West Indian can't turn fast food into good, tasty food in true Caribbean style—remember there is always the famous hot pepper sauce!

Whatever food you enjoy—hot, spicy, or simple—you'll find it in the Caribbean. See for yourself. Why not make yourself a rum punch, let the sunshine in and get down to cooking some Caribbean food. Grab that bag and head for the markets...

APPETIZERS

I n the West Indies, a meal is not usually started with an appetizer. Many of the recipes that appear in this section are commonly served as snacks or pre-dinner nibbles, but they would serve well as a first course. There is a huge variety of appetizers to appeal to all tastes—subtle or spicy, vegetarian or meat-loving.

Carnival time in the West Indies brings out the best goodies such as tamales and pastelles, but tasty snacks such as phulourie, chicharrones de pollo, and accras de morue are available all year round at the ever-present roadside foodstalls. Dishes range from the very quick and simple to prepare, such as plantain chips, to those using more involved techniques, such as aloo pie.

Salty nibbles such as chicharrones, tostones and coconut chips make excellent accompaniments to drinks, while others such as channa or stamp-and-go can be eaten on their own or served as a side dish. Those made from pastry or dough with a meat or vegetable filling make excellent picnic food. Still others, such as stuffed crab backs, make an impressive opener when entertaining friends and family. Whichever you choose, I'm sure you will enjoy them all!

Souskaï de Mangues Vertes, page 37

JAMAICAN BEEF PATTIES

MAKES 24

Pastry:

4 cups (1 lb/450 g) all-purpose (plain) flour

1 teaspoon yellow (powdered) food coloring

1 teaspoon salt

10 oz (280 g) shortening or suet

about 2/3 cup (5 fl oz/150 ml) ice water

Filling:

1 onion, coarsely chopped

2 large shallots, chopped

2 hot peppers, seeded and chopped

1 tablespoon vegetable oil

2 lb (1 kg) ground (minced) beef

1 tablespoon curry powder

2 1/2 teaspoons chopped fresh thyme

2 cups (8 oz/250 g) coarse fresh breadcrumbs

1/2 teaspoon MSG, optional

1 1/2 teaspoons salt

1 egg, separated

For pastry: Sift together flour, food coloring, and salt. Cut in shortening until mixture resembles coarse crumbs. Add ice water by the tablespoon, mixing just until dough holds together. Wrap dough in waxed (greaseproof) paper or foil and refrigerate for at least 12 hours or overnight.

For filling: Mince onions, shallots, and peppers in a blender or food processor. Heat oil in a large saucepan over medium heat. Add meat, curry powder, and thyme and cook for 15 minutes. Stir in onion mixture and cook 5 minutes longer. Add breadcrumbs, MSG, and salt, cover, and simmer 20 to 30 minutes or until the beef is tender. Cool before filling the pastry.

Preheat oven to 400°F (200°C/Gas 6) and position rack in top third of oven. Roll out dough to 1/8-inch (3 mm) thickness and cut out 5-inch (12 cm) circles. Place a tablespoon of filling in the middle of each. Moisten edges with lightly beaten egg white, fold into half-circles, and press edges together to seal. Glaze with lightly beaten egg yolk. Bake on ungreased baking sheets for 35 minutes or until golden brown. Serve hot or warm.

EMPANÁ

These empaná from the Dutch Antilles are made from a cornmeal dough and filled with beef. For instructions for boiling plantains, see page 185.

Dough:

4¹/2 cups (36 fl oz/1.125 l) water

1 teaspoon salt

3¹/2 cups (14 oz/440 g) yellow cornmeal

4 cups (32 fl oz/1 l) additional cold water

4 tablespoons grated cheddar cheese

1 green plantain, boiled for 10 minutes, mashed

about 1 cup (4 oz/125 g) all-purpose (plain) flour

Filling:

3 tablespoons butter

1 medium onion, finely chopped

1 lb (500 g) ground (minced) beef

2 medium tomatoes

¹/2 green bell pepper, chopped

1 small hot pepper, seeded and minced

1 tablespoon drained capers, finely chopped

8 green olives, chopped

1 tablespoon seedless raisins, finely chopped

¹/4 teaspoon freshly grated nutmeg or ground nutmeg

salt and freshly ground black pepper

3 to 4 cups (24 to 32 fl oz/750 ml to 1 l) vegetable oil for deep frying

For dough: Mix 4¹/2 cups water and salt in a saucepan and bring to boil. Combine cornmeal and 4 cups cold water and slowly add to the boiling salted water. Cook, stirring constantly, until the mixture thickens and almost forms a dough. Remove from heat and let cool. Blend in cheese, plantain, and enough flour to form a pliable dough.

For filling: Melt butter in a frying pan over medium heat and sauté onion until translucent. Add beef and sauté until browned. Add tomatoes, green bell pepper, and hot pepper and simmer until liquid is completely absorbed, 10 to 15 minutes. Add capers, olives, raisins, nutmeg, and salt and pepper to taste and mix well.

Place 1 heaping tablespoon of dough on a damp cloth and roll out to ¹/4-inch (5 mm) thickness. Place 1 tablespoon filling on one half of the circle, fold over, and seal edges by pressing down with a fork. Repeat with remaining dough and filling.

Heat oil in a deep pan until hot, about 360°F (185°C). Deep fry empaná until golden brown on all sides. Drain on paper towels. Serve warm.

Tamales

MAKES 30

This recipe was given to me by the chef of one of Miami's best Cuban restaurants, El Viajante. It's a popular Christmas treat. The corn can be grated straight from the cob, or canned creamed corn can be substituted. I have made this a rather special filling but it can be as simple as you like—just garlic, for example, or chicharrones (see page 28), which can be stirred directly into the corn dough.

Dough:

1/4 cup (2 fl oz/60 ml) water

4 cups (2 lb/1 kg) freshly grated corn

1/2 cup (3 oz/90 g) stoneground yellow cornmeal

2 teaspoons sugar

2 teaspoons salt

1 tablespoon butter

Filling:

1 clove garlic

2 teaspoons chopped fresh oregano or 1/2 teaspoon dried

salt and black pepper

1 lb (500 g) ground beef, pork, or chicken

2 teaspooons olive oil

1 teaspoon wine vinegar

1 tablespoon vegetable oil

1 onion, finely chopped

1/2 green bell pepper (capsicum), seeded and chopped

2 hard-cooked eggs, chopped

6 prunes, pitted and chopped

2 tablespoons seedless raisins, optional

8 pimiento-stuffed olives, sliced

1 tablespoon tomato paste (puree)

1 teaspoon drained capers

2 tablespoons annatto oil (see page 285)

To cook:

30 cornhusks or, if unavailable, 30 5-inch (12 cm) foil squares

1 bay leaf

1 sprig cilantro (fresh coriander)

1 teaspoon ground cumin

For dough: Blend water and grated corn to form a paste. Place in a saucepan with cornmeal, sugar, salt, and butter. Bring to boil and cook, stirring, until mixture thickens and almost forms a dough, about 20 minutes. Set aside for at least 1 hour.

For filling: Mash garlic, oregano, and salt and pepper together thoroughly to make a paste. Mix into meat with olive oil and vinegar. Set aside.

Heat vegetable oil in a saucepan over medium heat. Add onion and bell pepper and cook, stirring occasionally, until onion is transparent, about 5 to 8 minutes. Add meat mixture and brown, about 10 minutes, stirring occasionally. Add eggs, prunes, raisins, olives, tomato paste, capers, and 1 tablespoon annatto oil. Reduce heat to low and cook for 5 more minutes.

Grease each cornhusk or piece of foil with remaining annatto oil. Place a heaping spoonful of the corn dough in the middle and spread to within 1/2 inch (1 cm) of the edges using the back of a spoon. Place a spoonful of the meat mixture in the middle of the dough, then fold the husk or foil so that the sides of the corn mixture seal in the meat. Fasten each parcel with a piece of string.

Bring 20 cups (5 l) salted water to boil with bay leaf, cilantro, cumin, and salt. Add tamales and simmer 1 hour over medium heat. Lift out with a slotted spoon, then unwrap and serve hot.

Tamales

PASTELLES

MAKES 12 TO 14

These appear at Carnival in Trinidad, which takes place every February on the streets of Port of Spain. There you can find an amazing array of Trinidadian treats and delights.

Dough:

2 cups (10 oz/300 g) cornmeal

1 tablespoon sugar

2 tablespoons salt or to taste

1 tablespoon butter

about 4 cups (1 l) boiling water

Filling:

2 oz (60 g) pork fat or lard

2 cloves garlic, minced

1 large onion, finely chopped

2 lb (1 kg) ground (minced) beef

1 tablespoon wine vinegar

2 sprigs thyme, finely chopped

2 teaspoons finely chopped fresh basil or 1/2 teaspoon dried

2 oz (60 g) drained capers

4 mixed green and red hot peppers, seeded and finely chopped

3/4 cup (4 oz/120 g) seedless raisins

6 green olives, finely chopped

1 tablespoon ketchup

1/2 teaspoon freshly ground black pepper

salt

about 1/4 cup (2 fl oz/60 ml) meat stock or water, if needed

To cook:

12 to 14 banana leaves or 8-inch (3 cm) square pieces of foil

annatto oil (see page 285), vegetable or corn oil

1 tablespoon salt

For dough: Combine cornmeal, sugar, salt, and butter in bowl. Stir in 3 cups (24 fl oz/750 ml) boiling water. Mixture should be moist enough to spread; if too thick, add more water a little at a time.

For filling: Heat fat in large saucepan over high heat. Add garlic and onion and sauté 1 minute. Add meat and cook until browned, about 15 minutes. Add all remaining ingredients except stock, reduce heat, and simmer until meat is tender, 20 to 30 minutes, adding meat stock or water if meat sticks to pan. Filling should be moist.

If using banana leaves, pour some boiling water over them to make them pliable. Brush one leaf or piece of foil with a little oil. Spoon 1 heaping tablespoon cornmeal dough onto the leaf or foil and spread out to a thickness of 1/4 inch (5 mm) by placing a piece of wet cheesecloth (muslin) over the dough and spreading gently with the back of a spoon. Place 1 tablespoon of meat filling on top. Lift one side of the leaf or foil and fold in half. If using a leaf, fold edges over to form a secure parcel and tie crosswise with string. If using foil, fold sides toward middle, bring edges up, and press tightly to form a parcel.

Fill large saucepan 3/4 full of water and bring to boil. Add salt. Drop parcels into water and cook 1 hour. Drain and serve.

Aloo Pie

Today in the West Indies, there are many snacks of East-Indian origin that are eaten throughout the region. Aloo pie is one such dish, and is most common in Trinidad and Guyana. This one comes from Trinidad and is best served with a chutney or kuchilla (see pages 269 to 272). Aloo means potato in Hindi.

Dough:

2 cups (8 oz/250 g) all-purpose
(plain) flour

1/4 teaspoon salt

1 teaspoon baking powder

about 1 cup (8 fl oz/250 ml) water

vegetable oil

Filling:

4 cups (32 fl oz/1 l) water

1/2 teaspoon salt

1 lb (500 g) potatoes,
peeled and quartered

1 small onion, finely chopped

2 cloves garlic, crushed

1 green onion,
very finely chopped

2 teaspoons ground cumin

1/4 teaspoon masala (see page 284)
or garam masala

1 hot red pepper,
seeded and minced

salt and freshly ground
black pepper

To cook:

4 cups (32 fl oz/1 l) vegetable oil
for deep frying

For dough: Combine flour, salt, and baking powder in bowl. Add enough water to form dough and knead. Rub a little oil over dough and let rest while preparing filling.

For filling: Bring water and salt to boil in saucepan and boil potatoes until tender. Drain. While still hot, mash potatoes with onion, garlic, green onion, cumin, masala, hot pepper, and salt and pepper to taste.

Divide dough into 6 parts and knead each for 1 minute to form a smooth ball. Let rest 5 minutes.

Heat oil in saucepan. Roll out one portion of dough on floured surface into circle 5 inches (12 cm) in diameter. Spoon 1 to 2 tablespoons of filling in middle and fold into semicircle. Dab a little cold water around edges and pinch to seal. Deep fry pies, a few at a time, until golden brown on all sides. Drain on paper towels and serve hot.

Following pages: Pastelles, Aloo Pie, Phulourie

PHULOURIE

MAKES ABOUT 36

An East Indian snack that goes well with mango chutney (see page 270). It's very popular in Guyana and Trinidad, where there are large East Indian communities. When my grandmother makes phulourie, you can't stop eating them until they're all finished!

2 cups (8 oz/250 g) split pea flour or besan

1 cup (4 oz/125 g) self-rising flour

1/4 teaspoon baking powder

1/2 teaspoon turmeric

1/2 teaspoon cumin

1 to 2 teaspoons salt or to taste

about 2/3 cup (5 fl oz/150 ml) water

1/2 small onion, minced

2 cloves garlic, minced

1 green onion, green part only, finely chopped

1/4 teaspoon minced hot pepper, optional

about 2 cups (16 fl oz/500 ml) vegetable oil for deep frying

Sift flours and baking powder into a mixing bowl. Stir in turmeric, cumin, and salt. Add enough water to form a very thick batter. Mix in onion, garlic, green onion, and hot pepper.

Heat oil in a deep saucepan until very hot, about 375°F (190°C). Drop in mixture by tablespoons and fry until golden brown on all sides. Drain on paper towels and serve warm.

CHANNA

SERVES 4

Channa refers to chick peas in Hindi. To make a 'crunchier' channa, don't simmer the chickpeas but do soak them overnight. This East Indian snack should be served warm or at room temperature in bowls as a side dish or snack.

8 oz (250 g) dried chickpeas, soaked overnight and drained, or canned chickpeas, drained

1/4 cup (2 fl oz/60 ml) vegetable oil

1 small onion, finely chopped

1/2 teaspoon cumin

1/4 teaspoon chili powder or paprika, optional

salt and freshly ground black pepper

If using dried chickpeas, cover with 4 cups (32 fl oz/1 l) boiling water, add 1/2 teaspoon salt, and simmer over medium heat until tender, about 45 minutes. Drain.

Heat oil in a frying pan until hot. Add onion and sauté until golden. Add chickpeas and seasonings and sauté 3 to 4 minutes.

ACCRAS DE MORUE

SERVES 4

From the French Caribbean, these salt fish fritters can be served as a snack or appetizer.

4 oz (125 g) salt cod

4 cups (1 lb/500 g) all-purpose (plain) flour

2 eggs

1 cup (8 fl oz/250 ml) milk

2 cloves garlic, finely chopped

2 green onions, finely chopped

2 sprigs parsley, finely chopped

1 sprig fresh thyme, chopped, or 1/4 teaspoon dried

1 small hot pepper, seeded and finely chopped

salt and freshly ground black pepper

1/2 teaspoon baking soda (bicarbonate)

about 3 cups (24 fl oz/750 ml) vegetable oil for deep frying

Soak fish in water to cover at least 4 hours, preferably overnight. Discard soaking water. Place fish in saucepan with 6 cups (1.5 l) fresh water and bring to boil. Boil until fish is soft, about 20 minutes. Drain. Discard skin and bones and flake fish into small pieces.

Sift flour into mixing bowl. Make a well in the middle and add eggs. Gradually add milk to the well, beating with a wooden spoon and incorporating flour bit by bit. Beat until batter is smooth. Blend in garlic, onions, parsley, thyme, hot pepper, and salt and pepper to taste. Stir in fish. Let stand for 1 hour for a richer flavor. Add baking soda.

Heat oil in a deep frying pan over high heat until very hot. Drop batter by the teaspoon into oil. Reduce heat slightly and fry until golden on all sides, about 3 to 5 minutes. Remove with slotted spoon and drain on paper towels. Serve hot.

COCONUT CHIPS

SERVES 8

In the West Indies chips are made from many different vegetables such as breadfruit and cassava. These are great nibbles for any time or occasion.

1 coconut (see glossary)

butter

salt

Preheat oven to 400°F (200°C/Gas 6). Butter baking sheets. Bore two holes in eyes of coconut using a clean skewer or pointed utensil. Drain liquid from coconut. Bake coconut until shell cracks, about 15 minutes.

Remove coconut meat from the shell and peel off brown skin. Using a vegetable peeler, shave coconut into thin slices. Arrange slices on prepared baking sheets and bake until light brown, turning occasionally, about 10 minutes. Sprinkle with salt. Serve warm or at room temperature.

SOUSE

Found everywhere in the Caribbean, this dish is made with varying parts of the pig. In Curaçao the pig's ears are included; in Barbados they use the pig's head. This is based on my mother's recipe, which uses 6 cleaned pig's trotters, but I have substituted lean pork for the traditional pig parts. If using trotters, simmer for about 2 hours. Serve chilled or at room temperature with drinks and bread or crackers.

1 lb (500 g) lean pork, cubed

2 cloves garlic, crushed

salt

1 whole large or 2 small hot peppers

1 medium onion, coarsely chopped

1 small onion, minced

2 tablespoons finely chopped fresh parsley

1 small cucumber, finely diced

3 green onions, finely chopped

1/2 stalk celery, finely chopped

2 sprigs thyme, finely chopped, or 1 teaspoon dried

1 tablespoon distilled vinegar

juice of 1 lime or lemon

Place pork in a large saucepan and add enough water to cover. Add garlic, 1 tablespoon salt, hot pepper and the medium onion. Bring to boil, then reduce heat, cover, and simmer 20 to 30 minutes. Drain, reserving half a hot pepper, and set aside until cool enough to handle. (If using trotters, cut meat into small pieces, discarding any bones.)

In a large bowl combine meat, the small onion, parsley, cucumber, green onions, celery, and thyme. Add the reserved hot pepper, finely chopped. Blend in vinegar, juice, and additional salt to taste. Let stand at least 1 hour for flavors to develop.

Souse

27

CHICHARRONES

SERVES 4 TO 6

These pork cracklings, from Puerto Rico, make great nibbles when served warm with drinks. They can also be used when making mofongo (see page 158)—you may wish to halve this amount if using it for mofongo—or added to tamales with tomato (see page 18). The pork rind should only have about 1/12 inch (2 mm) of fat on it.

1 lb (500 g) pork rind, trimmed of excess fat

2 teaspoons salt or to taste

1/4 cup (2 fl oz/60 ml) vegetable oil

Soak pork rind in cold water to cover in a saucepan for 1 hour. Cover pan and bring to boil; boil 10 minutes. Chop into 1/2 x 1/4 inch (10 x 5 mm) pieces. Sprinkle with salt and let stand 10 minutes.

Heat oil in a frying pan over medium heat. Add salted pork rinds, cover, and fry 10 to 15 minutes, then partially uncover and continue to cook until they are light brown, crisp, and bubbly on the surface. Drain on paper towels and serve immediately.

CHICHARRONES DE POLLO

SERVES 4

Made with small pieces of chicken, this is from the Dominican Republic. It is a popular snack food sold by street vendors.

2 lb (1 kg) mixed chicken parts

1/4 cup (2 fl oz/60 ml) soy sauce

3 tablespoons lime or lemon juice

1/2 teaspoon salt

2 cloves garlic, crushed

1/2 cup (4 fl oz/125 ml) vegetable oil

all-purpose (plain) flour

freshly ground black pepper

Cut chicken breasts into 4 and wings into 2 pieces. Combine soy sauce, lime juice, and salt in a wide, shallow dish. Stir in garlic. Add chicken to the soy sauce mixture and marinate in refrigerator for at least 2 hours, turning chicken after 1 hour.

Heat oil in a large, heavy frying pan to medium hot, about 325°F (170°C). Season flour with pepper. Drain chicken pieces and wipe off excess marinade. Coat chicken with flour mixture. Fry in oil, in batches if necessary, until golden brown, about 5 to 7 minutes on each side. Drain on paper towels and serve hot.

PLANTAIN CHIPS

SERVES 4 TO 6

Serve as a snack or with drinks. The chips will keep in an airtight container for two or three days.

10 green plantains

about 2 cups (16 fl oz/500 ml) vegetable oil for deep frying

salt

Peel plantains and slice into very thin rounds. Heat oil in a deep pan until hot, about 360°F (185°C). Add about 1 dozen plantain slices at a time and fry, turning once, until crisp and golden brown. Drain chips on paper towels. Sprinkle with salt and toss to distribute evenly.

TOSTONES DE PLÁTANO VERDE

SERVES 4

Tostones are served in the Spanish-speaking islands of Cuba and Puerto Rico as a snack or an accompaniment to any meal. For a robust garlic flavor, try drizzling the cooked tostones with a mixture of 1/4 cup (2 oz/60 ml) olive oil mixed with 2 crushed cloves of garlic, or sprinkle with garlic salt (see page 288). In Puerto Rico a special utensil called a pilón is used to flatten the plantain, but I use a filled bottle.

2 cups (16 fl oz/500 ml) water

2 teaspoons salt

3 green plantains, peeled and cut diagonally into 1-inch (2.5 cm) slices

about 2 cups (16 fl oz/500 ml) vegetable or corn oil for deep frying

Combine water and salt in a bowl. Drop plantain slices into the salted water and let stand 10 minutes.

Heat oil in a deep frying pan until hot, about 360°F (185°C). Drain the plantains and fry until tender but not crisp, about 8 minutes. Remove from oil with a slotted spoon, arrange plantain pieces on several layers of paper towel, and press down to flatten. Return to hot oil and fry again until crisp and golden brown, about 5 to 6 minutes. Drain on paper towels and serve hot.

DUCANA

SERVES 4

These tempting little parcels, known as ducana, are from Antigua. They can be topped with syrup (such as those on pages 280 to 282) and eaten as a dessert, or served as an appetizer with a sauce made from salt cod, such as the one below. They are traditionally cooked in banana leaves; if you cannot obtain them, foil is a good substitute.

1½ cups (6 oz/175 g) all-purpose (plain) flour

salt

½ teaspoon ground or freshly grated nutmeg

2 cups (12 oz/350 g) grated sweet potato

2 cups (12 oz/350 g) grated fresh coconut or 1²⁄₃ cups (10 oz/315 g) dried

1 to 2 teaspoons brown sugar or to taste

1 cup (8 fl oz/250 ml) milk or water

¼ teaspoon vanilla extract

24 banana leaves or 5-inch (12 cm) square pieces of foil

Sift flour, a pinch of salt, and nutmeg into a mixing bowl. Add sweet potato, coconut, and sugar and mix well. Combine milk and vanilla and add gradually, stirring until mixture forms a soft dough. Roll 1-tablespoon portions of dough into sausage shapes; this quantity should make about 24 parcels. Place each on a leaf or piece of foil and wrap securely. Tie each parcel closed with string.

Bring about 24 cups (6 l) salted water to boil. Drop in the ducana parcels and cook until firm, about 15 minutes.

Unwrap ducana and serve hot with sauce or syrup.

SALT COD SAUCE

SERVES 4

This sauce can be eaten with ducana (see above) or bakes (see page 193).

6 oz (185 g) salt cod

2 tablespoons corn oil

1 small onion, chopped

1 green onion, chopped

½ red bell pepper (capsicum), seeded and chopped

½ tablespoon chopped fresh parsley

1 sprig fresh thyme or ¼ teaspoon dried

1 medium tomato, chopped

freshly ground black pepper

Soak salt cod in water to cover for 4 hours, preferably overnight. Drain, cover in fresh water in a saucepan, and bring to boil. Boil until soft, about 10 minutes. Drain. Discard skin and bones, and shred fish.

Heat oil in a large frying pan over medium heat. Add onions and bell pepper and sauté until onion is soft, about 4 minutes. Add parsley, thyme, tomato, salt cod, and pepper and simmer 15 minutes.

To serve, spoon hot sauce over cooked ducana.

Ducana with Salt Cod Sauce

STAMP-AND-GO

SERVES 8

This recipe was given to me by Devon Singleton, one of Kingston, Jamaica's best cooks! To serve the fritters as an hors d'oeuvre, make them bite size and serve on toothpicks. Or serve larger versions as a snack.

8 oz (250 g) salt cod

2 cups (8 oz/250 g) all-purpose (plain) flour

1 teaspoon salt

1¼ cups (10 fl oz/300 ml) water or milk

½ teaspoon baking powder

1 green onion, finely chopped

1 small onion, finely chopped

½ teaspoon finely chopped garlic

1 hot pepper, seeded and finely chopped

about ½ cup (4 fl oz/125 ml) vegetable oil

Soak salt cod overnight in water to cover generously. Drain, cover with fresh water in a saucepan, and bring to boil. Boil until soft, about 10 minutes. Drain. Discard skin and bones and shred fish finely.

Combine flour and salt in a mixing bowl. Gradually add water or milk and stir to form a soft, sticky batter. Add baking powder. Blend in onions, garlic, hot pepper, and fish.

Heat oil in a frying pan until hot, about 360°F (185°C). Drop in the fish mixture by the tablespoonful and fry until golden brown on all sides, about 2 to 3 minutes. Drain on paper towels and serve warm.

SALT FISH CAKES

SERVES 4

Every country in the Caribbean has its own version of these. This is a recipe of my mother's.

8 oz (250 g) salt cod

1 onion, finely chopped

2 green onions, finely chopped

2 cloves garlic, minced

2 teaspoons finely chopped fresh parsley

1 sprig fresh thyme, finely chopped, or ¼ teaspoon dried

1 small hot red pepper, seeded and minced

salt and ground black pepper

1 lb (500 g) baking potatoes, boiled and mashed

¾ cup (3 oz/90 g) all-purpose (plain) flour

vegetable oil for deep frying

Soak fish overnight in water to cover generously. Drain. Place fish in a saucepan with fresh water to cover and bring to boil. Boil until soft, about 10 minutes. Drain. Discard skin and bones and flake fish into small pieces.

In a large bowl combine fish, onions, garlic, parsley, thyme, hot pepper, black pepper, and potatoes and mash together. Add flour and mix to form a firm dough. Season with salt if necessary.

Heat oil in a deep saucepan over high heat. Using floured hands and on a floured surface, flatten heaping tablespoons of dough to thickness of ½ inch (1 cm). Deep fry until golden brown, 3 to 4 minutes. Drain on paper towels and serve hot or warm.

BOL JUL

Also known as brule johl, this cold appetizer from Barbados has a slightly hot and tangy taste, and is ideal to eat on a hot day. It can be prepared 1 or 2 days in advance and left in the refrigerator to marinate. Serve with lettuce, sliced avocado, and crackers.

1 lb (500 g) salt cod

2 medium onions,
finely chopped

2 ripe but firm medium tomatoes

$1/2$ red bell pepper (capsicum),
finely chopped

1 hot pepper,
seeded and finely chopped

$1/4$ cup (2 fl oz/60 ml) olive oil

2 tablespoons lime juice

1 sprig fresh thyme, finely
chopped, or $1/2$ teaspoon dried

freshly ground black pepper

Soak salt cod overnight in water to cover. Drain, rinse, and remove skin and bones. Flake fish into very small pieces. In a large bowl combine fish with remaining ingredients, seasoning to taste with black pepper. Serve chilled.

FÉROCE D'AVOCAT

As its name suggests, this dish can be fierce—depending on the amount of hot pepper that you use. It's a very popular appetizer in Martinique and Guadeloupe. To serve as finger food, shape into balls.

8 oz (400 g) salt cod

1 tablespoon vinegar

juice of 1 lime

2 tablespoons vegetable oil

2 cloves garlic, finely chopped

4 shallots, finely chopped

4 green onions, chopped

1 to 3 hot peppers,
seeded and minced

4 avocados,
peeled, seeded, and diced

1 cup (4 oz/125 g) manioc flour
(tapioca or cassava meal)

extra lime juice for serving

Soak salt cod in water to cover for at least 4 hours, preferably overnight. Drain and pat dry.

Broil (grill) fish on both sides until browned. Cool, then remove skin and bones. Shred fish into small pieces. Add vinegar, lime juice, oil, garlic, shallots, and green onions. Mix in hot pepper (as much as you desire). Mash avocado with manioc flour, add to fish mixture, and blend to form a thick paste. Spoon into individual serving dishes, or roll into balls and arrange on a plate. Sprinkle with lime juice just before serving.

GRATIN DE CHRISTOPHENE

SERVES 8

This recipe is from the French Caribbean. Serve it with a small salad.

4 christophenes
(chayote squash/chokos)

1 teaspoon salt

2 tablespoons vegetable oil

2 onions, chopped

2 cloves garlic, finely chopped

4 green onions

1 tablespoon chopped
fresh parsley

1 tablespoon all-purpose
(plain) flour

1/4 cup (2 fl oz/60 ml) milk

1 cup (4 oz/125 g) grated cheese

1/2 cup (1 oz/30 g)
fresh breadcrumbs

butter

freshly ground black pepper

Halve each christophene lengthwise to make two wide, shallow shells. Remove the core. Place christophenes in a saucepan, adding 1 teaspoon salt and enough water to cover. Boil until tender, about 20 to 30 minutes. Scoop out the flesh, leaving a 1/4-inch (5 mm) shell; be careful not to break the skin. Mash or puree the flesh until smooth.

Heat oil over medium heat and sauté onions, garlic, green onions, and parsley until onions are golden brown. Stir in flour and cook for 1 minute, stirring constantly. Add milk, stirring vigorously to prevent lumping. Stir in half the cheese. Add mashed christophene and half the breadcrumbs.

Preheat oven to 400°F (200°C/Gas 6). Spoon the mixture into the empty christophene shells and arrange on a baking sheet. Sprinkle with pepper and the remaining breadcrumbs and cheese. Dot with butter. Bake until lightly browned, about 10 to 15 minutes. Serve immediately.

Gratin de Christophene

KESHI YENA

A Curaçao classic that embodies a multitude of tastes: Dutch Edam cheese is hollowed out and then filled with seasoned meat, capers, olives, raisins, and more! This is great to prepare for company because it is unusual and scrumptious. I have chosen chicken for the filling but you can use beef or shrimp. An alternative version is given for using slices of Edam or Gouda rather than the whole cheese.

1 whole 4-lb (2 kg) Edam cheese

2 lb (1 kg) chicken breasts and/or thighs

salt and freshly ground black pepper

2 tablespoons butter

2 medium onions, chopped

1 green bell pepper (capsicum), seeded and finely chopped

1 small hot pepper, seeded and finely chopped

2 tomatoes, peeled and chopped

1 tablespoon seedless raisins, chopped

1 tablespoon chopped prune

2 tablespoons pickle relish or finely chopped sweet gherkins

1 tablespoon ketchup

8 pimiento-stuffed olives, sliced

1 tablespoon drained capers

1/4 cup (2 fl oz/60 ml) dry vermouth, optional

Remove red wax from the cheese and cut a 1-inch (2.5 cm) slice off the top of the cheese; reserve for use as "lid." Hollow out the inside, leaving a 1-inch (2.5 cm) shell. Set aside.

Season chicken with salt and pepper. Melt butter in a large frying pan over medium heat. Add chicken and onions and sauté until chicken is golden and onions are translucent, about 4 to 5 minutes. Add peppers and tomatoes and simmer 40 minutes, stirring occasionally.

Remove and shred the chicken meat, discarding skin and bones. Return chicken to the frying pan. Add raisins, prune, relish, ketchup, olives, capers, and vermouth and simmer 15 minutes. Taste and adjust seasoning.

Spoon meat mixture into hollowed-out cheese and place the lid on top.

Preheat oven to 350°F (180°C/Gas 4). Butter a baking dish large enough to hold the cheese. Place cheese in the dish and bake until cheese is soft, 25 to 30 minutes (do not overcook, or the cheese will toughen). Carefully transfer the cheese to a serving dish and cut into wedges.

To use sliced cheese: Grease 6 small ovenproof dishes (or an 8 x 8 inch/20 x 20 cm baking dish) and line with 1/4-inch (5 mm) thick slices of cheese. Spoon in the filling and cover with more slices of cheese. Bake 15 minutes for individual dishes, or 20 to 25 minutes if using a larger baking dish.

STUFFED CRAB BACKS

SERVES 6

Stuffed crab backs are popular in Guadeloupe, Martinique, and Dominica.

6 fresh crabs, cleaned
butter
2 cups (8 oz/250 g) coarse fresh breadcrumbs
1/4 cup (2 fl oz/60 ml) water
3 green onions
2 cloves garlic, finely chopped
2 tablespoons finely chopped fresh parsley
3 sprigs thyme, finely chopped
1 hot pepper, seeded and finely chopped
1 tablespoon lime juice
salt and freshly ground black pepper

Drop crabs into a large pot of boiling water and boil for 10 minutes. Drain. Remove meat; clean and reserve crab backs.

Melt 1½ tablespoons butter in medium frying pan over medium heat and sauté crabmeat until lightly browned, about 3 to 4 minutes. Mix two-thirds of the breadcrumbs with the water and mash with crabmeat.

Melt ½ tablespoon butter in the frying pan and sauté onions and garlic. Add parsley, thyme, hot pepper, crabmeat mixture, lime juice, and salt and pepper to taste.

Preheat oven to 350°F (180°C/Gas 4). Stuff crab backs with the mixture, sprinkling each with some of the remaining breadcrumbs. Dot with more butter. Bake until golden brown, about 20 minutes. Serve warm.

SOUSKAÏ DE MANGUES VERTES

SERVES 4

These marinated mangoes are made from green, unripe fruit. From the French-speaking islands, they are served on toothpicks with drinks.

1 clove garlic, crushed
1 hot pepper, seeded and minced
salt to taste
2 green mangoes, peeled, seeded, and cubed
juice of 2 limes

Combine garlic, hot pepper, and salt in bowl. Stir in mangoes. Add lime juice and let stand at least 1 hour.

SOUPS

In the Caribbean many soups are served as one-pot meals, unlike European soups which are usually served as a first course. Virtually every country in the region has its own thick and hearty broth, and some are rather similar. They are traditionally eaten on Saturday afternoons as a substantial lunch, a tradition that my family continued in London.

The many Africans who were enslaved and shipped to the Caribbean not only introduced some of the everyday foods known and loved throughout the region, they also brought many of their cooking methods. In Cuba, for example, cast iron pots were commonly found in slave kitchens. Today, similar pots are still used: the "dutchie" in Jamaica, "buck pot" in Barbados, or "karahee" in Guyana. Clay pots and earthenware casseroles are still widely used and thoroughly recommended as fine cooking utensils—they absorb the flavors of seasonings and continue to add flavor to the soups and stews cooked in them.

An even older tradition that continues today is the making of the Amerindian preservative, cassareep. The end product makes an excellent seasoning for meat stews and soups alike, including Guyana's pepperpot soup.

One crucial component to any West Indian soup is the hot pepper. The whole pepper is added to all soups, the amount depends on your preference. Great care should be taken not to pierce the flesh so that just the flavor is present in the soup and not the potency. Don't forget to remove the pepper just before serving so that a poor unsuspecting guest doesn't end up eating it.

Callaloo Soup, page 40

CALLALOO SOUP

SERVES 4

This is a one of the best-known soups of the Eastern Caribbean, although it varies from island to island—in Jamaica a similar dish is known as pepperpot (see page 42). You may see it spelled calaloo, calalou, callalu or callilu, but they all refer to the same callaloo. This recipe is from Dominica. Chinese spinach, bok choy, or English spinach make good substitutes for callaloo. Salted pig's tail is sometimes used in place of the salt beef.

4 oz (125 g) salt beef or salt pork

4 cups (32 fl oz/1 l) water

1 oz (25g) dried shrimp, optional

8 oz (250 oz) callaloo leaves, washed, stemmed, and chopped

1 small onion, chopped

2 green onions, chopped

1 clove garlic, finely chopped

2 sprigs thyme or
1/2 teaspoon dried

6 okras, washed

2 whole cloves

1/2 cup (4 fl oz/125 ml) coconut milk (see page 289)

4 oz (125 g) cooked fresh or canned crabmeat

salt and freshly ground black pepper

In a heavy saucepan cover the salt meat with 3 cups (24 fl oz/750 ml) water and bring to boil. Boil about 1 hour or until meat is almost tender. Meanwhile, soak shrimp in the remaining cup of water for 1 hour. Drain and add to the saucepan with meat. Add callaloo, onions, garlic, thyme, okra, and cloves, and simmer 45 minutes.

When meat is tender, remove from water and chop into small pieces. Return to saucepan. Add coconut milk, crabmeat, and salt and pepper and simmer 5 minutes to blend flavors.

Puree mixture in a blender or food processor until smooth. Return to saucepan and reheat. Serve hot.

CALALOU AUX CRABES

In Guadeloupe they make a callaloo soup similar to the Dominican one, except it includes crab pieces and very tiny dumplings. This recipe was given to me by a wonderful cook in Point-à-Pitre. Again, Chinese spinach, bok choy, or English spinach make good substitutes for callaloo, and salted pig's tail can replace the salt beef or salt pork. Serve very hot with white rice or bakes (see page 193).

8 oz (250 g) salt beef or salt pork, washed

2 medium onions

4 green onions, chopped

3 cloves garlic

3 sprigs thyme

2 tablespoons vegetable oil

6 teaspoons chopped fresh parsley

freshly ground black pepper

4 to 5 crabs, cleaned and chopped into pieces

1 lb (500 g) callaloo leaves, washed and chopped

salt

3 whole cloves

4 okras, trimmed, and thinly sliced

1 tablespoon lemon juice

spinners (see page 145, use half the quantity and make them half the size of a walnut)

In a saucepan bring to boil enough water to cover meat. Add meat, 1/2 onion, 1 green onion, 1 clove garlic, and 1 sprig thyme. Reduce heat to medium and cook until meat has softened, about 30 minutes. Drain, discarding seasonings but reserving meat and stock. Chop meat into very small pieces.

Chop 1 onion, 1 clove garlic, and 1 spring thyme. Heat oil in a large saucepan and sauté chopped onion, thyme, and garlic with 1 green onion, 2 teaspoons parsley, and black pepper for 1 minute. Add crab pieces and sauté for 3 minutes. (A lot of liquid will appear from the crab; this is fine as it will add to the flavor of the soup.) Set aside.

Heat 1 tablespoon water in a saucepan. Add remaining onion, green onions, garlic, thyme, and parsley along with callaloo and salt to taste. Cook until callaloo has wilted, about 3 to 4 minutes. Strain callaloo and seasonings and puree in a blender or by passing through a sieve.

Add meat to pan with crab pieces followed by callaloo puree and cloves. Heat through slowly, stirring with a wooden spoon. Add okra, lemon juice and spinners and stir well. (There should not be a lot of liquid in this dish but there should be a little at the bottom of the pan. If too dry, add some reserved meat stock.) Cook, covered, over low heat for 20 more minutes.

PEPPERPOT

SERVES 6

There are many pepperpots in the West Indies. The first originated with Amerindians in Guyana, who discovered the magic ingredient that goes into it, cassareep. You can use any meat in this dish—chicken, pork, beef, or duck, for example. Often pig's trotters and cow heel are added, which also help to thicken it. Try 2 lb (1 kg) lean beef with 8 oz (250 g) oxtail. Serve it hot with rice.

about 4 cups (32 fl oz/1 l) water

2 1/2 lb (1.25 kg) lean meat, cubed

1/2 cup (4 fl oz/125 ml) cassareep (see page 282)

1 cinnamon stick

2 teaspoons raw sugar

1/2 teaspoon grated fresh ginger

4 cloves garlic

2 whole cloves

2 sprigs fresh thyme, chopped, or 1/2 teaspoon dried

2 whole red or orange hot peppers, optional

salt and ground black pepper

Bring water to boil in a medium saucepan. Add all remaining ingredients, adding more water if necessary to cover meat. Reduce heat and simmer until meat is tender, about 2 hours. Remove hot pepper before serving.

JAMAICAN PEPPERPOT SOUP

SERVES 6

8 cups (2 l) water

8 oz (250 g) pig's tail, optional

8 oz (250 g) stewing beef, cubed

1 1/2 lb (750 g) callaloo leaves, spinach, or bok choy, finely chopped

12 oz (375 g) kale, spinach, or bok choy, finely chopped

8 oz (250 g) taro, eddoes or yams, peeled and sliced

1 1/2 cups (12 fl oz/375 ml) coconut milk (see page 289)

10 okras, trimmed and thinly sliced

1 sprig thyme, chopped

1 small onion, finely chopped

2 shallots, chopped

1 whole hot green pepper

salt and ground black pepper

Bring water to boil in a large, heavy saucepan. Add pig's tail and stewing beef and cook over medium heat until meat is nearly tender, about 1 1/2 hours. Add greens, taro, and coconut milk and simmer 1 hour.

Remove greens and puree in blender with 3 tablespoons soup. Return to saucepan and add okra, thyme, onion, shallots, and hot pepper and simmer until very thick, 20 to 25 minutes, stirring frequently. Remove thyme and whole pepper. Season with salt and pepper.

Jamaican Pepperpot Soup

METAGEE

Almost every country in the Caribbean has its own hearty soup, a one-pot meal. Metagee, also known as mettem, from Guyana, is one such dish. This is a special recipe of my Aunty Golin's. You can substitute meat for the fish and add any vegetables you choose, depending on your tastes and what is available at the time.

2 lb (1 kg) fillets of snapper or
other white-fleshed fish,
cut into pieces

2 teaspoons lemon juice

salt

2 teaspoons chopped fresh parsley

1 sprig fresh thyme or
1/4 teaspoon dried

2 cups (16 fl oz/500 ml) water

2 green plantains or
green bananas, peeled and
cut into thirds

8 oz (250 g) yam,
peeled and cubed

1 lb (500 g) sweet potatoes,
peeled and cubed

1 lb (500 g) cassava,
peeled and cubed

6 black peppercorns

1/2 teaspoon finely chopped fresh
thyme or 1/4 teaspoon dried

4 cloves garlic, crushed

4 cups (32 fl oz/1 l) coconut milk
(see page 289)

2 carrots, sliced

1 large onion, sliced

dumplings (see page 154)

Rub fish with lemon juice, salt, parsley, and thyme; set aside. Bring the water to boil in a large saucepan. Add plantain, yam, sweet potatoes, cassava, peppercorns, additional thyme, garlic, and coconut milk and cook over medium heat until liquid reduces a little, about 15 to 20 minutes. Add carrots, onion, and fish and cook 5 minutes. Add dumplings, cover, and cook 10 more minutes; do not lift the lid during that time or the dumplings will not be soft and fluffy. Serve immediately.

SANCOCHE

A traditional Trinidadian Saturday lunch or one-pot meal. This soup is made from odds and ends, so it can incorporate practically any ingredients you wish. Traditionally, pickled pig's tail or snout is used in place of salt pork.

Dumplings:

1 cup (4 oz/125 g) all-purpose (plain) flour

1/2 teaspoon baking powder

1/3 cup (2 oz/60 g) cornmeal

1/8 teaspoon salt

1/2 tablespoon butter or lard

about 1/2 cup (4 fl oz/125 ml) cold water

Soup:

4 oz (125 g) dried pigeon peas, soaked overnight and drained

8 cups (2 l) water

4 oz (125 g) salt beef or corned beef, soaked 1 hour and drained

8 oz (250 g) salt pork or corned beef, cubed, soaked 1 hour, and drained

2 sprigs thyme

1 large onion, coarsely chopped

1/2 stalk celery, chopped

8 cups (2 l) coconut milk (see page 289)

2 1/2 lb (1.25 kg) tannia, eddoes, yam, cassava, and/or sweet potatoes, peeled and cut into 1 1/2-inch (4 cm) pieces

1 whole green hot pepper

2 green plantains, peeled and cut into 1 1/2-inch (4 cm) slices

12 oz (375 g) pumpkin, peeled, cleaned, and cubed

6 okras, trimmed and cut into 1/4-inch (5 mm) slices, optional

salt and freshly ground black pepper

1 tablespoon butter

For dumplings: Sift flour, baking powder, and cornmeal into mixing bowl. Add salt and butter. Gradually blend in water and knead to form stiff dough (you may not need all the water). Roll dough into small balls and set aside.

For soup: Cover pigeon peas with 8 cups water and bring to boil. Reduce heat to medium and simmer until soft, about 1 hour. Cut meat into small pieces and add to pan with remaining ingredients. Drop in dumplings and simmer over medium low heat until vegetables are cooked, about 20 minutes. Discard whole pepper and thyme before serving. Serve hot.

Following page: Sancoche, Jamaican Red Pea Soup, Sopa de Amendoim

Jamaican Red Pea Soup

SERVES 4

A traditional soup that uses Mexican chili beans, but red kidney beans are a good substitute. Taro, a root vegetable native to the Pacific region, is used to thicken the soup; potatoes could just as easily be used. Salted pig's tail, salt beef, bacon, or ham hocks could be used instead of salt pork, if desired.

10 oz (315 g) dried red kidney beans

8 oz (250 g) salt pork

1 lb (500 g) stewing beef, cubed

water

1 medium onion, chopped

3 green onions, chopped

1 sprig thyme

1 whole hot pepper

4 oz (125 g) taro or coco

8 to 10 spinners or dumplings (see page 154)

salt and freshly ground black pepper

Soak beans and pork overnight in water to cover. Drain.

In a large saucepan combine the beans, pork, and beef in 8 cups (2 l) water and bring to boil. Boil until meats are tender and beans are soft but not mushy, about 2 hours. Add onions, thyme, hot pepper, taro, and spinners and cook for 15 minutes.

Take one-third of the soup (without any spinners) and puree. Return to the pan and stir well. Discard thyme and hot pepper. Season with salt and pepper. Serve hot.

Sopa de Amendoim

SERVES 4

This peanut and chicken soup from Curaçao can be found at the Caribana in Willemstad, Otrabanda, where you can sit, eat, and enjoy the sight of the island's unique floating bridge.

8 oz (250 g) salt beef or corned beef

water

2 lb (1 kg) chicken parts

3 tablespoons peanut butter

1 onion, finely chopped

1 clove garlic, crushed

1/2 hot green pepper, seeded and finely chopped, optional

1/4 teaspoon freshly ground black pepper

salt

Boil salt beef in about 3 cups (24 fl oz/750 ml) water until tender, about 1 hour. Strain, cool, and cut into small pieces. Discard beef stock or reserve for another recipe.

Bring 4 cups (32 fl oz/1 l)water to boil, add chicken, and cook 40 minutes.

Remove chicken and discard bones; reserve stock. Whisk peanut butter into chicken stock. Add onion, garlic, hot pepper, black pepper, and salt to taste and simmer 20 minutes. Add beef and chicken to stock and heat through, about 5 to 8 minutes. Serve hot.

PUMPKIN SOUP

SERVES 6

6 oz (175 g) salt beef
or 6 oz (175 g) corned beef,
cut into small pieces

garlic salt (see page 288)

about 10 cups (2.5 l) water

2 lb (1 kg) pumpkin,
peeled, seeded, and diced

1 whole hot green hot pepper

2 sprigs thyme

1 small onion, minced

1/4 teaspoon ground or
freshly grated nutmeg

If using salt beef, soak in cold water to cover for at least 1 hour. Drain. Sprinkle meat with garlic salt and let stand at least 30 minutes.

Place meat and 8 cups (2 l) water in saucepan and simmer 1 hour over medium heat. Add pumpkin, hot pepper, thyme, and onion and cook over medium low heat until meat is tender, about 45 minutes, stirring occasionally. Add up to 2 cups (8 fl oz/250 ml) water if soup is too thick. Remove thyme and hot pepper. Stir in nutmeg and serve.

GIRAUMON SOUP

SERVES 4

Many of the French-speaking Caribbean countries have a version of this pumpkin soup with rice. This one comes from Haiti. Giraumon is the name given to pumpkin in the French Antilles.

1 lb (500 g) salt beef

water

1 1/2 lb (750 kg) pumpkin,
peeled and diced

1 small onion, finely chopped

2 green onions or 1 shallot,
finely chopped

1 sprig parsley

1 sprig thyme

2 cloves garlic, crushed

1 cup (8 fl oz/250 ml) milk

1/8 teaspoon ground or
freshly grated nutmeg

1 tablespoon butter

3/4 cup (4 oz/125 g) rice, washed

salt and freshly ground
black pepper

butter

Place salt beef in saucepan with water to cover generously. Bring to boil and cook over medium low heat, partially covered, for 1 hour. Drain and chop into small pieces.

Bring 4 cups (32 fl oz/1 l) water to boil in medium saucepan. Add pumpkin, beef, onions, parsley, thyme, and 1 clove garlic and simmer until pumpkin is tender, about 15 minutes.

Discard thyme and parsley. Transfer pumpkin to blender or food processor with 1/4 cup (2 fl oz/60 ml) stock and puree. Return to saucepan and heat through. Add milk, nutmeg, butter, and rice and cook until rice is tender, about 15 to 20 minutes. Season with salt and pepper. Stir through remaining garlic. Serve hot with a knob of butter.

SOPA DE POLLO

SERVES 4

This is a traditional Cuban chicken soup recipe given to me by Angélica Suárez, one of Cuba's best cooks. I remember spending one afternoon in Havana at Angélica's place, hoping to discover some of the secrets of Cuban cuisine. I found her energy and enthusiasm an inspiration. I hope you enjoy this as much as I did.

10 cups (2.5 l) water

2 lb (1 kg) chicken parts

1 teaspoon salt or to taste

2 cloves garlic, crushed, or
1 teaspoon garlic salt
(see page 288)

2 onions, sliced

2 teaspoons finely chopped fresh
oregano or 1/4 teaspoon dried

2 tomatoes, finely chopped

2 tablespoons tomato paste
(puree) or sofrito
(see page 276)

1 stalk celery, chopped

1 whole hot red pepper

8 oz (250 g) taro,
peeled and cubed

8 oz (250 g) sweet potato,
peeled and cubed

2 green plantains, peeled and
cut into 1 1/2-inch (4 cm) slices

8 oz (250 g) pumpkin,
peeled, cleaned, and cubed

4 oz (125 g) carrots, diced

1 chicken bouillon (stock) cube

1 teaspoon seasoned salt, optional

1 tablespoon butter

1/2 teaspoon cumin

5 oz (150 g) vermicelli, optional

Bring water to boil in large saucepan. Add chicken and salt and cook over medium heat until chicken is tender, about 20 minutes.

Add garlic, onions, oregano, tomatoes, tomato paste, celery, and hot pepper and simmer 10 minutes.

Add taro, sweet potato, plantains, pumpkin, carrots, bouillon cube, and seasoned salt and cook over low heat until vegetables are tender, about 40 to 45 minutes.

Stir in butter and cumin. Add noodles and immerse in liquid, then cover and cook until noodles are soft, about 4 to 6 minutes. Serve hot.

Sopa de Pollo

PEANUT SOUP

SERVES 6

The salt beef in this recipe gives it that distinctively Caribbean flavor. If unavailable, stewing beef makes a good substitute. Serve hot as a first course.

4 oz (125 g) salt beef or
8 oz (250 g) stewing beef

water

1 cup (8 fl oz/250 ml) chicken
stock (see page 285)

1 medium onion, chopped

1 hot red pepper,
seeded and minced

1/2 cup (4 oz/125 g) peanut butter

1 cup (8 fl oz/250 ml) milk

Soak salt beef in 4 cups (32 fl oz/1 l) water for 1 hour. Drain. Place soaked beef or stewing beef in saucepan with 3 cups (24 fl oz/750 ml) water and bring to boil, then simmer until meat is tender, about 1 hour.

Drain meat, reserving 1 cup (8 fl oz/250 ml) stock. Cut beef into small pieces and set aside.

Heat chicken stock with reserved beef stock. Add onion and hot pepper and simmer 10 minutes. Whisk in peanut butter and cook 15 minutes. Stir in milk and simmer 5 minutes, stirring until smooth. Serve hot.

CREAM OF GARBANZO SOUP

SERVES 4

A Surinamese chef living in Curaçao, Erwin Singodiojo, first told me of this soup. At first I was a bit unsure about what it would taste like, but when I tried it I was more than pleasantly surprised. It's delicious!

8 oz (250 g) chickpeas, soaked
overnight and drained

5 cups (40 fl oz/1.25 l) water

1 onion, finely chopped

2 cloves garlic, crushed

1/2 teaspoon white pepper

1/2 teaspoon cumin

salt

3/4 cup (6 fl oz/180 ml)
evaporated milk

Place chickpeas and water in saucepan and cook over medium heat, partially covered, until chickpeas are just tender, about 40 to 45 minutes.

Add onion, garlic, pepper, cumin, and salt and cook until chickpeas are soft but not mushy, about 40 more minutes.

Add evaporated milk and simmer 5 minutes. Remove soup from heat and puree in food processor or blender. Return to saucepan and stir over low heat 3 to 4 minutes. Serve hot.

BREADFRUIT SOUP

SERVES 4 TO 6

This versatile fruit appears in a multitude of Caribbean dishes and snacks. Trinidadian breadfruit soup makes a good lunchtime meal. It traditionally uses salt beef or salted pig's tail and 6 cups (1.5 l) water but you can use corned beef, chopped ham, or one smoked ham hock and 4 cups (32 fl oz/1 l) water.

8 oz (250 g) meat (see note above)

water (see note above)

1 yellow breadfruit,
peeled, cored, and sliced

4 cups (32 fl oz/1 l) coconut milk
(see page 289)

1 sprig thyme

1 medium onion, chopped

2 green onions, chopped

1 whole hot pepper

salt

chopped parsley to garnish

If necessary, boil salt meat in water until tender, about 1 hour. Drain, reserving stock. Cut meat into small pieces.

Add breadfruit to reserved stock and boil until soft, about 15 to 20 minutes. Mash until smooth or puree in food processor or blender with 1/3 cup (3 fl oz/80 ml) of the stock. Return to saucepan and add coconut milk, thyme, onions, hot pepper, and salt. Simmer 15 minutes. Discard thyme and hot pepper just before serving. Serve hot, garnished with parsley.

CONCH CHOWDER

SERVES 4 TO 6

Conch meat is very tough and has to be thoroughly pounded and marinated before cooking. This chowder is popular on St. Kitts and Nevis. There is no real substitute for conch, but abalone or the meat of other large sea mollusks will do.

2 lb (1 kg) conch meat

juice of 2 limes

water

2 large tomatoes, peeled and diced

2 medium onions, diced

1 stalk celery, chopped

1 tablespoon paprika

1 whole hot red pepper

1 tablespoon tomato paste (puree)

1/2 teaspoon ground allspice

1 bay leaf

1 sprig thyme

1/2 teaspoon salt

salt

2 tablespoons dry sherry

Pound conch meat to tenderize. Pour lime juice over and leave for 1 hour.

Place conch in saucepan with boiling salted water to cover and cook 5 minutes over medium heat. Let cool. Chop conch into 1/2-inch (1 cm) pieces.

Bring 6 cups (1.5 l) water to boil in large saucepan. Add conch, tomatoes, onions, and celery and stir well. Add all remaining ingredients except sherry, bring to boil, then simmer over low heat until conch is tender, about 1 hour. Add sherry and cook 5 more minutes. Remove whole pepper and thyme, and serve hot.

AVOCADO SOUP

SERVES 4

2 ripe avocados,
peeled, seeded, and cubed

1 clove garlic, crushed

3 cups (24 fl oz/750 ml) chicken
stock (see page 285)

1 tablespoon fresh lime juice

1 tablespoon sour cream, optional

salt and freshly ground
black pepper

1/2 to 1 teaspoon hot pepper sauce
(see page 274) or a few drops
Tabasco sauce

3 chives, finely chopped

Combine avocado, garlic, half the chicken stock, lime juice, sour cream, and salt and pepper in a blender or food processor and puree. Mix in the remaining chicken stock until smooth. Stir in hot pepper sauce. Chill the soup for at least 1 hour. Garnish with chopped chives just before serving.

FISH CHOWDER

SERVES 4 TO 6

Similar to conch chowder (see page 53), this is a favorite from Bermuda.

2 lb (1 kg) heads from non-oily fish

1 tablespoon lime juice

1 lb (500 g) fillets of red snapper or
other firm white-fleshed fish

salt and 1/2 teaspoon white pepper

1/2 teaspoon paprika

6 cups (1.5 l) water

1 onion

1 carrot, diced

1 small hot red pepper,
seeded and minced

1 stalk celery, sliced

2 sprigs thyme

2 bay leaves

1/8 teaspoon ground or
freshly grated nutmeg

1 tablespoon tomato paste (puree)

1 large tomato, peeled and chopped

1 to 2 tablespoons dry sherry,
optional

chopped fresh parsley

Clean fish heads and sprinkle with lime juice. Cut fish fillets into 2-inch (5 cm) pieces and sprinkle with salt, white pepper, and paprika.

Bring water to boil in large saucepan and add fish heads. Simmer 30 minutes. Strain, and discard fish heads.

Return fish stock to saucepan. Add onion, carrot, hot pepper, celery, thyme, bay leaves, nutmeg, tomato paste, and tomato. Simmer 20 minutes over low heat. Add fish pieces and cook for 10 more minutes. Add sherry. Garnish with parsley before serving.

Avocado Soup

54

SOPITU

SERVES 4

This soup can be found in Curaçao, St. Martin, and Aruba. Use coconut milk from the recipe on page 289, but add an extra cup of water. Use any firm, white-fleshed fish. Serve with funchi (see page 150).

1¹/₂ lb (750 g) whole fish, cleaned

lime juice

salt

2 cloves garlic, crushed

1 lb (500 g) salt beef or 8 oz (250 g) corned beef, finely chopped

4 oz (125 g) salt cod, optional

water

1 bay leaf

2 medium onions, 1 quartered and 1 finely chopped

1 stalk celery

4 cups (32 fl oz/1 l) coconut milk (see note above)

1 green bell pepper (capsicum), seeded and minced

small piece of hot pepper

¹/₈ teaspoon ground or freshly grated nutmeg

1 large tomato, peeled and finely diced

3 tablespoons cornstarch

Marinate fish in lime juice, salt, and garlic; set aside.

In separate bowls, cover beef and cod generously with water and let stand at least 1 hour to remove excess salt. Drain. Place beef and cod in saucepan with 4 cups (32 fl oz/1 l) water, bay leaf, quartered onion, and celery stalk. Bring to boil, then simmer until meat and cod are soft, about 1 hour.

Remove meat and cod and cut into ¹/₂-inch (1 cm) pieces, discarding any fish bones. Reserve 2 cups (16 fl oz/500 ml) stock, discarding vegetables.

Slowly bring coconut milk to boil in separate saucepan. Add chopped onion, bell pepper, hot pepper, nutmeg, and tomato and simmer on low heat 10 minutes. Add whole fish with garlic and simmer until cooked through, about 20 to 25 minutes.

Lift fish from stock and discard bones. Cut fish crosswise into 1¹/₂-inch (4 cm) chunks. Add reserved beef/cod stock to soup. Mix cornstarch with a little cold water and whisk into soup. Add beef, cod, and fish chunks and heat through, about 5 to 8 minutes. Season with salt and serve hot.

CORN SOUP

SERVES 6

2 lb (1 kg) chicken pieces

1 clove garlic, crushed

1 hot pepper, seeded and minced

salt

6 cups (1.5 l) water

2 sprigs thyme

1 onion, finely chopped

1 teaspoon sugar

10 ears corn, grated, or 14-oz (440 g) can creamed corn

salt and ground black pepper

2 green onions, chopped

Marinate chicken in garlic, hot pepper, and salt for 30 minutes.

Bring water to boil in large saucepan. Add chicken with marinade, thyme, onion, and sugar and cook over medium heat until chicken is cooked, about 30 minutes.

Remove chicken. Add corn and salt and pepper and simmer over medium low heat, 10 minutes if using canned corn, 15 minutes if using fresh.

Meanwhile, shred chicken into small pieces and return to soup. Add green onions and cook 5 more minutes. Remove thyme before serving. Serve hot.

Mondongo Soup

SERVES 8

It's not surprising to find that the Spanish word for tripe is the same as the name of this soup from Curaçao. The language spoken in the vast majority of the Dutch Antilles is Papiamento; it is an amazing amalgam of Spanish and Dutch with some Amerindian, Portuguese, and English as well as African syntax. In fact, nearly everyone in the Dutch Caribbean speaks more than one language.

juice of 2 limes

1 lb (500 g) tripe, cleaned

2 calf's feet, cleaned

1 large onion, coarsely chopped

1 stalk celery

1 whole hot green pepper

2 shallots, chopped

1 bay leaf

2 cloves garlic, bruised

2 large tomatoes, chopped

water

4 oz (125 g) salt beef

2 carrots, cut into strips

1 plantain, peeled and cut into 1-inch (2.5 cm) rounds, optional

1 sweet potato, peeled and cubed

3 potatoes, peeled and cubed

8 oz (250 g) pumpkin, peeled, cleaned, and cubed

1 tablespoon seedless raisins

2 teaspoons drained capers

1 beef bouillon (stock) cube

1 tablespoon dry sherry, optional

salt and freshly ground black pepper

Squeeze lime juice over tripe and calf's feet and let stand 10 minutes.

Combine tripe, calf's feet, onion, celery, hot pepper, shallots, bay leaf, garlic, tomatoes, and 6 cups (1.5 l) water in large saucepan and bring to boil. Simmer until meat is tender, about 2 to 2$^{1}/_{2}$ hours.

Meanwhile, place salt beef and 4 cups (32 fl oz/1 l) water in medium saucepan and bring to boil. Simmer 1 hour.

Remove cooked tripe and calf's feet from stock and let cool. Cut tripe into $^{1}/_{2}$-inch (1 cm) pieces and slice meat off feet, cutting it into small pieces. Strain tripe stock and discard vegetables.

Strain salt beef stock and combine with tripe stock. Cut beef into small pieces and return to stock. Add carrots, plantain, sweet potato, potatoes, and pumpkin and cook until nearly tender, 10 to 15 minutes. Add raisins, capers, bouillon cube, tripe, and meat from calf's feet and simmer 10 minutes. Add sherry and simmer 5 more minutes. Season with salt and pepper and serve.

57

SOPA DE QUINGOMBOS

SERVES 4

Although the okra is native to Africa, it has found its way into every Caribbean country in one way or another. This okra soup comes from Puerto Rico.

3 cups (24 fl oz/750 ml) chicken stock (see page 285)

1 lb (500 g) white yam or potatoes, peeled and cubed

1 tablespoon butter

1 small onion, minced

1 clove garlic, crushed

2 oz (60 g) salt pork or leg ham, finely chopped

1 tomato, peeled and finely chopped

1 whole hot red pepper, optional

8 oz (250 g) okra, trimmed and cut into 1/4-inch (5 mm) rounds

2 teaspoons tomato paste (puree)

salt

Parmesan cheese to garnish

Bring stock to boil in saucepan, add yam, and cook 10 minutes. Melt butter in frying pan over medium heat. Add onion and garlic and sauté 1 minute. Add salt pork, tomato, and hot pepper and sauté until onion is tender, about 3 to 4 minutes. Add mixture to stock with okra, tomato paste, and salt and simmer until okra is tender, about 15 minutes, stirring occasionally. Serve sprinkled with Parmesan cheese.

GIAMBO SOUP

SERVES 6

This soup from Curaçao has an unusual texture, but it is extremely tasty. The locals use an herb called yerba di hole, but basil makes a good substitute, and salted pig's tail is often used instead of salt beef. The soup makes a filling meal when eaten with funchi (see page 150).

8 oz (250 g) salt beef, salt pork, or corned beef

water

1 oz (30 g) dried shrimp (prawns)

2 onions, quartered

1 clove garlic, peeled

1 sprig basil

3 sprigs parsley

1 bay leaf, bruised

1 lb (500 g) red snapper, perch, or other white-fleshed fish, cut into large pieces

2 lb (1 kg) okra, trimmed and sliced

1/2 teaspoon ground black pepper

Cover salt meat with water and soak overnight. Drain. Cover shrimp with water to soak while preparing soup.

Bring 8 cups (2 l) water to boil in medium saucepan. Add drained meat, onions, garlic, basil, parsley, and bay leaf and simmer over low heat 1 1/2 hours.

Add fish and simmer until cooked, 10 to 15 minutes.

Remove fish. Discard bones, flake fish, and set aside. Remove meat from saucepan, cool, and chop into bite-size pieces. Strain stock, discarding vegetables and herbs, and return it to saucepan. Add okra, drained shrimp, meat, and pepper. Simmer 10 minutes. Add fish pieces and heat through. Serve hot.

Sopa de Quingombos

PÂTÉ EN POT

SERVES 10 TO 12

This thick, robust traditional soup is cooked in Martinique on special occasions and for parties. If you prefer, substitute 4 to 5 lb (2 to 2 1/2 kg) stewing lamb or mutton for the sheep parts.

12 cups (3 l) water

salt

1 lb (500 g) sheep tripe

1 sheep's head

14 oz (400 g) sheep's liver

4 sheep's feet

1 sheep's heart

2 onions, quartered

3 cloves garlic, crushed

4 whole cloves

2 bay leaves

2 sprigs thyme

1/4 cup (2 fl oz/60 ml) vegetable oil

2 onions, finely chopped

1 lb (500 g) potatoes, peeled and diced

1 lb (500 g) carrots, diced

1 lb (500 g) pumpkin, peeled, cleaned, and diced

10 oz (300 g) cabbage, washed and chopped

4 leeks, washed and chopped

4 turnips, peeled and diced

2 stalks celery, chopped

1 lb (500 g) smoked bacon, finely chopped

salt and freshly ground black pepper

2 cups (16 fl oz/500 ml) dry white wine

1/4 cup (1 oz/60 g) drained capers

Pour the water into a stockpot, add salt, and bring to boil. Add all the meat (adding more water to cover if necessary), quartered onions, garlic, cloves, bay leaves, and thyme and boil 1 hour, skimming off the fat.

Pour off stock; strain and reserve, discarding vegetables and seasonings. Remove meat from the head and feet and chop into small pieces. Dice the liver and heart.

In another saucepan large enough to hold the soup, heat oil over medium high heat. Add chopped onions and vegetables and sauté until onion is translucent. Add cooked meat and bacon and sauté until golden brown. Add reserved stock and season to taste with salt and pepper. Simmer 2 hours. Add white wine and simmer 10 minutes longer. Garnish the soup with capers and serve hot.

MANNISH WATER

SERVES 15 TO 20

This very traditional Jamaican soup is served on festive occasions and so is made in large quantities.

2 lb (1 kg) mixed goat head, feet, and tripe

water

8 oz (250 g) yam, peeled and cut into 1½-inch (4 cm) slices

1 lb (500 g) potatoes, peeled and cut into 1½ inch (4 cm) pieces

6 green bananas, peeled and cut into 1½-inch (4 cm) slices

8 oz (250 g) pumpkin, peeled and cut into 1½-inch (4 cm) slices

8 oz (250 g) christophene (chayote squash/choko), peeled and cubed

2 onions, chopped

4 cloves garlic, crushed

4 shallots, chopped

2 sprigs thyme

2 whole hot peppers

salt and ground black pepper

spinners (see page 154)

1 teaspoon ground allspice

Wash meat well and chop into very small pieces using a meat cleaver. Cover meat generously with water in large stockpot and bring to boil, then reduce heat and simmer 2 hours.

Add yam, potatoes, green bananas, pumpkin, christophene, onions, garlic, shallots, thyme, hot peppers, and salt and pepper and simmer 20 minutes. Add spinners and allspice and cook 20 more minutes. Discard hot peppers and thyme before serving. Serve hot.

TANNIA SOUP

SERVES 4 TO 6

Tannia is a hardy root vegetable that can be replaced by eddo or taro (see glossary).

2 tablespoons butter

2 lb (1 kg) tannia, peeled and cubed

1 onion, sliced

4 cups (1 l) chicken stock (see page 285)

1 teaspoon sugar

2 shallots, chopped

1 sprig thyme

1 tablespoon margarine

1 tablespoon all-purpose (plain) flour

1 cup (8 fl oz/250 ml) milk

salt and white pepper

Melt butter in deep saucepan and lightly fry tannia and onion. Add chicken stock, sugar, shallots, and thyme, bring to boil, and simmer until tannia is very soft, about 25 minutes. Discard thyme. Mash tannia until smooth, or puree in food processor or blender with about ¼ cup (2 fl oz/60 ml) soup, then return to saucepan.

Melt margarine in small saucepan over medium low heat. Add flour and cook, stirring constantly, until light brown. Slowly stir in milk and cook until mixture is thickened and smooth. Add to soup and heat through. Serve hot.

MEAT AND POULTRY

Meat and poultry play a fairly major role in the main meal of the day. Those unfamiliar with West Indian cooking will notice that salted, smoked, and pickled meats are ubiquitous in the following recipes (and, in fact, in soups). This stems from the days of early European settlement and slavery, when refrigeration was not an option for preserving and keeping meat.

Today, West Indian food would not have the same distinctive flavor without its use of salted meats. As an excess of salt can be a health hazard, many people are leaving out this component. However, for authenticity, I have left it in the recipes, providing substitutes where possible. Even though the meat is rinsed or boiled to rid some of the salt, enough remains to add the flavor essential to many dishes.

Smoking is another method still used in the region to preserve meat. In French Guiana, smoked chicken, duck, pork, and the like, are very popular and very good. The Portuguese brought the method of pickling meat to Guyana and the recipe for garlic pork in this book is a reminder of those days gone by.

Marinating meat is still of great importance in every Caribbean country. It is usually left overnight, in preparation for the next day's meal. Traditionally, spices were ground with a mortar and pestle. Seasonings were minced the same way, or by crushing them with a rolling pin on a wooden board (a technique still used in parts of the region). Perhaps the best known example of this process is Jamaica's jerk meat—try the jerk chicken recipe in this book for a sensational introduction to a very old seasoning method.

Bajan Fried Chicken, page 72

CHICKEN CURRY

SERVES 4

A favorite of mine, which I would often help my grandmother and mother to prepare for the family.

3 tablespoons vegetable oil

1 large onion, chopped

2 green onions, chopped

1/4 green bell pepper (capsicum), seeded and chopped

1/4 red bell pepper (capsicum), seeded and chopped

2 to 3 cloves garlic, finely chopped

1 tablespoon curry powder

1/4 teaspoon turmeric

1/2 teaspoon cumin

1/4 teaspoon garam masala

1 sprig thyme or 1/2 teaspoon dried thyme

1/4 teaspoon celery salt (see recipe on page 288)

1 cup (8 fl oz/250 ml) water

11/2 lb (750 g) chicken pieces

1 medium potato, peeled and cut into 11/2-inch (4 cm) cubes

1/4 teaspoon salt

1/4 teaspoon freshly ground black pepper

1 teaspoon tomato paste (puree)

Heat oil in a medium saucepan and sauté onions, bell peppers, and garlic until onion is tender and golden.

In a small bowl mix curry powder, turmeric, cumin, garam masala, thyme, and celery salt with enough water (from the 1 cup) to form a smooth paste. Add to the onion mixture; rinse out the bowl with a bit more of the water and add to the mixture. (Reserve remaining water.) Fry over high heat until the curry paste is quite dry, stirring frequently to prevent burning.

Add chicken and stir well. Fry over high heat for a few minutes, then reduce to medium heat. Add potato, salt, pepper, and tomato paste and cook 5 minutes. Add remaining water and stir to immerse potatoes in liquid. Cover and cook over medium low heat until chicken and potatoes are cooked, about 25 minutes, stirring occasionally. Serve hot.

BAKED CHICKEN

SERVES 4

Serve with boiled rice (see page 174) or rice and peas (see page 145).

2 lb (1 kg) chicken parts

1 onion, minced

2 cloves garlic, crushed

1/2 green bell pepper (capsicum), seeded and minced

2 tablespoons malt vinegar

1 tablespoon tomato paste (puree)

1 tablespoon soy sauce

1 hot green pepper, seeded and minced, optional

1/2 teaspoon ground allspice

salt and freshly ground black pepper

1 tablespoon butter

Place chicken in large bowl. Add onion, garlic, bell pepper, vinegar, tomato paste, soy sauce, hot pepper, allspice, and salt and pepper and marinate 2 hours or refrigerate overnight.

Preheat oven to 350°F (180°C/Gas 4). Place chicken and marinade in large baking dish and dot with butter. Cover and bake 30 minutes. Increase heat to 400°F (200°C/Gas 6), uncover, and bake until the chicken is browned, about 10 minutes longer. Pour the sauce from bottom of pan over chicken to serve.

FRICASSÉE DE POULET

SERVES 4 TO 6

This dish from the French Antilles can be served with boiled rice and haricots rouges (see page 141) or yams and sweet potatoes (see page 185).

3 tablespoons vegetable oil

juice of 2 limes

3 sprigs thyme, chopped

1/4 teaspoon ground allspice

2 cloves garlic

1 hot pepper, seeded and minced

salt

2 lb (1 kg) chicken parts

1 tablespoon butter or margarine

1 onion, minced

1 cup (8 fl oz/250 ml) water

1 bouquet garni (thyme, green onion, and parsley wrapped in cheesecloth/muslin)

2 bay leaves

freshly ground black pepper

Combine 1 tablespoon oil, lime juice, thyme, allspice, 1 chopped garlic clove, hot pepper, and salt in large dish. Add chicken and marinate in refrigerator 2 hours, turning pieces occasionally. Drain chicken, reserving marinade.

Melt butter with 2 tablespoons oil in large frying pan over medium heat. Add chicken and onion and sauté until chicken is browned and onion is tender. Pour in marinade. Add water, bouquet garni, and bay leaves; season with salt and pepper. Simmer 45 minutes.

Before serving, remove bouquet garni and bay leaves and add remaining clove of garlic, crushed. Stir well and serve hot.

Poulet au Lait de Coco

SERVES 4 TO 6

Served with rice, this dish appears in the French-speaking islands of Guadeloupe, Martinique, and Haiti, with some variation from island to island. To make the bouquet garni, wrap the herbs in a cheesecloth (muslin) pouch.

2 tablespoons butter

2 lb (1 kg) chicken pieces

1 large onion, finely chopped

2 cloves garlic, finely chopped

2 teaspoons curry powder

pinch saffron

1 1/2 cups (12 fl oz/375 ml) coconut milk (see page 289)

1/4 cup (2 fl oz/60 ml) chicken stock (see page 285)

bouquet garni (1 sprig thyme, 1 green onion, 8 parsley leaves)

1/2 teaspoon salt

freshly ground black pepper

Melt butter in a deep frying pan over medium heat and brown chicken on all sides. Add onion, garlic, curry powder, and saffron and cook for a few minutes. Add coconut milk, chicken stock, bouquet garni, salt, and pepper. Mix well, cover, and simmer until chicken is tender, about 40 minutes, stirring occasionally. Remove bouquet garni before serving.

Colombo de Poulet

SERVES 4 TO 6

This chicken curry from Martinique and Guadeloupe should be served with white rice.

1/4 cup (2 fl oz/60 ml) peanut oil

2 lb (1 kg) chicken pieces

1 medium onion, finely chopped

2 green onions, finely chopped

2 cloves garlic, minced

2 tablespoons curry powder

1/2 teaspoon ground allspice

2 cups (16 fl oz/500 ml) water

1 tablespoon white wine vinegar

3 sprigs thyme, finely chopped, or 1 teaspoon dried

1 tablespoon minced fresh parsley

1/4 cup (1 oz/30 g) dried chickpeas, soaked overnight and drained

1 large carrot, diced

2 zucchini (courgettes), sliced

1 hot pepper, seeded and finely chopped

Heat oil in large, deep saucepan over high heat and brown chicken. Reduce heat to medium high, add onions and garlic, and cook until soft. Add curry powder, allspice, water, vinegar, thyme, parsley, and chickpeas. Reduce heat to low, cover, and cook 40 minutes.

Add carrot, zucchini, and hot pepper and cook until vegetables are tender. Serve hot.

Poulet au Lait de Coco

JERK CHICKEN

SERVES 6

This recipe is from Jamaica, where it is enormously popular. The technique of "jerking" is very old and traditionally pork was used. It is the process of marinating meat with hot peppers and spices. The meat would be roasted over a fire made up of fresh allspice branches and leaves, whose smoke added an extra sweet and aromatic character to an already tasty dish—in some parts of the countryside this method is still used. Nevertheless, roasting in the oven still produces a good "jerk". This recipe can be used to jerk pork if you wish.

1 1/2 teaspoons ground allspice or 1/2 oz (15 g) dried allspice berries

1/4-inch (5 mm) cinnamon stick or 1/4 teaspoon ground cinnamon

1 medium onion, coarsely chopped

3 green onions, coarsely chopped

3 cloves garlic, coarsely chopped

2 hot peppers, seeded and chopped

2 sprigs fresh thyme or 1/2 teaspoon dried

1/4 teaspoon chopped fresh ginger

2 tablespoons soy sauce

1 1/2 teaspoons salt

1/2 teaspoon freshly ground black pepper

2 tablespoons water

3 lb (1.5 kg) chicken pieces

6 tablespoons vegetable oil

If using whole spices, grind allspice berries and cinnamon stick to a powder in a spice mill.

If using a food processor, mince onions, garlic, hot peppers, thyme, and ginger. Transfer to mixing bowl. Add ground spices, soy sauce, salt, pepper, and water and mix thoroughly.

If not using a food processor, mince onions, garlic, hot peppers, thyme, and ginger. Transfer to mortar and add soy sauce. Grind to a paste with pestle. Add ground spices, salt, pepper, and water and mix thoroughly.

Place chicken in a large baking dish and coat evenly with spice mixture. Cover and refrigerate 3 hours.

Preheat oven to 350°F (180°C/Gas 4). Sprinkle oil over chicken pieces. Bake uncovered until cooked through, about 50 minutes.

ESSEQUIBO CHICKEN

SERVES 4

This playfully entitled dish is named after Guyana's mighty Essequibo River which, along with the Berbice and Demarara rivers, helps to make Guyana the land of many waters. Serve with white boiled rice (see page 174), ground provisions (see page 185), or plantain.

3 tablespoons vegetable oil

1 teaspoon raw sugar

2 lb (1 kg) chicken parts

3 cloves garlic, crushed

1 onion, chopped

1/4 teaspoon garlic salt
(see page 288)

1/4 teaspoon celery salt
(see page 288)

2 sprigs thyme, finely chopped

2 green onions, chopped

1/4 red bell pepper (capsicum),
seeded and cut into thin strips

1 medium tomato, chopped

1 bay leaf, bruised

1 tablespoon tomato paste (puree)

1 1/4 cups (10 fl oz/300 ml) water

2 teaspoons cornstarch

1/4 teaspoon freshly ground
black pepper

Heat oil in large saucepan over medium heat until hot. Sprinkle with sugar and let bubble about 30 seconds. Add chicken pieces and fry, browning evenly.

Add garlic and onion and fry 1 minute. Stir in garlic salt, celery salt, thyme, green onions, and bell pepper. Add tomato and bay leaf and cook 2 minutes. Add tomato paste and all but 2 tablespoons water. Reduce heat to simmer and cook 20 minutes.

Combine cornstarch and remaining water and stir into chicken mixture. Season with pepper. Cook until sauce is thickened. Serve hot.

Following page: Essequibo Chicken, Bajan Fried Chicken, Fricasseed Chicken

BAJAN FRIED CHICKEN

SERVES 4 TO 6

From Barbados, this fried chicken has a distinctively Bajan flavor. Roadside fruit and vegetable stalls on the island sell "seasoning"—which usually refers only to green onion.

1 onion, minced

2 green onions, including some of green part, minced

1/2 green bell pepper (capsicum), seeded and minced

1 hot pepper, seeded and minced, optional

1 sprig fresh thyme, minced, or 1/4 teaspoon dried

2 teaspoons fresh marjoram, minced, or 1 teaspoon dried

2 cloves garlic, minced

2 tablespoons water

1 tablespoon ketchup

2 lb (1 kg) chicken parts

about 2 cups (16 fl oz/500 ml) vegetable or corn oil for frying

1 cup (4 oz/125 g) all-purpose (plain) flour

1/2 teaspoon baking powder

salt

1/2 teaspoon freshly ground black pepper

Combine minced ingredients, water, and ketchup in large bowl. Rub into chicken and marinate 1 hour or longer.

Heat oil in frying pan until hot. Combine flour, baking powder, salt, and pepper. Pat chicken pieces dry with paper towels and coat with flour mixture. Fry chicken over medium heat until cooked and golden brown on both sides, 15 to 20 minutes. Serve hot.

FRICASSEED CHICKEN

SERVES 4 TO 6

Originally Spanish, this dish can be found in all parts of the West Indies; this recipe comes from Jamaica. Serve with rice and peas (see page 145) and fried yellow plantain (see page 170).

3 lb (1.5 kg) chicken parts

salt and 1/2 teaspoon freshly ground black pepper

1/2 teaspoon garlic salt (see page 288)

1/2 green bell pepper (capsicum), seeded and minced

1/4 cup (2 fl oz/60 ml) vegetable oil

1 large onion, chopped

1 clove garlic, finely chopped

2 medium tomatoes, chopped

1 sprig thyme, finely chopped

1/2 teaspoon paprika

1 whole hot pepper

1/4 cup (2 fl oz/60 ml) water

Sprinkle chicken with salt, black pepper, garlic salt, and bell pepper and marinate 2 hours or refrigerate overnight.

Heat oil in deep frying pan over medium high heat. Scrape off marinade from chicken and fry chicken until golden brown on both sides. Drain excess oil from pan. Add onion, garlic, tomatoes, thyme, paprika, and hot pepper and sauté until tomatoes are soft, 3 to 4 minutes. Add water and bring to boil, then cover and simmer over low heat until chicken is cooked, about 20 minutes, stirring occasionally. Serve hot.

BAJAN BROWN STEW

SERVES 4

A good brown stew can be had in Baxter's Road, Barbados, but if you can't get there, try making this one. Serve with white rice, rice and peas (see page 145), or ground provisions (see page 185).

2 lb (1 kg) stewing beef, cubed

2 cups (16 fl oz/500 ml) water

2 tablespoons browning sauce

1/2 teaspoon garlic powder or garlic salt (see page 288)

1 tablespoon butter

1 small onion, minced

2 shallots, finely chopped

1/2 green bell pepper (capsicum), seeded and chopped

1 hot green pepper, seeded and finely chopped

1 sprig thyme, finely chopped

2 sprigs marjoram, finely chopped

1 clove garlic, minced

pinch of sugar

salt

Place beef and water in a saucepan and bring to boil. Add browning sauce and cook until beef has browned, about 10 to 15 minutes. Add remaining ingredients and cook over medium low heat until meat is tender, about 45 minutes. Serve hot.

Arroz con Pollo

Literally rice with chicken, this typical Cuban dish is excellent for lunch or dinner. If you have an earthenware pot, use it for an authentic touch in this recipe. The seasonings used to make up the sofrito form the basis of countless dishes from the Spanish-speaking islands. The chicken stock should be made to the recipe on page 285 but with the addition of 1 sprig parsley, 1/4 green bell pepper (capsicum), 1 small onion, quartered, and 1 teaspoon salt. Try garnishing this dish with a handful of cooked green beans, thinly sliced red bell pepper (capsicum), or slices of hard-cooked egg.

3 lb (1.5 kg) chicken pieces

2 cloves garlic, crushed

juice of 1 lemon

freshly ground black pepper

1/4 teaspoon cumin

1/4 teaspoon dried oregano

3 tablespoons vegetable oil

1 medium onion, finely chopped

3/4 green bell pepper (capsicum), seeded and chopped

1/4 cup (2 fl oz/60 ml) tomato paste (puree) or 1 cup (8 fl oz/250 ml) canned tomatoes or 2 tomatoes, finely chopped

1/4 teaspoon paprika

1 cup (2 fl oz/60 ml) dry white wine

4 cups (32 fl oz/1 l) chicken stock (see note above)

1 bay leaf

2 cups (10 oz/300 g) rice

Season chicken with garlic, lemon juice, pepper, cumin, and oregano. Heat oil in an earthenware pot or large saucepan over medium heat. Add onion and bell pepper and sauté until onion is translucent. Add seasoned chicken pieces and brown on all sides. Pour off excess fat. Stir in tomato, paprika, wine, stock, and bay leaf and bring to boil. Reduce heat and simmer for 10 minutes. Taste and adjust seasoning.

Add rice and boil 3 minutes. Reduce heat, cover, and cook until rice and chicken are tender, about 20 to 25 minutes. Serve hot.

Arroz con Pollo

CHICKEN CHOW MEIN

SERVES 4 TO 6

The Chinese workers in the Caribbean brought with them many excellent dishes that have become everyday food throughout the region. Beef or pork can be substituted for chicken.

3 tablespoons peanut or corn oil

1 lb (500 g) chicken breast, cut into 1-inch (2.5 cm) pieces

1/2 teaspoon garlic salt (see page 288)

1 tablespoon soy sauce

1 onion, chopped

1 green onion, chopped

2 cloves garlic, finely chopped

1 sprig thyme, finely chopped

1 hot pepper, seeded and minced

1/2 stalk celery, finely chopped

1 shallot, chopped

1/2 teaspoon tomato paste (puree)

1/2 cup (2 oz/60 g) cooked green beans, cut into 1/2-inch (1 cm) pieces

1/2 cup (2 oz/60 g) diced cooked carrots

2 tablespoons water

8 oz (250 g) egg noodles, cooked, drained, and rinsed

Heat oil in large saucepan or wok over high heat and stir-fry chicken with garlic salt until browned on all sides. Stir in soy sauce. Add onions, garlic, thyme, hot pepper, and celery and stir-fry until onions are cooked but slightly crispy. Add tomato paste, beans, carrots, salt to taste, and water. Reduce heat to low and cook for 4 minutes. Add noodles and combine well. Serve hot.

BAMI

SERVES 4

These fried noodles are a popular dish in Suriname, formerly a Dutch colony. Dutch dominance in the region provided the pathway for Indonesian influence on the cuisine. This would traditionally be served with sambal, a red chili condiment.

1/4 cup (2 fl oz/60 ml) vegetable oil

8 oz (250 g) pork, cubed

3 1/2 oz (100 g) dried shrimp (prawns), soaked in 1 cup (8 fl oz/250 ml) water and drained

1 large onion, finely chopped

1 leek, sliced

4 cloves garlic, finely chopped

1/4 teaspoon trasi (dried shrimp paste)

2 hot red peppers, seeded and minced

2 fresh bay leaves or 1 dried

8 oz (250 g) fine vermicelli noodles, cooked and drained

2 tablespoons soy sauce

3 1/2 oz (100 g) cabbage, finely chopped

3 oz (90 g) bean sprouts, washed

2 green onions, chopped

Heat oil in medium frying pan over high heat and stir-fry pork 1 to 2 minutes until browned. Add shrimp and cook 1 more minute.

Add onion, leek, garlic, trasi, hot peppers, and bay leaves and sauté until onion is translucent, about 2 minutes. Add noodles and stir well. Add soy sauce, cabbage, bean sprouts, and green onions and heat through, stirring frequently. Serve hot.

GRIOT

This marinated fried pork is a popular Haitian dish. It can be eaten as a main meal or as a snack.

2 lb (1 kg) pork loin, cubed

2 cloves garlic, crushed

2 medium onions, finely chopped

4 green onions, finely chopped

2 hot peppers,
seeded and finely chopped

salt and freshly ground
black pepper

juice of 2 limes

1/2 cup (4 fl oz/125 ml)
fresh juice from underripe or
Seville oranges

about 1 cup (8 fl oz/250 ml) water

about 1 cup (8 fl oz/250 ml)
vegetable oil

Place pork in bowl and add garlic, onions, hot peppers, salt, pepper, and citrus juices. Marinate at least 1 hour.

Transfer pork with marinade to large saucepan and add just enough water to cover meat. Bring to boil. Immediately reduce heat to simmer and cook until meat is tender and most of the liquid is evaporated, about 1 hour.

Drain meat. Heat oil in saucepan over medium high heat. Add pork and fry until well browned. Drain on paper towels and serve hot.

CHOP SUEY

Another popular Chinese dish that is very quick and easy to prepare. Although this recipe is from Jamaica, it can be found in many Caribbean countries. Serve with boiled white rice (see page 174).

1 chicken breast, boned
and cut into small pieces

1 teaspoon grated fresh ginger

2 cloves garlic, crushed

salt and freshly ground pepper

2 tablespoons soy sauce

1 teaspoon sugar

5 tablespoons water

3 tablespoons vegetable oil

2 carrots, diced

1 large onion, thinly sliced

1 celery stalk, chopped

1 small can bamboo shoots, drained

2 teaspoons cornstarch

6 oz (185 g) bean sprouts, washed

2 green onions, green part only,
chopped

Combine chicken, ginger, garlic, salt, pepper, soy sauce, sugar, and 1 tablespoon of the water in bowl and marinate 1 hour. Drain, reserving marinade.

Heat oil in medium saucepan or wok over high heat and stir-fry chicken until browned. Add carrots and stir-fry for 1 minute. Add onion, celery, and bamboo shoots and cook over low heat 4 minutes, stirring frequently. Stir in marinade. Mix cornstarch with remaining water and add to pan. Add bean sprouts and green onions and stir-fry until cooked, about 2 more minutes. Serve immediately.

Chop Suey

TRINIDAD PILAU

This recipe is from my Trinidadian aunt, Seeta. Parboiled rice is sold commercially and is easily obtainable. This type of rice is parboiled while still in the husk.

5 cloves garlic, crushed

1 medium onion, finely chopped

1 large green onion, chopped

8 celery leaves, minced

2 sprigs thyme, chopped

2 tablespoons ketchup

2 tablespoons soy sauce

1 hot pepper, chopped

salt

2 lb (1 kg) chicken parts

5 tablespoons vegetable
or corn oil

2 tablespoons raw
or brown sugar

3 cups (1 lb/500 g) rice,
parboiled

4 tablespoons margarine
or butter

2 1/2 cups (20 fl oz/600 ml) water

1/2 cup (2 oz/60 g)
cooked green peas

1/2 cup (2 oz/60 g)
cooked diced carrots

Combine garlic, onion, green onion, celery leaves, thyme, ketchup, soy sauce, hot pepper, and salt to taste in large bowl. Add chicken and coat with marinade. Cover and refrigerate at least 2 hours, preferably overnight. Scrape off and reserve marinade.

Heat oil in a large, heavy saucepan over medium heat. Add sugar and cook until it is dissolved and syrup darkens. Add chicken pieces and brown over medium high heat, 4 to 5 minutes. Add marinade. Add a little water to the bowl to rinse out marinade; set aside. Cover saucepan, reduce heat to medium low, and cook chicken 15 minutes.

Rinse rice in strainer until water runs clear. Add to chicken along with margarine and stir constantly until rice begins to stick. Add water and reserved marinade-water, stir, cover, and simmer until rice is cooked, 15 to 20 minutes. Stir in peas and carrots. Serve warm.

Pelau Rice

Also known as "seasoned rice," this is very popular in Antigua. Serve it with a green salad (see page 160).

8 oz (250 g) salt beef or corned beef, cubed

¼ cup (2 fl oz/60 ml) vegetable oil

1 lb (500 g) chicken parts

1 large onion, chopped

2 green onions, chopped

2 cloves garlic, crushed

1 sprig thyme, chopped

½ red bell pepper (capsicum), seeded and chopped

6 oz (185 g) pumpkin, peeled and cleaned

3 cups (1 lb/500 g) rice, rinsed until water runs almost clear

1 tablespoon soy sauce

2 tablespoons margarine

1 tablespoon ketchup

salt and freshly ground black pepper

1 cup (6 oz/175 g) dried red peas or pigeon peas, soaked overnight and drained

about 6 cups (1.5 l) water

Soak salt beef 1 hour in water to cover. Drain.

Heat oil in a large saucepan over medium high heat. Add chicken and fry 2 minutes. Add beef, then onions, garlic, thyme, bell pepper, and pumpkin. Stir in rice, then soy sauce, magarine, ketchup, and salt and pepper and fry 3 minutes. Add peas and fry for 1 more minute. Add water to cover and bring to boil for 3 minutes, then reduce heat, cover, and simmer until all liquid is absorbed, about 25 minutes.

ASOPAO DE POLLO

SERVES 6

This dish from Puerto Rico can be cooked with chicken, pork, shrimp, or lobster. It is a thick stew—precisely what asopao means.

1 cup (8 oz/250 g) rice

2 cloves garlic, crushed

1 teaspoon finely chopped fresh oregano or 1/4 teaspoon dried

2 teaspoons salt

1/8 teaspoon paprika

2 teaspoons olive oil

1 teaspoon white vinegar

1 cup (8 fl oz/250 ml) sofrito II (see page 276)

8 pimiento-stuffed olives

1 medium tomato, chopped

1 tablespoon drained capers

2 tablespoons tomato paste (puree)

3 1b (1.5 kg) chicken pieces

8 cups (2 l) chicken stock (see page 285)

Garnish:

1/2 cup (4 oz/125 g) cooked green peas

1/2 cup (4 oz/125 g) cooked asparagus tips

1 red bell pepper (capsicum), seeded and sliced

Soak rice in enough cold water to cover by 1 inch (2.5 cm). Let stand while preparing asopao.

In a small bowl combine garlic, oregano, salt, paprika, oil, and vinegar. Rub into chicken and set aside for 30 minutes if possible.

Combine sofrito, olives, tomato, capers, and tomato paste in a large saucepan over medium heat. Add chicken. Reduce heat, cover, and cook 20 minutes, turning occasionally.

Add stock, increase heat to high, and bring to boil. Drain rice and stir into saucepan. Return to boil, then reduce heat to low, cover, and cook until rice is tender, 15 to 20 minutes, stirring occasionally. Serve immediately, garnished with peas, asparagus tips, and slices of red pepper.

Asopao de Pollo

SANCOCHO

SERVES 6

Sancocho is found on all the Spanish-speaking islands. Any meat, such as pork, chicken, beef, even goat's head, can be used in this stew instead of the salt pork and stewing beef combination. Spinach, Chinese spinach, or bok choy can be substituted for callaloo. This recipe is from the Dominican Republic; although almost a meal in itself, it is eaten with boiled white rice (see page 174).

12 oz (375 g) salt pork, cubed

12 oz (375 g) stewing beef

about 3 cups
(24 fl oz/750 ml) water

2 onions, chopped

2 cloves garlic, chopped

2 stalks celery, chopped

1 green bell pepper (capsicum),
seeded and minced

1 tablespoon finely chopped
fresh parsley

1 tablespoon finely chopped
cilantro (fresh coriander leaves)

1 whole hot pepper

4 cups (32 fl oz/1 l) meat stock

2 green plantains, peeled and
cut into 2½-inch (7 cm) pieces

4 oz (125 g) cassava, peeled and
cut into 1-inch (2.5 cm) pieces

4 oz (125 g) yautia, taro, or yam,
peeled and cut into
1-inch (2.5 cm) pieces

4 oz (125 g) sweet potato, peeled
and cut into 1-inch (2.5 cm) pieces

4 oz (125 g) pumpkin, peeled and
cut into 1-inch (2.5 cm) pieces

1 tablespoon olive oil

salt and freshly ground
black pepper

8 oz (250 g) callaloo leaves,
washed, stemmed,
and coarsely chopped

1 tablespoon dry sherry

Place salt pork and beef in a large saucepan with the water, adding more if necessary to cover meat. Bring to boil, then reduce heat to low and simmer 45 minutes.

Add all remaining ingredients except callaloo and sherry, cover, and continue to simmer 15 minutes.

Add callaloo and sherry and simmer until meat and all vegetables are tender, about 20 more minutes. Serve hot.

MARINATED BEEF STEW

SERVES 4

My mother used to serve this for Sunday lunch with a Jamaican-style rice and peas (see page 145).

1 large onion, chopped

3 cloves garlic, chopped

1/2 red bell pepper (capsicum), seeded and chopped

1/2 green bell pepper (capsicum), seeded and chopped

2 tomatoes, chopped

2 teaspoons chopped fresh thyme or 3/4 teaspoon dried

1/2 teaspoon ground allspice or 10 dried allspice berries, crushed

1/4 teaspoon celery salt (see page 288) or handful of chopped celery leaves

1/4 teaspoon garlic salt (see page 288)

freshly ground black pepper

1 1/2 lb (750 g) lean stewing beef, cut into 1-inch (2 cm) cubes

3 to 4 tablespoons vegetable oil

1 teaspoon brown sugar

2 small hot red peppers, seeded and chopped, optional

1 beef bouillon (stock) cube, dissolved in 1 1/2 cups (12 fl oz/ 375 ml) hot water

Combine onion, garlic, bell peppers, tomatoes, thyme, allspice, celery salt, garlic salt, and pepper in a large container with lid. Add beef and stir to coat with marinade. Cover and refrigerate overnight.

Remove beef from marinade; set marinade aside. Heat oil until hot in large frying pan. Add sugar and cook until it begins to bubble. Add beef and sauté over high heat until very brown, stirring frequently to prevent sticking. Pour off excess oil. Add marinade, reduce heat to medium, and sauté, stirring frequently, until onion is soft. Add hot peppers and stock and bring to boil. Cover and simmer over medium low heat until beef is tender, 30 to 40 minutes. Serve hot.

Following page: Marinated Beef Stew, Picadillo, Ropa Vieja

PICADILLO

This is a very popular Cuban dish and should be served with boiled rice (see page 174) and frijoles negros (see page 142).

2 lb (1 kg) lean
ground (minced) beef

2 teaspoons salt

1/4 cup (2 fl oz/60 ml) annatto oil
(see page 285) or vegetable oil

1 large onion, finely chopped

2 cloves garlic, finely chopped

1 green bell pepper (capsicum),
seeded and finely chopped

2 hot peppers,
seeded and finely chopped

1/4 teaspoon cumin

1 tablespoon finely chopped
cilantro (fresh coriander leaves)

1 teaspoon chopped fresh oregano
or 1/2 teaspoon dried

1 tablespoon chopped
fresh parsley

1 tablespoon tomato paste (puree)

1 tablespoon vinegar, lemon juice,
or dry white wine

1/4 cup (2 fl oz/60 ml) beef stock

8 pimento-stuffed olives

2 oz (60 g) seedless raisins

Boil meat with 1 teaspoon salt in water to cover until meat is tender, about 20 minutes. Drain.

Heat oil in a large frying pan over medium heat. Add onion, garlic, peppers, and cumin and sauté until onion is soft, about 4 minutes. Stir in meat, herbs, tomato paste, vinegar, stock, olives, raisins, and remaining 1 teaspoon salt, and cook over low heat for 10 minutes.

Ropa Vieja

SERVES 4 TO 6

A dish found throughout the Spanish-speaking islands; its name literally translates as "old clothes". This traditionally uses leftover vegetables and meat, such as roast. Serve with rice or fried potatoes.

2 lb (1 kg) leftover meat, cubed

1 teaspoon salt or to taste

2 cloves garlic, finely chopped

1/4 cup (2 fl oz/60 ml) olive oil

1 large onion, finely chopped

1/2 green bell pepper (capsicum), seeded and chopped

1 teaspoon chopped fresh oregano or 1/4 teaspoon dried

1 large tomato, chopped

1 tablespoon tomato paste (puree)

1 hot pepper, seeded and finely chopped

1 tablespoon drained capers

Season meat with salt and garlic. Heat oil in medium saucepan over medium high heat. Add onion and bell pepper and sauté until onion is translucent, 1 minute. Stir in oregano, tomato, and tomato paste and cook for 5 minutes. Add meat, hot pepper, and capers, reduce heat to low, and cook for 8 more minutes, stirring occasionally. Serve hot.

Ragoût de Boeuf

SERVES 4 TO 6

Enjoy this stew from Martinique with boiled rice (see page 174) or ground provisions (see page 185).

3 tablespoons vegetable oil

2 lb (1 kg) beef, cubed

1 small onion, chopped

2 green onions, chopped

2 cloves garlic, crushed

1/2 cup (4 fl oz/125 ml) water

1 whole hot pepper

3 sprigs fresh thyme or 1 teaspoon dried

2 tablespoons finely chopped fresh parsley

1 bay leaf

1/4 teaspoon ground allspice

1 tablespoon tomato paste (puree)

1 tablespoon white vinegar

1 teaspoon lime juice

salt and white pepper

Heat oil in a deep frying pan over medium high heat. Add beef and sauté until well browned on all sides. Add onions and garlic and sauté until onion is translucent. Add water, whole pepper, herbs, allspice, tomato paste, vinegar, lime juice, and salt and pepper. Stir well. Simmer over low heat until meat is tender, about 45 to 60 minutes. Remove hot pepper, thyme sprigs, and bay leaf and serve hot.

GOAT CURRY

SERVES 4 TO 6

Jamaica is one of the best places to get this curry. Many other islands also have curries, and naturally they vary from island to island. Mutton or lamb is often used and requires a shorter cooking time. This is one of my mother's recipes. If you have time, it is well worth marinating overnight. The bones are left in because they add a rich sweetness. Serve the curry with white rice or rice and peas (see page 145).

2 lb (1 kg) goat
(with bones), cubed

1 medium onion, finely chopped

4 green onions, finely chopped

2 cloves garlic, finely chopped

1/2 red bell pepper (capsicum), seeded and finely chopped

1/2 green bell pepper (capsicum), seeded and finely chopped

3 sprigs fresh thyme, finely chopped, or 3/4 teaspoon dried

2 tablespoons curry powder

2 teaspoons cumin

1 teaspoon finely grated fresh turmeric or 1/2 teaspoon powdered

1 teaspoon garam masala

3 tablespoons vegetable oil

4 large celery leaves, finely chopped, or 1/4 teaspoon celery seed, or 1 to 2 teaspoons celery salt (see page 288)

freshly ground black pepper

3/4 to 11/4 cups (6 to 10 fl oz/ 175 to 300 ml) water

1 medium potato, peeled and cut into 11/2-inch (4 cm) cubes

Combine meat, onions, garlic, bell peppers, and thyme in a large nonmetal container. Combine curry powder, cumin, turmeric, and garam masala and rub into meat to coat well. Cover and refrigerate overnight.

Heat oil in a large saucepan over medium high heat. As much as possible, scrape chopped ingredients from meat and sauté these in hot oil until onions are soft, 3 to 4 minutes, stirring constantly. Add meat and cook 10 minutes, stirring frequently. Add celery leaves and pepper. Reduce heat to low, add 3/4 cup water, and cook 11/2 hours, stirring occasionally.

Cut one-third of the potato cubes in half (these will thicken the curry). Add potatoes to pan and, if water has evaporated, add enough water to cover. Cover pan and simmer until potatoes are tender, about 15 minutes. Serve hot.

Goat Curry

STOBÁ DI CABRITO

SERVES 6

Stobá is a meat stew eaten in the Dutch-speaking islands. This recipe uses lamb, although traditionally kid may be used instead. This version, from Curaçao, should be served with boiled white rice (see page 174).

$2^{1}/_{2}$ cups (20 fl oz/625 ml) beef stock, or 4 oz (125 g) salt beef cooked in $2^{3}/_{4}$ cups (22 fl oz/680 ml) water

2 tablespoons vegetable or corn oil

2 lb (1 kg) lean lamb, cubed

1 medium onion, finely chopped

2 cloves garlic, crushed

1 green bell pepper (capsicum), seeded and finely chopped

1 hot pepper, seeded and finely chopped

2 medium tomatoes, peeled and diced

1 tablespoon fresh lime juice

$^{1}/_{4}$ teaspoon ground or freshly grated nutmeg

2 tablespoons annatto oil (see page 285)

salt and freshly ground black pepper

2 potatoes, peeled and cubed

If using salt beef, soak overnight in water to cover. Drain, discarding water. Combine salt beef and 4 cups fresh water in large saucepan, cover, and simmer 1 hour. Strain and reserve stock. Cube beef and set aside.

Heat oil in same saucepan over high heat and brown the lamb. Add onion, garlic, and peppers and cook until onion is tender, reducing heat as necessary to prevent burning. Stir in tomatoes, lime juice, nutmeg, annatto oil, cubed beef (if using), and salt and pepper to taste and simmer 15 minutes.

Add reserved beef stock, cover, and simmer 30 minutes. Add potatoes and cook until tender, about 15 minutes. Serve hot.

LAMB CURRY

SERVES 4

This is one of my family's recipes. Serve with white rice (see page 174), rice and peas (see page 145), or roti (see page 196).

1 tablespoon curry powder

1/4 teaspoon turmeric

1/2 teaspoon cumin

1/2 teaspoon garam masala

1/2 teaspoon garlic salt (see page 288)

4 to 6 tablespoons water

3 tablespoons vegetable oil

1 large onion, finely chopped

3 green onions, chopped

3 cloves garlic , crushed

6 celery leaves, finely chopped, or 1/4 teaspoon celery salt (see page 288)

3 sprigs fresh thyme or 1/2 teaspoon dried

1/4 green bell pepper (capsicum), seeded and chopped

1/4 red bell pepper (capsicum), seeded and chopped

2 lb (1 kg) lamb or mutton, trimmed and cubed

salt

1/4 teaspoon freshly ground black pepper

1 teaspoon tomato paste (puree)

about 3/4 cup (6 fl oz/175 ml) water

1 medium potato, peeled and cubed

Combine curry powder, turmeric, cumin, garam masala, and garlic salt in a small bowl. Add enough of the 4 to 6 tablespoons water to form a smooth paste.

Heat oil in a large deep saucepan over high heat. Add onions, garlic, celery leaves, thyme, and bell peppers and fry until onion is golden brown. Add curry paste, rinsing out bowl with a little water and adding it to saucepan. Fry for a few minutes until mixture resembles a dry paste, stirring frequently to prevent burning.

Add lamb, mix well into the paste, and cook over high heat for 5 minutes, stirring constantly.

Add salt, black pepper, and tomato paste, reduce heat to medium, and cook 5 minutes. Add enough of the 3/4 cup water just to cover meat. Cover and simmer over low heat 30 minutes, stirring occasionally.

Add potato and press down into sauce. Cook over low heat until meat is tender, 20 to 30 minutes, stirring occasionally. Serve hot.

Karni Kabritu Stobá

SERVES 4 TO 6

For this dish from the Dutch Antilles, goat is traditionally used and the cooking time is longer (about 1 to 1½ hours). Serve hot with funchi (see page 150) and fried yellow plantains (see page 170).

2 lb (1 kg) goat or lamb, cubed
1 tablespoon lime juice
3 tablespoons butter
1 medium onion, finely chopped
2 cloves garlic, crushed
1 medium tomato, finely chopped
2 teaspoons tomato paste (puree)
1 whole hot pepper,
seeded and finely chopped
¼ teaspoon paprika
⅔ cup (5 fl oz/160 ml) water
1 tablespoon white
distilled vinegar
salt and freshly ground
black pepper

Place meat in bowl and sprinkle with lime juice. Melt butter in large, deep saucepan over medium heat and fry meat until lightly browned on all sides. Add onion and garlic and fry 1 minute. Add remaining ingredients and cook 5 minutes.

Preheat oven to 350°F (180°C/Gas 4). Transfer mixture to casserole, cover, and bake until meat is tender, about 45 minutes. Serve hot.

Garlic Pork

SERVES 6 TO 8

This Guyanese dish is popular at Christmastime. It makes a lovely snack eaten with freshly baked rolls.

2 lb (1 kg) cubed pork leg
or shoulder
juice of ½ lime
2 oz (60 g) garlic, chopped
1 teaspoon chopped fresh thyme
or ¼ teaspoon dried
1 hot pepper, seeded and chopped
2 teaspoons salt or to taste
about 1 cup (8 fl oz/250 ml)
white vinegar
¼ cup (2 fl oz/60 ml) vegetable oil

Place pork in bowl and squeeze lime juice over. Add garlic, thyme, hot pepper, and salt and stir to coat pork. Pour vinegar over pork, making sure the meat is fully covered. Cover bowl tightly and refrigerate 5 to 6 days.

Drain pork, discarding marinade. Heat oil in frying pan until very hot. Add pork, cover, and cook over medium high heat until lightly browned on all sides, about 10 minutes. Serve hot.

Garlic Pork

COLOMBO DE PORC

SERVES 6

Martinique's Indian community brought their curries and spices with them when they arrived in the Caribbean. A Martinican curry is prepared with more vegetables than a traditional Indian curry. Serve with white rice (see page 174).

2 lb (1 kg) lean pork, cubed

salt and freshly ground black pepper

2 cloves garlic, crushed

1 hot pepper, seeded and minced

1 tablespoon fresh lemon juice

1/4 cup (2 fl oz/60 ml) peanut oil

3 green onions

1 medium onion, chopped

2 tablespoons curry powder

1/4 teaspoon ground allspice

2 whole cloves

1 tablespoon finely chopped fresh parsley

2 sprigs fresh thyme or 1/4 teaspoon dried

2 cups (16 fl oz/500 ml) water

1 small eggplant (aubergine), peeled and diced

1 zucchini (courgette), sliced

1 christophene (chayote squash/ choko), peeled and sliced

Season meat with salt, pepper, garlic, hot pepper, and lemon juice; let stand while preparing vegetables.

Heat oil in large saucepan over medium high heat. Add onions and pork (along with marinade seasonings but not the liquid, which should be reserved for later) and brown pork on all sides. Add curry powder and allspice and stir well. Add cloves, parsley, thyme, and water. Reduce heat, cover, and simmer 30 minutes. Season with salt and pepper. Add vegetables and reserved marinade liquid. Cover and cook until vegetables are tender, about 15 minutes. Serve hot.

CUBAN PORK FILLETS

SERVES 6

This is a quick and easy dish I came across at a local family restaurant in Havana. Serve with fried or boiled sweet potatoes (see page 185), yams with mojo criollo (see page 277), and fried plantains (see page 170).

2 lb (1 kg) lean pork fillets

juice of 2 lemons or 3 limes

1 teaspoon salt or to taste

3 cloves garlic, crushed

1/2 teaspoon paprika

1/4 cup (2 fl oz/60 ml) corn oil

In a bowl marinate pork with citrus juice, salt, garlic, and paprika for 2 hours.

Heat oil until hot in shallow frying pan. Scrape marinade from pork fillets and fry meat until lightly browned on both sides. Serve hot.

SWEET AND SOUR PORK

SERVES 6

One of the many excellent Chinese dishes brought to the region. Serve with boiled white rice (see page 174).

2 lb (1 kg) pork loin, cubed
1/2 teaspoon minced hot pepper
1 clove garlic, crushed
salt
6 tablespoons vegetable oil

Sauce:
3 tablespoons corn or peanut oil
1 onion, sliced
2 green onions, chopped
2 tablespoons white distilled vinegar
3 tablespoons raw sugar
2 tablespoons soy sauce
3 tablespoons ketchup
1 teaspoon salt
1 cup (8 fl oz/250 ml) water
2 tablespoons cornstarch

Place pork in bowl. Add hot pepper, garlic, and salt to taste and mix to coat meat. Cover and let stand 1 to 2 hours or refrigerate overnight.

Heat oil in large pan over high heat. Add pork and stir-fry until evenly browned. Drain on paper towels and set aside while preparing sauce.

For sauce: Heat oil in small saucepan over high heat. Add onions and stir-fry until golden. Add vinegar, sugar, soy sauce, ketchup, salt, and 3/4 cup (6 fl oz/ 175 ml) of the water and bring to boil. Cook 2 minutes. Dissolve cornstarch in remaining water. Add to sauce and stir well over high heat until sauce thickens. Add sauce to pork, reduce heat to medium, and heat through. Serve hot.

LECHON ASADO

SERVES 10 TO 12

Roast pig is a traditional Puerto Rican Christmas dish that is often prepared at home for parties and large gatherings. In the countryside a suckling pig is usually roasted over an open fire, but it can also be cooked in the oven. Serve with moros y cristianos (see page 144), and boiled cassava and yams (see page 185). Sliced onions sautéed in a little oil and vinegar or citrus juice often accompany this meat.

10 cloves garlic, minced

2 tablespoons finely chopped fresh oregano or 1 tablespoon dried

4 hot red peppers, seeded and finely chopped

2 to 4 tablespoons salt or to taste

2 tablespoons sour orange juice

2 tablespoons finely chopped marjoram or 1 tablespoon dried

2 tablespoons water

12 to 15 lb (6 to 8 kg) suckling pig, cleaned (or substitute large pork pieces)

Combine all ingredients except meat to make a paste. Wash meat and make deep gashes in it. Press seasoning paste into gashes and, if using a whole pig, inside the body cavity. Refrigerate overnight.

Preheat oven to 325°F (170°C/Gas 3). Set meat on rack in roasting pan and cover with foil. Roast 4 to 5 hours, basting occasionally, until juices run clear when a skewer is inserted into the meat. Remove foil and cook for a further 20 to 30 minutes until the meat is browned. Let meat rest at room temperature 10 to 15 minutes before carving.

MARINATED ROAST PORK

SERVES 6

On many of the English-speaking Caribbean islands a version of the English roast dinner exists in one form or another. Even Yorkshire pudding can be found in Dominica. You can substitute a leg of lamb for the pork in this recipe if you wish. Serve this pork roast with roast vegetables such as potatoes or yams.

3 green onions, minced

1 small onion, minced

4 cloves garlic, minced

4 celery leaves, finely chopped

2 sprigs thyme, finely chopped

1 hot red pepper, seeded and minced

3/4 teaspoon salt or to taste

1/4 teaspoon freshly ground black pepper

2 tablespoons olive or vegetable oil

4 lb (2 kg) leg of pork

Combine all ingredients except oil and meat in small bowl.

Wash meat and make deep gashes all around the leg. Pack two-thirds of seasoning mixture into gashes; rub remainder on outside of leg. Place in roasting pan and marinate 2 to 3 hours.

Preheat oven to 350°F (180°C/Gas 4). Pour oil into pan, add meat, cover with foil, and roast 2 1/2 hours, basting occasionally and removing foil for last 30 minutes of roasting time to enable meat to brown. Let meat rest at room temperature 10 to 15 minutes before carving.

Lechon Asado

MOKSIE ALESIE

SERVES 4 TO 6

This translates to "mixed rice"; it comes from Suriname. Cooked meat left over from another meal can be used. Be sure the cooked rice isn't too soft, as it will cook further.

3¹/2 oz (100 g) salt beef or corned beef

6 cups (1.5 l) water

3 tablespoons vegetable oil

1 onion, sliced

1 clove garlic, minced

3¹/2 oz (100 g) dried shrimp (prawns), soaked in 1 cup (8 fl oz/250 ml) water and drained

6¹/2 oz (200 g) cooked beef or pork, diced

1 tablespoon tomato paste (puree)

1 lb (500 g) cooked rice

1 beef bouillon (stock) cube, dissolved in ¹/2 cup (4 fl oz/125 ml) boiling water

5 oz (150 g) cabbage, chopped

¹/2 cup (2 oz/60 g) cooked green peas

¹/2 red bell pepper (capsicum), seeded and chopped

2 hot red peppers, seeded and finely chopped

salt and freshly ground black pepper

Boil salt beef in the water 30 minutes. Drain. Cut salt beef or corned beef into ¹/2-inch (1 cm) cubes.

Heat oil in saucepan over high heat. Add onion and garlic and fry 2 minutes. Add shrimp, cooked beef, and salt beef and cook 2 more minutes. Stir in tomato paste, cooked rice, and stock and cook over medium heat until most of the liquid is evaporated. Add remaining ingredients, reduce heat to low, cover, and cook, stirring occasionally, for 10 more minutes. Serve hot.

enne L. Cymbala

Blind date [videorec
ID: 39550004376074
5/2/2013

Autumn spring [video
ID: 39550004277611
5/2/2013

A fistful of lentils
ID: 39550003200531
5/23/2013

Authentic Vietnamese
ID: 39550002946738
5/23/2013

The Africa cookbook
ID: 39550002818432
5/23/2013

The complete Caribbe
ID: 39550002328879
5/23/2013

BÉBÉLÉ

SERVES 4 TO 6

This one-pot meal comes from the French Caribbean. To speed up the cooking time you can cook the tripe in a pressure cooker if you wish. Some people prefer to make a bouquet garni by tying up the thyme, parsley, and green onions in a small piece of cheesecloth (muslin) and removing it before serving, because it is visually more pleasing. I have chopped the herbs in this version.

14 oz (400 g) tripe, cut into
1-inch (2.5 cm) pieces

water

juice of 1 large lemon

1 andouille (French pork sausage),
cut into 1/4-inch (1 cm) cubes,
optional

3 cloves garlic, crushed

1 whole hot pepper

3 green onions

2 sprigs thyme, finely chopped

2 sprigs parsley, finely chopped

1 tablespoon vegetable oil

1 breadfruit, peeled and cut into
1-inch (2.5 cm) cubes

4 lb (2 kg) plantains, peeled and
cut into 1-inch (2.5 cm) rounds

4 oz (125 g) yams,
peeled and cubed

salt

Dumplings:

2 1/4 cups (10 oz/300 g)
all-purpose (plain) flour

1/4 teaspoon salt

1/2 teaspoon baking powder

about 1 cup (8 fl oz/250 ml) water

Place tripe in saucepan, cover with water, and add three-quarters of the lemon juice. Boil until tender, 1 to 1 1/2 hours. Drain and return to saucepan.

Add 6 cups (1.5 l) water, andouille, 2 cloves garlic, and hot pepper, being careful not to puncture the pepper. Add green onions, thyme, parsley, oil, breadfruit, plantains, yams, salt, and remaining lemon juice and simmer, partially covered, 25 to 30 minutes.

For dumplings: Combine flour, salt, and baking powder in bowl. Add enough water to make a smooth, firm dough. Break off small pieces of dough (about 1 teaspoonful), roll into smooth balls, and add to the pot. Add remaining garlic and cook until mixture is very thick, 20 to 30 more minutes. Serve immediately.

CREOLE CHICKEN

SERVES 4 TO 6

This recipe is typical of French Caribbean fare; the viniagrette-style sauce, known as sauce chien, is common to many Creole dishes. Creole chicken also makes an excellent appetizer in small portions.

2 lb (1 kg) chicken drumsticks, wings, and breasts

3 cloves garlic, crushed

1 small hot red pepper, seeded and minced

1/2 teaspoon ground allspice

3 tablespoons lime juice

water

salt and freshly ground black pepper

4 green onions, finely chopped

1 shallot, chopped

1 teaspoon finely chopped parsley

1/2 hot red or orange pepper, seeded and finely sliced

1 tablespoon olive or vegetable oil

5 tablespoons boiling water

Place chicken in bowl with 2 cloves garlic, hot pepper, allspice, 1 tablespoon lime juice, 1 tablespoon water, and salt and pepper. Marinate 3 hours.

Preheat broiler (grill) to low. Remove chicken pieces from marinade and cook 20 to 30 minutes, turning occasionally and basting frequently with marinade. Keep chicken warm while preparing sauce.

Place green onions, shallot, parsley, hot pepper, and remaining garlic in small bowl. Mix in oil, salt, and pepper. Pour on the boiling water and let stand for 10 minutes. Add remaining lime juice and serve warm with the chicken pieces.

OIL DOWN

SERVES 4-6

The name of this Grenadian recipe comes from the dish being "boiled down," which over time became "oil down." Pig's tail is often used as the meat in this dish.

8 oz (250 g) salt beef, salt pork, or corned beef

1 large breadfruit, peeled and cored

3 cups (24 fl oz/750 ml) coconut milk (see page 289)

6 celery leaves, finely chopped

1 sprig thyme, finely chopped

1 sprig parsley, finely chopped

1 whole hot green pepper

1 small onion, finely chopped

1 green onion, chopped

1 clove garlic

1 teaspoon turmeric

salt

Boil salt meat in saucepan in water to cover until almost tender, about 20 minutes, changing water halfway during cooking to eliminate excess salt. Drain. Cut salt meat or corned beef into small pieces.

Cut breadfruit into slices about 2 inches (5 cm) thick. Combine meat, breadfruit, and coconut milk in deep saucepan and bring to boil. Reduce heat to low, add remaining ingredients (being careful not to puncture hot pepper), and simmer until meat is tender and liquid is absorbed, about 20 to 30 minutes, stirring occasionally. Remove hot pepper before serving. Serve hot.

Creole Chicken

MARINATED CHICKEN LIVERS

SERVES 4 AS A SIDE DISH

Serve on a bed of lettuce with diced tomatoes and cucumber slices.

1 lb (500 g) chicken livers

1/2 teaspoon celery salt

2 sprigs fresh thyme or
1/2 teaspoon dried

1/4 teaspoon freshly ground
black pepper

salt

juice of 1/2 small lemon

2 cloves garlic, chopped

1 small onion, chopped

4 large green onions, chopped

1 hot red pepper, seeded
and finely chopped, optional

1/4 cup (2 fl oz/60 ml) vegetable oil

Combine all ingredients except oil in medium bowl. Cover and refrigerate at least 1 hour.

Heat oil in frying pan until hot. Scrape as much marinade as possible from livers and reserve. Fry livers on all sides over medium heat for 10 minutes or until almost cooked. Add garlic, onion, and shallots from marinade and cook until onion is tender. Raise heat to medium high and brown livers on both sides. (To speed up cooking, gently press livers a few times with the back of a fork during cooking.)

CHICKEN LIVER CURRY

SERVES 4

This is a dry curry, so there should not be much liquid in the pan when it is finished. Serve with dhal (see page 153) and boiled rice or roti (see page 196), or on its own with boiled rice (see page 174).

3 tablespoons vegetable oil

1 medium onion, chopped

4 large green onions, chopped

3 cloves garlic, chopped

2 sprigs fresh thyme or
1/2 teaspoon dried

1 hot red pepper, seeded and
finely chopped, optional

2 lb (1 kg) chicken livers

1 1/2 tablespoons curry powder

1/2 teaspoon turmeric

1/2 teaspoon celery salt
(see page 288)

1/2 teaspoon garam masala plus
1/2 teaspoon cumin, or
1 teaspoon masala (see page 284)

1/3 cup (3 fl oz/80 ml) water

salt and 1/4 teaspoon freshly
ground black pepper

Heat oil in saucepan over medium high heat. Add onions, garlic, thyme, and hot pepper and fry until onion is golden brown. Add livers, followed by curry powder, turmeric, celery salt, and garam masala/cumin. Cook 5 minutes over medium high heat, stirring frequently. Add water, reduce heat to low, and simmer until livers are cooked, 15 to 20 minutes (they should be firm and no longer pink when cut open). Season with salt and pepper and serve hot.

GOAT WATER

SERVES 6

This stew from Montserrat is similar to Jamaica's mannish water (see page 61). In Montserrat the essential herbs for a good goat water are green onions and thyme, known locally as chible. In the Caribbean a commercially sold browning sauce is used in the soup; if it is unavailable, gravy browning is a good substitute. Serve hot with rice or fresh bread, and a small piece of hot pepper.

3 lb (1.5 kg) goat, kid, lamb or mutton (with bones), cubed

water

2 onions, chopped

3 green onions, chopped

3 sprigs thyme

3 cloves garlic, crushed

4 whole cloves

1 whole hot pepper

2 tablespoons browning sauce

salt

freshly ground black pepper

2 tablespoons all-purpose (plain) flour

1/3 cup (3 fl oz/80 ml) water

Place meat in a large saucepan and add just enough water to cover. Bring to boil; simmer 5 minutes. Skim. Add onions, thyme, garlic, cloves, whole hot pepper, browning sauce, and salt to taste. Cover and simmer until meat is tender, 1 to 2 hours depending on type of meat.

Add pepper. Combine flour with water to form a paste. Gradually add to stew and cook, stirring until lightly thickened. Be careful not to pierce the pepper.

MOUNTAIN CHICKEN

SERVES 4

Also known as crapaud, mountain chicken is in fact a very large frog found only on Dominica and Montserrat. This is a very popular local recipe, if you can get hold of the main ingredient!

2 lb (1 kg) mountain chicken, skinned and cut into quarters

1 small onion, minced

2 green onions, finely chopped

1 clove garlic, minced

2 sprigs thyme, chopped

1 cup (4 oz/125 g) all-purpose (plain) flour

1/2 teaspoon paprika

salt and ground black pepper

about 4 cups (32 fl oz/1 l) vegetable oil

Combine meat, onions, garlic, and thyme in bowl and marinate at least 1 hour.

Combine flour, paprika, and salt and pepper on plate. Heat oil until very hot. Coat meat in flour mixture, then deep fry over medium heat until golden. Drain on paper towels and serve.

FISH AND SEAFOOD

Fish and shellfish can be found in abundance throughout the Caribbean, with as much variety on offer as there are ways of cooking it: baking, barbecuing, frying, currying, stewing, soup, fritters, the list goes on.

As with meat, fish was traditionally salted as a way of preserving it, in a manner that is thought to have originated with the Portuguese. While the need to preserve fish in this way is no longer so crucial, people in the region still enjoy "salt fish", which usually refers to salted cod, and use it to create some of their tastiest fish dishes. There are many methods for salting fish and they are practised on many of the islands, although today it is much easier to buy it already salted. Be careful when choosing because some contain more salt than others and will need to be soaked or boiled for longer before using them.

One very popular shellfish found in salads, stews, chowders, and barbecues is conch—a large mollusc inside a beautiful, pink shell. Other widely used fish include red snapper, grouper, jack, mackerel, and cutlass. And if I didn't mention the famous flying fish of Barbados, there would be trouble next time I venture into Bridgetown! Crabs are also very popular, particularly in the French-speaking islands and Dominica—look out for matatou crabs, crabs aux callalou, and stuffed crab backs. Less popular is hassar or cascadura. Perhaps it's the prehistoric, armor-plated appearance that puts people off, but it tastes great.

When choosing fish make sure that the eyes are clear, the gills have a bright, red color, and flesh is firm. Be wary of any fish that has a high, unpleasant smell.

Poisson Frit, page 108

POISSON FRIT

SERVES 4 TO 6

I was introduced to these marinated fried fish in Martinique by Josette Paruta. You can use red snapper or any white-fleshed fish, either whole or in pieces. A green salad makes a good accompaniment (see page 160). You can also try a different dressing: steep 2 dried allspice berries and a small piece of hot pepper in 1/3 cup (3 fl oz/80 ml) of salted boiling water for 5 to 10 minutes (remove berries before serving).

2 tablespoons water

2 cloves garlic, crushed

1 medium onion, sliced

juice of 2 limes

1 whole hot red pepper, seeded
and crushed, optional

1/4 teaspoon ground allspice

salt and freshly ground
black pepper

1 1/2 to 2 lb (750 g to 1 kg) fish

1/4 cup (2 fl oz/60 ml) vegetable
or corn oil

1 tablespoon all-purpose (plain)
flour

Vinaigrette:

2 tablespoons white wine vinegar

1/4 cup (2 fl oz/60 ml)
vegetable or soy oil

1/4 hot red pepper,
seeded and minced

1/2 small onion, sliced

salt to taste

Combine water, garlic, onion, lime juice, hot pepper, allspice, and salt and pepper. Coat fish with mixture and marinate 1 to 2 hours.

Heat oil in a frying pan until very hot. Remove fish from marinade and pat dry with paper towel. Coat fish with flour. Fry over medium heat until golden brown on both sides.

For vinaigrette: Heat vinegar in a small saucepan then pour over oil, hot pepper, onion, and salt in a small bowl. Stir. Serve hot over fish.

Fried Flying Fish

SERVES 4 TO 6

This fish is so named because it normally swims just below the water's surface and, when disturbed, leaps out of the water in a way that makes it appear to be flying. Though not widely eaten throughout the Caribbean, this is the national dish of Barbados. Any tasty white-fleshed fish is a good substitute.

1 onion, minced

2 green onions, minced

1/2 green bell pepper (capsicum), seeded and minced

2 cloves garlic, minced

1 hot pepper, seeded and finely chopped, optional

1 sprig fresh thyme, finely chopped, or 1/4 teaspoon dried

2 teaspoons finely chopped fresh marjoram or 1 teaspoon dried

salt and freshly ground black pepper

1/2 cup (4 fl oz/125 ml) water

juice of 2 limes

6 fish fillets, about 8 oz (250 g) each

vegetable oil for shallow frying

1 cup (4 oz/125 g) all-purpose (plain) flour

1/2 teaspoon baking powder

Combine minced vegetables, herbs, and salt and pepper in a bowl large enough to marinate fish. Stir in water and lime juice. Add fish fillets and press seasoning mixture firmly into the flesh. Marinate at least 1 hour.

Heat oil in frying pan over high heat. Pat fish dry with paper towels. Combine flour and baking powder and coat fish with mixture. Fry on both sides for 1 minute to brown, reduce heat to medium high, and cook through about 5 minutes. Drain on paper towels and serve hot.

FRIZZLE SALT COD

SERVES 4

This dish from Barbados is served with rice and peas (see page 145).

8 oz (250 g) salt cod
1 onion, finely chopped
2 green onions, chopped
1/4 teaspoon ground white pepper
2 sprigs thyme, finely chopped,
    or 1/2 teaspoon dried
1 clove garlic, crushed, optional
4 to 6 tablespoons vegetable oil
chopped fresh parsley to garnish

Soak salt cod in water to cover for at least 4 hours, preferably overnight. Drain.

Place fish in saucepan with enough fresh water to cover. Bring to boil, then simmer until soft, about 10 to 15 minutes. Flake or mince fish very finely.

Combine fish, onions, white pepper, thyme, and garlic in a bowl. Heat oil in frying pan over high heat and cook fish mixture until golden brown, about 5 minutes, stirring constantly. Serve hot, garnished with freshly chopped parsley.

CARIBBEAN FRIED FISH

SERVES 6

Fried fish is eaten everywhere in the Caribbean; it is always highly seasoned. Here is one of those recipes.

6 fish pieces, cleaned
juice of 1 lime
1/4 cup (2 fl oz/60 ml)
fish seasoning (see page 286)
1/2 teaspoon celery salt
(see page 288), optional
2 1/2 tablespoons all-purpose
(plain) flour
1/2 cup (4 fl oz/125 ml) cold water
about 1/2 cup (4 fl oz/125 ml)
vegetable oil

Sprinkle fish with lime juice. Season with fish seasoning, and celery salt, and let stand at least 10 minutes. Combine flour, water, and pepper to make a smooth, thin batter. Add fish pieces and turn to coat all sides. Heat oil in shallow frying pan over medium high heat. Fry a few fish pieces at a time on both sides until golden brown. Drain on paper towels and serve hot.

Frizzle Salt Cod

Escovitch Fish

SERVES 4 TO 6

This technique for pickling meat and fish (known as escabeche) comes from the Spanish. Popular in Jamaica, this recipe was given to me by Rosewell Robbs in Kingston. Use snapper, kingfish, or sprats. Serve hot with bammies or johnny cakes (see pages 190 and 193).

2 lb (1 kg) fish, cut into pieces 1 inch (2.5 cm) thick

juice of 2 limes

1 teaspoon garlic salt (see page 288)

1 teaspoon onion salt

1 teaspoon celery powder or celery seed, ground

1/2 teaspoon freshly ground black pepper

1/2 cup (4 fl oz/125 ml) vegetable oil

1/2 hot pepper, seeded and cut into strips

1 cup (8 fl oz/250 ml) cane or malt vinegar

1 carrot, cut into thin strips 2 inches (5 cm) long

1 large onion, sliced

1 christophene (chayote squash/choko), peeled and cut into thin strips

4 dried allspice berries or 1/4 teaspoon ground allspice

4 peppercorns

salt

Wash fish in a large bowl of water to which lime juice has been added. Drain. Rub garlic salt, onion salt, celery powder, and pepper into fish. Let stand while preparing vegetables.

Heat oil in medium saucepan until very hot. Pat fish dry with paper towels and fry over medium heat until crisp and brown on both sides. Drain on paper towels. Arrange fish pieces in a deep dish and keep warm.

Combine all remaining ingredients in saucepan and bring to boil. Simmer until vegetables are tender, about 3 minutes. Pour over fish while hot. Serve immediately, or cover and refrigerate overnight and serve chilled.

BAKED WHOLE FISH

SERVES 6

Use snapper, salmon, bream, or any kind of whole white-fleshed fish.

juice of 1 lime or 1/2 lemon

3 cloves garlic, crushed

1 hot pepper,
seeded and finely chopped

1 teaspoon salt or to taste

4 lb (2 kg) whole fish, cleaned

2 tablespoons butter

4 teaspoons finely chopped
fresh parsley

2 sprigs thyme, finely chopped

1 large onion, finely chopped

6 tablespoons water

1 bay leaf

3 tomatoes

Preheat oven to 400°F (200°C/Gas 6). Combine lime juice, garlic, hot pepper, and salt and rub into fish. Place fish in baking dish, adding pieces of butter, parsley, thyme, onion, water, bay leaf, and two of the tomatoes, chopped, over fish and around pan. Slice the remaining tomato and arrange over fish. Bake uncovered on middle shelf of oven until fish is opaque, 30 to 40 minutes, basting once while cooking. Serve hot.

FILETE DE CHILLO EN SALSA

SERVES 4 TO 6

Chillo is a type of local fish. Any white-fleshed fish can be used in this Puerto Rican dish.

6 fish fillets

1 tablespoon butter

1/4 cup (2 fl oz/60 ml) beer

3 cloves garlic, crushed

juice of 1 lime

3 tablespoons vegetable oil

1 onion, sliced

2 teaspoons finely chopped fresh
oregano or 1 teaspoon dried

1/2 green bell pepper (capsicum),
seeded and chopped

1 tablespoon tomato paste (puree)

3/4 cup (6 fl oz/175 ml)
chicken stock (see page 285)

1/4 cup (2 fl oz/60 ml)
dry white wine

Preheat oven to 350°F (180°C/Gas 4). Place fish in baking dish; dot with butter. Add beer, 1 clove garlic, and lime juice and bake 30 minutes, basting occasionally.

Meanwhile, heat oil in frying pan over high heat. Add onion, remaining garlic, oregano, and bell pepper and sauté until onion is tender. Add tomato paste, stock, and wine and cook 10 to 15 minutes. Add fish to sauce and cook over medium low heat until fish is heated through and infused with the flavor of the sauce, about 5 to 8 more minutes. Serve hot.

Following page: Jamaican Roast Fish, Curried Baked Sprats, Poisson Grillé

JAMAICAN ROAST FISH

SERVES 4

On many a roadside in Jamaica you can find fish wrapped in foil with a tasty stuffing and roasted over coals. If this method is inconvenient, you can also use the oven. Snapper or another white-fleshed fish is suitable for this recipe. Chinese spinach, bok choy, or English spinach make good substitutes for callaloo. Serve with fresh bread or rolls.

4 lb (2 kg) whole fish, cleaned

2 tablespoons lime or lemon juice

salt and freshly ground black pepper

4 oz (125 g) callaloo leaves, washed and finely chopped

1 small onion, minced

2 green onions, chopped

2 cloves garlic, crushed

1 hot pepper, seeded and finely chopped

Prepare barbecue or preheat oven to 400°F (200°C/Gas 6) if using. Place fish in large bowl. Rub inside and out with lime juice and sprinkle with salt and pepper. Let stand briefly while preparing other ingredients.

Combine remaining ingredients in small bowl. Pat fish dry. Stuff with callaloo mixture. Wrap in foil. If using oven, cook for about 30 to 40 minutes until flesh is opaque. If roasting over hot coals, cook about 20 minutes and turn occasionally. Unwrap (at the table if you prefer) and serve hot.

CURRIED BAKED SPRATS

SERVES 4

This is one of my grandmother's specialities. Whitebait, frays, or jacks also work well in this recipe.

3 tablespoons vegetable oil

juice of 1/2 lime

1 lb (500 g) sprats, cleaned and scaled

1 tablespoon curry powder

1/2 teaspoon garam masala

1/2 teaspoon cumin

1/4 teaspoon turmeric

salt and freshly ground black pepper

2 sprigs thyme, finely chopped

1 clove garlic, finely chopped

1/4 cup (2 fl oz/60 ml) water

2 tomatoes, finely chopped

Preheat oven to 350°F (180°C/Gas 4). Oil a shallow baking dish. Squeeze lime juice over fish. Blend dry ingredients, thyme, garlic, and water to make a paste. Add tomatoes. Coat fish with mixture. Arrange in prepared baking dish and bake until fish is opaque, 30 to 40 minutes.

POISSON GRILLÉ

SERVES 4

This recipe from Martinique was shared with me by Josette Paruta. You can use red snapper or any white-fleshed fish, either whole or in pieces. Serve with boiled rice (see page 174).

Marinade:

1 medium onion, sliced

2 cloves garlic, crushed

1/4 teaspoon ground allspice

1 hot red pepper, seeded and crushed, optional

juice of 2 limes

2 tablespoons water

salt and freshly ground black pepper

1 1/2 to 2 lb (750 g to 1 kg) fish

Vinaigrette:

2 tablespoons white vinegar

1/4 cup (2 fl oz/60 ml) water

2 dried allspice berries or 1/8 teaspoon ground allspice

1 small hot red pepper, seeded and finely chopped

salt

Combine marinade ingredients in bowl. Add fish and coat with marinade. Let stand 1 to 2 hours.

Prepare barbecue or preheat broiler (grill). Remove fish from marinade and cook at moderate heat until golden brown and cooked on both sides, about 10 minutes.

Meanwhile, combine vinaigrette ingredients in small nonaluminum saucepan and simmer over low heat 1 minute. Pour over fish just before serving.

COURT BOUILLON DE POISSON

SERVES 4

In Guadeloupe and Martinique red snapper is commonly used for this, but if snapper is unavailable, any white-fleshed fish is a good substitute. Leave the heads on. Serve with rice, avocado slices, and green or yellow plantains, yams, or sweet potatoes.

1 1/2 lb (750 g) white-fleshed fish, scaled and cleaned, cut in halves

juice of 2 limes

2 cloves garlic, crushed

1/2 bell pepper (capsicum), seeded and thinly sliced

1/4 teaspoon ground allspice

salt

3 tablespoons vegetable or corn oil

1 small onion, sliced

3 green onions

1 sprig fresh parsley or 1/2 teaspoon dried

1 sprig fresh thyme or 1/4 teaspoon dried

2 tomatoes, chopped, or 2 teaspoons tomato paste (puree)

1 whole hot red pepper

about 1 cup (8 fl oz/250 ml) water

Combine fish, lime juice, 1 clove garlic, bell pepper, allspice, and salt in a bowl and let stand at least 1 hour.

Heat oil in a frying pan over high heat. Fry onions and remaining garlic for 1 minute. Add parsley, thyme, and tomatoes and cook 3 minutes. Add fish with marinade, hot pepper, salt, and just enough water to cover fish (be careful not to pierce the pepper). Simmer gently until fish is done, about 15 minutes. Remove parsley, thyme, and hot pepper just before serving.

Court Bouillon de Poisson

BLAFF

SERVES 4

This French Antillean dish is so called because the fish is supposed to make a sound like "blaff" when it is dropped into the water in the cooking pot. Serve with white rice or French bread.

1¹/₂ to 2 lb (750 g to 1 kg) whole red snapper or other white-fleshed fish

2 cloves garlic, crushed

juice of 2 limes

salt

¹/₂ teaspoon ground allspice

¹/₄ red bell pepper (capsicum), seeded and thinly sliced

6 cups (1.5 l) water

1 small onion, sliced

4 green onions, chopped

1 sprig thyme

3 sprigs parsley

1 whole hot red pepper, seeded and crushed

Place fish in a bowl and marinate with 1 clove garlic, lime juice, salt, half the allspice, and bell pepper for 1 to 2 hours.

In a saucepan bring water to boil and add onions, thyme, 2 sprigs parsley, hot pepper, and remaining garlic and allspice. Return to the boil and add fish with marinade (did you hear the "blaff"?). Reduce heat and simmer for 15 to 20 minutes. Remove whole pepper, thyme, and parsley. Garnish with remaining sprig parsley, finely chopped, before serving.

FISH "TEA"

SERVES 4

A tasty Jamaican soup that may include many vegetables, such as pumpkin, potatoes, and turnips. Fish heads may be used to make the stock.

6 cups (1.5 l) water

1 lb (500 g) fish pieces with bones

1 carrot, diced

1 small christophene (chayote squash/choko), peeled and diced

2 whole green hot peppers

1 sprig thyme or ¹/₄ teaspoon dried

2 green onions, chopped

1 clove garlic

1 chicken bouillon (stock) cube, optional

1 green banana, cut into 2-inch (5 cm) pieces

4 spinners (see page 154), optional

salt and ground black pepper

Bring water to boil in saucepan. Add fish and simmer over low heat 30 minutes. Drain, reserving stock. Cut fish flesh away from the bones and set aside; discard bones and scraps.

Heat fish stock in saucepan and add diced vegetables, hot peppers, thyme, green onions, garlic, bouillon cube, banana, and spinners. Bring to boil, then reduce heat to medium low and simmer until vegetables and spinners are cooked, about 30 minutes, adding reserved fish flesh during the last 5 minutes of cooking. Add salt and pepper to taste. The soup should not be thick; if it is, add up to ¹/₂ cup (4 fl oz/125 ml) more water. Serve hot, removing hot peppers and thyme before serving.

POISSON AU FOUR

SERVES 4

This recipe for oven-baked fish is from Martinique. Whole snapper works very well, but you can use any white-fleshed fish. Serve with avocado slices and rice.

1¹/₂ to 2 lb (750 g to 1 kg) whole fish

2 cloves garlic, crushed

juice of 2 limes

¹/₂ hot red pepper, seeded and crushed, optional

¹/₄ teaspoon ground allspice or 1 leaf bois d'inde

salt and freshly ground black pepper

1 medium onion, sliced

4 spring onions

2 sprigs fresh thyme or ¹/₄ teaspoon dried

2 sprigs parsley

¹/₄ cup (2 fl oz/60 ml) dry white wine

1 tablespoon vegetable or corn oil

¹/₄ red bell pepper (capsicum), seeded and thinly sliced

Season fish with 1 garlic clove, lime juice, hot pepper, allspice, and salt and pepper. Marinate 1 to 2 hours.

Preheat oven to 350°F (180°C/Gas 4). Place fish in baking dish with remaining garlic, onions, thyme, parsley, wine, and oil. Bake until fish is opaque, about 30 minutes. Remove thyme and parsley, and garnish with slices of bell pepper before serving.

RUN DOWN

SERVES 4

A classic Jamaican dish eaten with boiled green bananas (see page 185) dipped into the coconut sauce. The term for such a meal is "dip and fall back."

2 lb (1 kg) pickled or salted mackerel

5 cups (40 fl oz/1.25 l) coconut milk (see page 289)

2 cloves garlic, crushed

1 large onion, chopped

3 green onions, finely chopped

3 tomatoes, chopped

2 sprigs fresh thyme, finely chopped, or 1/4 teaspoon dried

1 to 2 whole hot peppers

1/8 teaspoon ground allspice, optional

salt and freshly ground black pepper

Cover mackerel with water and let soak at least 6 hours.

Bring coconut milk to simmer in a deep frying pan. Add garlic, onions, tomatoes, thyme, peppers, and allspice and simmer until coconut milk has thickened and a custard begins to form on the milk, about 15 minutes.

Meanwhile, drain fish and remove fins, heads, and bones. Cut fish into pieces 2 inches (5 cm) thick. Add fish pieces to coconut milk mixture and season with salt and pepper to taste. Simmer a further 10 minutes. Serve hot with bananas.

FISH CURRY WITH GREEN MANGOES

SERVES 6

If using large fillets of fish, cut into 4 x 3-inch (10 x 8 cm) pieces. Serve with boiled white rice, sada roti, or roti (see pages 174, 192, and 196).

2 teaspoons lemon juice

2 lb (1 kg) fish fillets

3 tablespoons vegetable oil

1 onion, finely chopped

3 cloves garlic, minced

1 1/2 tablespoons curry powder

1 teaspoon cumin

1 hot pepper, seeded and minced, optional

2 green mangoes or green papaya (pawpaw), peeled, seeded, and sliced

1 large tomato, finely chopped

1/4 cup (2 fl oz/60 ml) water

salt and freshly ground black pepper

Sprinkle lemon juice over fish. Heat oil in large saucepan over medium heat. Add onion and garlic and sauté until onion is tender. Add curry powder and cumin and fry 3 minutes, stirring frequently. Add hot pepper, mangoes, and tomato and cook 3 minutes. Add fish fillets, water, and salt and pepper. Cover, reduce heat, and simmer gently until fish is cooked, about 10 minutes. Serve hot.

Run Down

HASSAR CURRY

SERVES 6

Hassar is the name given to an unusual armor-plated fish eaten in Guyana; in Trinidad it is known as cascadura. There is no real substitute for its distinctive taste, but if hassar is unavailable, you could use tuna fillets. This is one of my cousin Sharmala's recipes. Serve it with boiled rice (see page 174) or roti (see page 196).

10 hassars, cleaned thoroughly

2 to 3 limes

8 cloves garlic, peeled

3 sprigs fresh thyme or
³/4 teaspoon dried

2 tablespoons curry powder

1/2 teaspoon cumin

1/2 teaspoon masala (see page 284)

1 onion, finely chopped

about 1/4 to 1/2 cup (2 to 4 fl oz/60 to 125 ml) water

1/4 cup (2 fl oz/60 ml) vegetable or corn oil

3 cups (24 fl oz/750 ml) coconut milk (see page 289)

Cover hassars with water. Squeeze in lime juice; drop in lime peels. Let soak while preparing remaining ingredients.

Puree garlic and thyme together in a food processor or crush with a rolling pin. Drain fish and spread with two-thirds of the puree, coating inside and out. In a bowl combine all dry ingredients and onion with just enough water to make a thin paste.

Heat oil in large saucepan until very hot. Add curry paste and fry 2 to 3 minutes, stirring constantly. Add remaining garlic puree and cook 4 minutes. Add fish and cook 3 minutes. Add coconut milk, cover, and cook until fish is done, about 20 to 25 minutes. Serve hot.

ACKEE AND SALT COD

SERVES 6

A Jamaican national dish. If using fresh ackees, make sure they are ripe—they should be split open, revealing light yellow flesh. Serve this dish for breakfast with bammies (see page 190) and roasted breadfruit, or as a main course garnished with sliced hard-cooked eggs and red bell pepper (capsicum).

8 oz (250 g) salt cod

water

2 dozen ripe fresh ackees or 15-oz (450 g) can

1/2 teaspoon salt

1/4 cup (2 fl oz/60 ml) vegetable oil

1 small onion, sliced

1 small hot pepper, seeded and minced

1 tomato, chopped

salt and freshly ground black pepper

Soak salt cod in water to cover for several hours or overnight. Drain. If using fresh ackees, remove flesh and discard pods. Wash flesh under cold water. In a pan, bring to boil enough water to cover ackees. Add salt, then ackees and cook until soft but still intact, about 12 minutes. Drain and set aside.

Cover fish with fresh water in saucepan. Boil until soft, about 10 minutes. Discard skin and bones; flake fish. Heat oil in another saucepan over medium heat. Add onion and hot pepper and sauté until onion is translucent. Add tomato and fish and stir 3 to 4 minutes. Add ackees and salt and pepper to taste. Cook, stirring gently, 5 more minutes.

CURRY SHRIMP

SERVES 4

In Kingston, Jamaica, I have tasted many wonderful meals prepared by one of the best cooks on the island, Rosewell Robbs. This is a dish he served me when we exchanged curry recipes—his Jamaican, mine Guyanese. It is very quick and easy to prepare. Serve with boiled rice (see page 174).

1 tablespoon butter

1 tablespoon curry powder

1 medium onion, finely chopped

1/2 green bell pepper (capsicum), seeded and finely chopped

1 hot pepper, seeded and finely chopped

1 lb (500 g) shrimp (prawns), peeled

2/3 cup (5 fl oz/160 ml) water

1/2 teaspoon MSG, optional

1 teaspoon sugar

2 teaspoons cornstarch mixed with 2 tablespoons cold water, optional

Heat butter in frying pan over low heat. Add curry powder and fry 1 minute, stirring constantly to prevent burning. Stir in onion, bell pepper, hot pepper, then shrimp. Add water, MSG, and sugar and simmer until shrimp are cooked, 10 to 12 minutes, stirring regularly. If sauce is too thin, stir in cornstarch paste and return to boil to thicken. Serve hot.

CURRY LOBSTER

SERVES 4

This is a variation of the Curry Shrimp recipe above.

Instead of shrimp:

rock (spiny) lobsters, total 4 lb (2 kg)

2 green onions

2 sprigs thyme

1 whole hot pepper

Drop lobsters into large pot of boiling water. Add remaining ingredients and boil for 2 minutes. Drain and discard seasonings. Remove meat from lobster and use instead of shrimp in Curry Shrimp recipe but reduce cooking time to 5 to 8 minutes.

TUNA IN BROWN STEW

SERVES 4

This tasty recipe is from Dominica.

4 tuna fillets, about 8 oz/200 g each

juice of 2 limes

2 tablespoons butter

1 medium onion, chopped

2 cloves garlic, minced

2 sprigs parsley, finely chopped

1 teaspoon celery salt
(see page 288)

1/2 teaspoon curry powder

1/2 tablespoon tomato paste
(puree)

1/2 red bell pepper (capsicum),
seeded and finely chopped

salt and ground black pepper

2 cups (16 fl oz/500 ml) water

1 tablespoon all-purpose
(plain) flour

Place fish in a bowl and squeeze lime juice over both sides.

Melt butter in deep saucepan over medium heat. Add onion, garlic, parsley, celery salt, curry powder, tomato paste, bell pepper, and salt and pepper and cook until onion is soft. Add fish and all but 2 tablespoons water, reduce heat, and simmer 15 minutes.

Combine flour with remaining 2 tablespoons water and stir to form a smooth paste. Slowly stir into stew and cook until sauce has thickened and fish is cooked, about 3 minutes.

FISH IN CREOLE SAUCE

SERVES 4

This dish from Martinique is good for a hot summer day. Red snapper is recommended, about 2 to 3 lb (1 to 1.5 kg).

2 white-fleshed fish of your
choice, halved if large

juice of 2 limes

1/2 teaspoon ground allspice

salt and ground black pepper

1 red bell pepper (capsicum),
seeded and finely chopped

1 medium onion, finely chopped

1 tablespoon drained capers

1 clove garlic, crushed

3 sprigs thyme, finely chopped

2 sprigs parsley, finely chopped

2 tablespoons vinegar

6 tablespoons olive oil

2 tomatoes, finely chopped

Prepare barbecue or preheat broiler (grill). Place fish in a bowl with lime juice and enough water to cover. Let stand 5 minutes.

Remove fish and pat dry. Season with allspice and salt and pepper. Cook until golden brown on both sides.

Meanwhile, combine remaining ingredients in a bowl. Spoon cold dressing over hot cooked fish and serve.

Tuna in Brown Stew

SHRIMP WITH CREOLE SAUCE

SERVES 4 TO 6

This tasty dish is great eaten with rice and peas (see page 145). It comes from Dominica, where the French and English influences on the cuisine are virtually equal—but this is definitely more French than English. In this dish I have used green onions, but if they are unavailable you can leave them out and add a little more onion.

lime juice

1 lb (500 g) shrimp (prawns), peeled

2 tablespoons butter

4 green onions, finely chopped

1 onion, finely chopped

3 cloves garlic, crushed

1/2 green bell pepper (capsicum), seeded and finely chopped

1/2 red bell pepper (capsicum), seeded and finely chopped

2 tablespoons finely chopped fresh parsley

8 celery leaves, finely chopped

1/4 teaspoon rosemary, optional

2 teaspoons chopped fresh lemon thyme or thyme

2 tablespoons tomato paste (puree)

salt and freshly ground black pepper

6 tablespoons water

1 tablespoon cornstarch

Rub a few drops of lime juice into shrimp. Heat butter in large frying pan over medium low heat until it begins to foam. Add onions, garlic, bell peppers, parsley, celery leaves, rosemary, and thyme and sauté until onion is soft.

Stir in tomato paste and salt and pepper. Add shrimp and 3 tablespoons water and bring to boil; boil, stirring constantly, 2 minutes. Reduce heat and simmer 5 to 10 more minutes or until shrimp are cooked.

Mix cornstarch with remaining water to form a paste. Stir into sauce just before shrimp are cooked and return to boil. Serve hot.

ENCHILADA DE CAMARONES

SERVES 4 AS MAIN COURSE OR 6 AS APPETIZER

A Cuban dish that is served with boiled white rice (see page 174).

lime juice

1 lb (500 g) shrimp (prawns), peeled

2 tablespoons vegetable or corn oil

1 onion, finely chopped

3 cloves garlic, minced

2 small hot peppers, seeded and finely chopped

2 tablespoons finely chopped fresh parsley

1/2 teaspoon chopped fresh oregano or 1/4 teaspoon dried

1/4 cup (2 oz/60 g) tomato paste (puree)

1 bay leaf

1/2 teaspoon cumin

2 teaspoons white wine vinegar

1/2 cup (4 fl oz/125 ml) water

1 teaspoon salt

1/4 teaspoon freshly ground black pepper

Squeeze just a few drops of lime juice onto shrimp and rub in.

Heat oil in large frying pan over medium heat and gently fry onion for 1 minute. Add garlic, hot peppers, parsley, and oregano and fry for 1 more minute. Stir in tomato paste and cook for 5 minutes. Add remaining ingredients and cook over medium low heat until shrimp are cooked through, about 10 to 15 minutes. Serve hot.

Following page: Enchilada de Camarones, Grilled Lobster, Shrimp, Rice, and Callaloo

GRILLED LOBSTER

SERVES 2 TO 4

4 tablespoons butter

2 cloves garlic, crushed

1/2 teaspoon minced
hot red pepper, optional

salt and freshly ground
white pepper

2 teaspoons lime juice

2 lb (1 kg) lobster, cleaned

lime wedges and chopped fresh
parsley for serving

Preheat broiler (grill). Melt butter in saucepan over medium heat. Add garlic and hot pepper and cook 2 minutes. Remove from heat and add salt and pepper.

Sprinkle 1 teaspoon lime juice over each lobster, followed by 1 to 2 tablespoons butter mixture. Cook just until golden brown, 20 to 30 minutes. Serve hot with lime wedges and sprinkled with parsley.

FRIED RICE WITH SHRIMP

SERVES 4

If you like, add a beaten egg after the shrimp and stir constantly until the egg is cooked.

1 tablespoon butter or margarine

1 tablespoon corn oil

1 large onion, chopped

2 green onions, finely chopped

2 cloves garlic, crushed

1 sprig thyme, finely chopped

1 sprig parsley, finely chopped

7 oz (200 g) dried shrimp (prawns)

1/2 teaspoon tomato paste (puree)

1 hot pepper,
seeded and minced

1 carrot, cut into 1/4-inch
(5 mm) cubes

3 tablespoons water

4 cups (1 lb/500 g) cooked rice

1 tablespoon soy sauce, optional

salt and freshly ground
white pepper

1 5-oz can (150 g) corn kernels

Melt butter with oil in large saucepan or wok over high heat. Add onions, garlic, thyme, parsley, and shrimp and sauté until onions are translucent. Add tomato paste, hot pepper, carrot, and water and simmer just until carrot is tender. Add rice, soy sauce, salt and pepper, and corn and heat through. Serve hot.

SHRIMP, RICE, AND CALLALOO

SERVES 4

8 oz (250 g) fresh raw shrimp (prawns), peeled

2 teaspoons lime juice

2 tablespoons butter or margarine

1 large onion, chopped

1 clove garlic, finely chopped

3 green onions, finely chopped

1 sprig thyme

1 sprig parsley

1 large tomato, finely chopped

12 oz (375 g) callaloo leaves and stems, washed and chopped

2 cups (10 oz/300 g) rice, rinsed until water runs almost clear

2 cups (16 fl oz/500 ml) chicken stock (see page 285)

1 hot pepper, seeded and sliced

salt and freshly ground black pepper

Sprinkle shrimp with lime juice and let stand.

Melt butter in a large, deep saucepan over high heat. Add onion and sauté 2 minutes. Add shrimp, garlic, green onions, thyme, parsley, tomato, and callaloo and stir-fry until callaloo has wilted, about 2 minutes. Stir in rice, chicken stock, hot pepper, and salt and pepper to taste. Boil 2 minutes, then reduce heat, cover, and cook over low heat until rice is tender and has absorbed all liquid, about 15 to 20 minutes.

CAMARONES A LA VINAGRETA

SERVES 4

1/2 cup (4 fl oz/125 ml) olive oil

1/4 cup (2 fl oz/60 ml) white vinegar

1 teaspoon salt

1 medium onion, finely chopped

1/4 green bell pepper (capsicum), seeded and finely chopped

1 sprig parsley, finely chopped

1/4 teaspoon paprika

2 lb (1 kg) cooked shrimp (prawns), peeled

Combine all ingredients except shrimp to make a vinaigrette. Pour over shrimp and chill well before serving.

Fricassée de Langouste

SERVES 4

The French-speaking islands use this sauce for lobster, but it can be used with any seafood. Serve hot with rice or boiled potatoes. Make a bouquet garni of the thyme, parsley, and green onion if desired.

1 large rock (spiny) lobster, about
1¹/₂ to 2 lb (750g to 1 kg), quartered

juice of ¹/₂ lime

2 tablespoons olive oil

1 onion, chopped

4 green onions

2 cloves garlic, crushed

1 whole hot pepper, optional

1 teaspoon finely chopped fresh
thyme or ¹/₄ teaspoon dried

2 teaspoons chopped fresh parsley

1 bay leaf

¹/₈ teaspoon ground allspice

1 tablespoon tomato paste (puree),
or 2 tomatoes, finely chopped

¹/₃ cup (3 fl oz/80 ml) dry white
wine or white wine vinegar

2 tablespoons water

salt and ground black pepper

Sprinkle lobster pieces with lime juice. Heat oil in a frying pan and sauté lobster until it turns pink, about 3 to 5 minutes. Add onions, 1 clove garlic, hot pepper, thyme, parsley, bay leaf, allspice, and salt and pepper. Add tomato paste and wine and simmer until lobster meat is soft and white, about 10 to 15 minutes. Just before serving, stir in remaining garlic.

Smoked Herring Choka

SERVES 4

This is popular among the East Indian community in both Trinidad and Guyana. A more traditional way of preparing this dish is to add onion and herring to oven- or coal-roasted tomatoes, scatter minced garlic on top, and pour about 2 to 3 tablespoons of very hot oil over before mixing. Often eaten for breakfast, it is usually accompanied by sada roti (see page 192). If you can't remove all the fish bones there is no need for concern, as they are soft and easily eaten.

3 dried smoked herrings

water

3 tablespoons vegetable or corn oil

1 lb (500 g) tomatoes, chopped

6 cloves garlic, crushed

1 medium onion, sliced

salt

Place herrings in a saucepan or deep frying pan and cover with water. Bring to boil, then simmer 10 minutes. Drain fish, cut off heads and tails, and remove skin and as many bones as possible. Flake the fish. Heat oil in frying pan over high heat. Add tomatoes, garlic, onion, and herring and cook until tomatoes are soft, 10 to 15 minutes, stirring occasionally. Season to taste with salt. Serve hot.

Smoked Herring Choka

SMOKED HERRING SALAD

SERVES 2

My grandmother used to make this, one of my favorite recipes as a child. Serve cold with hot boiled rice (see page 174), or as an accompaniment to a meal for four.

1 smoked herring,
about 8 oz (250 g)

1 head lettuce, washed

1 large tomato, finely chopped

salt and freshly ground
black pepper

1/4 cucumber, thinly sliced

Discard skin and bones from herring. Coarsely chop half the lettuce. Place fish in a shallow medium bowl with chopped lettuce, tomato, and salt and pepper. Using your hand or a fork, mash ingredients together until fish and tomatoes are almost a paste and lettuce is well combined. Serve on top of remaining lettuce leaves, garnished with cucumber.

SEAFOOD IN "GROS" SAUCE

SERVES 2

In Dominica, seafood is in abundance and tastes superb, especially when it is accompanied by a sauce such as this one. This recipe was given to me by Yolande Cools-Lartigue, a well-known Dominican cook and writer. The sauce can be used with any seafood. I have chosen to use lobster, lightly sautéed in butter first; the blend of flavors is mouthwatering. Serve this dish with boiled white rice (see page 174) or with fresh bread or vegetables (e.g plantain, yams).

2 tablespoons butter

1 lb (500 g) lobster meat

2 large cloves garlic,
finely chopped

3/4 cup (6 fl oz/175 ml)
boiling water

1 small onion, chopped

4 green onions

1 medium tomato, chopped

1 tablespoon finely chopped
fresh parsley

1 teaspoon finely chopped fresh
thyme or 1/4 teaspoon dried

1 hot pepper,
seeded and minced

1 tablespoon lime juice

Melt butter in a frying pan over medium heat and sauté lobster until lightly golden. Set aside.

Drop garlic into boiling water over moderate heat. Add onions, tomato, parsley, thyme, and hot pepper and simmer 15 minutes over low heat. Add lobster and lime juice and heat through.

MATÉTÉ CRAB

SERVES 6

This Easter specialty from the French Caribbean is also known as matoutou crab. There are many variations of this dish, which is traditionally served on the beach at a large gathering of friends.

4 fresh crabs, about 10 to 12 oz (300 to 350 g) each

juice of 1/2 lemon

2 tablespoons butter

1 small onion, minced

2 green onions, finely chopped

2 shallots, chopped

1 hot pepper, seeded and chopped

3 cloves garlic, crushed

2 sprigs thyme, finely chopped

1 sprig parsley, finely chopped

2 medium tomatoes, quartered

3 cups (1 lb/500 g) rice, rinsed until water runs almost clear

4 cups (32 fl oz/1 l) water

2 whole cloves

2 bay leaves

salt and black pepper

Separate legs from crabs. Remove shell from backs and cut crabmeat from backs and legs into smaller pieces. Sprinkle with lemon juice.

Melt butter in saucepan over medium high heat. Add onions, shallots, hot pepper, garlic, thyme, parsley, crablegs and crabmeat and and sauté 4 minutes.

Add tomatoes, rice, water, cloves, bay leaves, and salt and pepper to taste. Bring to boil, then lower heat, cover, and cook until rice is tender and has absorbed all liquid, about 20 minutes. Serve hot.

STEWED CONCH

SERVES 4

There is no real substitute for conch but abalone comes very close.

2 lb (1 kg) conch or abalone

water

2 limes

2 tablespoons butter

1 onion, sliced

1 clove garlic

2 green onions, chopped

1 hot red pepper, seeded and finely chopped, optional

1 tablespoon ketchup

2 tomatoes, sliced

1 whole clove

1 sprig thyme, chopped

salt and ground black pepper

Wash conch with water, rub with lime halves, then squeeze lime juice over. Pound with a meat mallet to tenderize. Cut conch into 1-inch (2.5 cm) pieces.

Place conch in large saucepan and add enough water to cover. Bring to boil, then simmer until conch is almost tender, about 2 hours. Drain.

Heat butter in saucepan until it begins to foam. Add onion, garlic, green onions, and hot pepper and sauté until onion is soft. Add conch meat, 1/2 cup (4 fl oz/ 125 ml) water, and remaining ingredients and simmer, covered, for 20 minutes.

VEGETABLES, SALADS, AND SIDE DISHES

Caribbean cuisine uses a wide variety of vegetables in cooking and in the preparation of salads, served either as side dishes or main meals. Many of these recipes owe much to the Chinese and Indian workers who brought to the region vegetables such as bok choy, eggplant, and chick peas, and dishes such as dhal, channa, and sautéed bora.

Peas and beans feature extensively around the Caribbean, either in rice dishes or as highly seasoned side dishes accompaning rice or ground provisions. Cuba's black beans and the red kidney beans of Puerto Rico, Martinique, and Guadeloupe are just a few examples in this chapter of their widespread use.

The ground provisions in this section refer to the many and varied root vegetables grown throughout the region which are usually served as an accompaniment to meat or fish dishes.

Larger salads have not traditionally been a major part of West Indian fare, particularly in the ex-British West Indian countries. There, salads accompany a meal and often consist of just lettuce, tomatoes, and cucumber or, in Trinidad, simply watercress. However, more complex salads are created in the Spanish-speaking islands, such as serenata from Puerto Rico. Commonly known salads such as coleslaw and potato salad can also be found.

The recipes in this chapter cover only part of a great range of possibilities. Feel free to experiment with the flavors of different ingredients such as okras, bora, plantains, breadfruit, yams, cassava, pumpkin, and sweet potato—to name only a few.

Yam Fritters, page 182

ARROZ CON GANDULES

SERVES 4

This is a Puerto Rican version of a rice and peas dish common to many Caribbean countries. Sofrito gives this one a Spanish taste.

8 oz (250 g) dried or
1 lb (500 g) fresh pigeon peas

8 cups (2 l) water

4 teaspoons salt

2 tablespoons olive oil

1 cup (8 fl oz/250 ml) sofrito II
(see page 276)

1/2 green bell pepper (capsicum),
seeded and minced

4 olives, pitted and chopped

1 teaspoon drained capers

2 cups (10 oz/300 g) rice, rinsed
until water runs almost clear

Soak dried peas overnight and boil in salted water until tender but not too soft, about 1 hour. If using fresh peas, boil in salted water until tender, about 20 minutes.

Heat oil in deep frying pan or medium saucepan over medium high heat. Add sofrito and bell pepper and cook 2 minutes. Add olives and capers and sauté 4 minutes.

Drain pigeon peas, reserving 2 1/2 cups (20 fl oz/600 ml) liquid. Add peas and rice to pan, stir well, and cook over high heat for 3 to 4 minutes. Add reserved liquid from peas and cook over medium heat until most but not all of water is absorbed, about 4 minutes. Stir, cover, reduce heat to low, and cook until rice is tender, about 20 minutes. Serve hot.

HARICOTS ROUGES

SERVES 4 TO 6

These stewed red beans are an accompaniment to boiled rice and vegetable dishes in the French-speaking Caribbean.

2 cups (13 oz/400 g) dried red kidney beans

about 5 to 6 cups water

1 beef or chicken bouillon (stock) cube or 8 oz (250 g) salt beef or pork, optional

1 large onion, chopped

2 green onions, chopped

1 sprig thyme, finely chopped

2 cloves garlic, crushed

1 tablespoon corn or peanut oil

salt

Soak beans overnight in the water in large saucepan.

Cook beans in same water over medium low heat, adding bouillon cube or salted meat, for about 2 hours or until beans are soft. Add onions, thyme, 1 clove garlic, oil, and salt to taste. Cook until beans are very soft and almost mushy, about 20 minutes. Just before serving, crush remaining garlic clove and stir into beans.

STEWED RED PEAS

SERVES 6

Pig's tail is traditionally used in place of corned beef in this Jamaican dish. It would be soaked along with the salt beef. The stew is thick and served hot with boiled rice and fried plantains (see page 170).

8 oz (250 g) salt beef or stewing beef, cubed

2 cups (12 oz/350 g) red peas, soaked overnight in 8 cups (2 l) water

4 oz (125 g) corned beef, cubed

1 sprig thyme

2 cloves garlic, crushed

2 green onions, chopped

1 whole hot pepper

salt and freshly ground black pepper

spinners (see page 154)

If using salt beef, soak in water to cover for 1 to 2 hours. Drain and cut into small pieces.

Bring peas to boil in the water in which they soaked. Add salt or stewing beef and corned beef and bring to boil again. Simmer over medium low heat until meat is tender and peas are soft but not mushy, about 2 hours.

Stir in thyme, garlic, green onions, hot pepper, and salt and pepper. Add spinners and simmer until spinners are cooked through, about 15 to 20 minutes (these will help thicken the stew). Remove whole pepper and thyme just before serving.

FRIJOLES NEGROS

This recipe was given to me by the chef of El Viajante, an excellent Cuban restaurant in Miami. It is usually served with white rice as an accompaniment to meat dishes.

1 lb (500 g) dried black kidney beans

1 tablespoon salt or to taste

18 cups (4.5 l) water

3 medium onions, finely chopped

2 cloves garlic, finely chopped

3 hot green peppers, seeded and chopped

1 teaspoon cumin, optional

3 bay leaves

1/4 cup (2 fl oz/60 ml) olive oil

Rinse and sort debris from beans. Place in large, deep saucepan with the salt and water and bring to boil. Add remaining ingredients and cook until beans are soft, about 1 hour, then continue to simmer over low heat until thickened, about 10 minutes longer.

JUG-JUG

Jug-jug is said to have come from the Scots who settled in Barbados until the 1680s, when they were exiled. Its origins appear to be in the Scottish haggis, a traditional dish made from oatmeal and offal. This Bajan specialty is served at Christmastime with roast pork (see page 98) or boiled ham.

6 oz (180 g) lean salt beef or corned beef

12 oz (375 g) stewing beef

2 lb (1 kg) dried pigeon peas

5 cups (40 fl oz/1.25 l) water

2 large onions, chopped

2 shallots, chopped

3 sprigs fresh thyme, chopped, or 3/4 teaspoon dried

1 whole hot red pepper, optional

salt and freshly ground black pepper

3 oz (90 g) Guinea corn flour or millet (see glossary)

2 tablespoons softened butter

If using salt beef, soak in water to cover overnight. Drain.

Cover salt or corned beef, stewing beef, and peas with water in a large saucepan and bring to boil. Simmer until all are tender, about 1 hour. Strain and reserve stock.

To half the stock add onions, shallots, thyme, hot pepper, and salt and pepper. Gradually add Guinea corn flour, stirring constantly until thoroughly blended.

Grind meat and peas in food processor. Combine with stock mixture to form a stiff paste; adding extra stock if required. Stir in butter, mound on a serving plate, and serve immediately.

Jug-Jug

MOROS Y CRISTIANOS

SERVES 6

Centuries ago the Spanish fought the Moors over Granada in Spain. At that time the Spanish were firmly entrenched in Cuba and loyalists named this rice dish after that struggle. Surprisingly, the name remains the same today.

1 cup (8 oz/250 g) dried black beans

water

2 tablespoons vegetable or corn oil

1 medium onion, finely chopped

2 cloves garlic, finely chopped

1 hot pepper, seeded and finely chopped

2 cups (10 oz/300 g) rice, rinsed until water runs clear

2 teaspoons salt

freshly ground black pepper

Soak black beans overnight in water to cover. Drain beans and place in saucepan. Add 2 cups (16 fl oz/500 ml) water. Bring to boil, then simmer 20 to 30 minutes over low heat until tender but not soft.

Heat oil in frying pan over high heat. Add onion, garlic, and hot pepper and sauté until onion is tender. Add to beans. Add rice to beans with salt and pepper and stir gently. Increase heat to medium high and cook until most of the water is absorbed. Reduce heat to very low, cover, and cook until rice is tender and all liquid is absorbed, about 20 more minutes. Serve hot.

RICE AND PEAS IN COCONUT

SERVES 6

Despite its name, this dish uses dried beans of one kind or another. It is eaten throughout the Caribbean, though the recipe varies slightly from country to country. Here is the Jamaican version, which uses kidney beans that give the rice a pinkish tinge. Black-eyed peas can also be used. Pigeon peas (also known as congo or gungo peas) are a good variation; they require less cooking time and need only be soaked for two hours before cooking.

8 oz (250 g) red kidney beans

water

2 cups (10 oz/300 g) long-grain rice, well rinsed

1 medium onion, chopped

2 long hot red peppers, seeded and finely chopped

1 teaspoon chopped fresh thyme or 1/2 teaspoon dried

2 cloves garlic, chopped

2 oz (60 g) creamed coconut or 1/2 cup (4 fl oz/125 ml) coconut cream (see page 289)

1 tablespoon butter or margarine

salt and freshly ground black pepper

Soak beans in water to cover overnight. Drain.

Place beans and 4 cups (32 fl oz/1 l) fresh water in large saucepan and boil until beans are cooked but still firm, 45 to 60 minutes. Stir in all remaining ingredients. If using creamed coconut, add 2 cups (16 fl oz/500 ml) water; if using coconut cream, add 1 1/2 cups (12 fl oz/375 ml) water. Boil until water is 1/2 inch (1 cm) deep above rice, about 5 minutes. Reduce heat, cover tightly, and simmer gently until rice is cooked, 25 to 30 minutes. Serve immediately.

Following page: Moros y Cristianos, Rice and Peas in Coconut, Habichuelas Rojas

HABICHUELAS ROJAS

SERVES 6 TO 8

These stewed red beans are from the Spanish-speaking islands. They are usually served as an accompaniment to a main dish but are tasty enough to form a vegetarian meal if served with rice (see page 174) or boiled yams or cassava (see page 185).

1 lb (500 g) dried red kidney beans, soaked overnight and drained

8 cups (2 l) water

2 tablespoons olive oil

4 oz (125 g) ham, optional

2 medium onions, finely chopped

1 green bell pepper (capsicum), seeded and finely chopped

8 oz (250 g) pumpkin, peeled and cubed

8 oz (250 g) potatoes, peeled and cubed

2 sprigs parsley, finely chopped

1 chicken bouillon (stock) cube

2 tablespoons tomato paste (puree)

$1/4$ teaspoon cumin

1 teaspoon chopped fresh oregano or $1/4$ teaspoon dried

salt and freshly ground black pepper

Combine beans and water in large saucepan with 1 tablespoon olive oil and ham. Cook over medium low heat until beans are tender but not mushy, about 2 to $2^1/2$ hours.

Add onions, bell pepper, pumpkin, potatoes, parsley, bouillon cube, and tomato paste and cook until beans are soft. Add cumin, oregano, remaining olive oil, and salt and pepper and cook 5 more minutes or until beans are very soft. Serve hot.

Arroz con Habichuelas

SERVES 4 TO 6

This dish from the Spanish-speaking islands translates literally as "rice with red kidney beans." Serve with any meat or fish dish, particularly stews.

1¹/₃ cups (8 oz/250 g) dried kidney beans

4 cups (32 fl oz/1 l) water

2 teaspoons salt or to taste

3 tablespoons vegetable oil

2 teaspoons annatto oil (see page 285)

2 oz (60 g) ham, chopped

1 oz (30 g) salt pork, chopped, optional

1 onion, chopped

2 cloves garlic, crushed

2 small hot peppers, seeded and finely chopped

2 teaspoons chopped fresh oregano or 1 teaspoon dried

2 teaspoons tomato paste (puree)

2¹/₂ cups (13 oz/400 g) rice

Soak beans in water overnight.

Bring beans and soaking water to boil with salt in medium saucepan. Reduce heat to medium low, partially cover, and cook until beans are tender but not mushy, about 1 hour.

Heat vegetable oil in frying pan over medium heat. Add annatto oil and sauté ham, pork, onion, garlic, hot peppers, and oregano until onion is soft, about 5 minutes. Stir in tomato paste and rice. Add rice mixture to beans and cook over medium heat until most of water has been absorbed, about 4 minutes. Reduce heat, cover, and cook until rice is tender and all water is absorbed, about 20 minutes. Serve hot.

SPINACH BHAJI

SERVES 4

Bhaji is the name given to Indian kale or calalloo and is sometimes known as Chinese spinach. Serve as an accompaniment with rice, dhal and roti (see pages 153 and 196), or fried rice (see page 174).

2 tablespoons vegetable oil

2 cloves garlic, minced

8 oz (250 g) spinach, callaloo leaves, or Swiss chard, washed, stemmed, and finely chopped

2 oz (60 g) dried shrimp (prawns), soaked in 1 cup (8 fl oz/250 ml) water, optional

1 hot pepper, seeded and finely chopped, optional

salt and freshly ground black pepper

Heat oil in heavy saucepan over high heat. Add garlic and greens and stir well. Drain shrimp and add to saucepan with hot pepper and salt and pepper to taste. Cook until greens are wilted and most of the liquid has evaporated, about 8 to 10 minutes. Serve hot.

FUNCHI

SERVES 4

Also known as funghi, this cornmeal dish from Curaçao and the Dutch-speaking islands is similar to Bajan cou-cou (see page 152). Serve with giambo soup (see page 58) or stobá di cabrito (page 92), or as an accompaniment to meat stews.

1¼ cups (10 fl oz/300ml) cold water

1½ cups (9 oz/275 g) cornmeal

butter

1½ cups (12 fl oz/375 ml) water

2 teaspoons salt

Combine cold water and cornmeal in small saucepan. Butter a serving bowl and set aside.

Bring 1½ cups water to boil in medium saucepan with salt and 1 tablespoon butter. Reduce heat to medium high and gradually add cornmeal paste, stirring constantly with a wooden spoon until mixture thickens. Continue to cook until the funchi leaves sides of pan. Transfer to prepared bowl and serve hot.

Spinach Bhaji

151

COU-COU

This side dish from Barbados has its origins in West Africa where a number of different vegetables are prepared this way. Cou-cou should be served hot; try it as an accompaniment to Bajan Brown Stew (page 73). Leftover cou-cou can be sliced and lightly fried to accompany another meal.

1 cup (6 oz/175 g)
yellow cornmeal

1 cup (8 fl oz/250 ml) cold water

butter

1¼ cups (10 fl oz/300 ml) water

6 okras, trimmed and cut into
¼-inch (5 mm) slices

1 teaspoon salt

Combine cornmeal and cold water in small bowl. Butter a serving bowl and set aside.

Bring 1¼ cups water to boil in deep medium saucepan. Add okra and boil 5 minutes. Reduce heat and add salt. Gradually add cornmeal paste, stirring constantly with a wooden spoon until mixture becomes very thick and begins to leave sides of pan. Transfer to prepared bowl and form a mound. Make a depression in the top and add 1 tablespoon butter. Serve hot.

BREADFRUIT COU-COU

butter

1 lb (500 g) ripe breadfruit, peeled,
cored, and cut into
2-inch (5 cm) cubes

3 oz (90 g) salted or corned
meat, finely chopped

water

3 green onions, chopped

1 tablespoon butter

freshly ground black pepper

Butter a serving bowl and set aside.

Place breadfruit and meat in deep saucepan and add enough water to cover by 1 inch (2.5 cm). Bring to boil, then cook until breadfruit is just tender, about 15 to 20 minutes, adding green onions near the end. Drain. Mash until smooth. Add about 3 tablespoons water, just enough so that you can stir the cou-cou with a wooden spoon. Mound in a bowl. Make a depression in the top of the mound and add 1 tablespoon butter. Serve warm.

DHAL

The word dhal is Hindi for split peas. This dish was brought to the Caribbean by the East Indian community. It should be a thick sauce but the consistency can vary depending on personal taste. There are various utensils made for pureeing the soft peas but a hand whisk or electric blender makes a good substitute. A good accompaniment to curries, spinach bhaji (page 150), smoked herring choka (page 134), baigan choka (page 164), and tomato choka (page 162).

2 cups (1 lb/500 g) yellow split peas

5 cups (1.25 l) water

1/2 teaspoon salt or to taste

1 teaspoon turmeric

1/2 teaspoon curry powder

2 whole hot peppers, optional

1 small onion, chopped

2 tablespoons vegetable oil

2 cloves garlic, finely chopped

1/2 teaspoon cumin seeds

Wash split peas thoroughly, removing any debris. Place in saucepan with water and bring to boil. Skim off froth. Add salt, turmeric, curry powder, hot peppers, and onion and cook covered on medium low heat until peas begin to soften, about 45 minutes. Using a wooden spoon, beat the dhal until it begins to thicken.

In a ladle or very small frying pan, heat oil until very hot. Add garlic and cumin and fry until garlic is golden brown and seeds are almost black. If you have used a ladle, quickly lower it into the dhal saucepan, partially covering the saucepan to keep oil from splattering. If you have used a frying pan, carefully spoon oil mixture into the dhal. Cook dhal until split peas have formed a sauce consistency, about 50 to 60 minutes, beating occasionally with a wooden spoon to help dhal thicken. You may need to add some water from time to time if dhal becomes too thick, as it should be only slightly thickened (although this may vary according to personal preference).

DUMPLINGS

SERVES 4

These Guyanese dumplings can be added to a soup or served as an accompaniment to any meal along with ground provisions (see page 185).

2 cups (8 oz/250 g) all-purpose (plain) flour

1/2 teaspoon baking powder

1/2 teaspoon salt

water

1/2 cup (4 fl oz/125 ml) vegetable oil

Sift flour, baking powder, and salt into large mixing bowl. Gradually mix in enough water to form a firm dough, about 1 cup (8 fl oz/250 ml). Knead dough for 2 minutes.

Bring 8 cups (2 l) water to boil in medium saucepan. Roll tablespoon-size portions of dough between your hands into sausage shapes about 3 inches (8 cm) long. Place in boiling water, cover, and cook 4 to 5 minutes.

Heat oil in frying pan over medium heat. Remove dumplings from saucepan with slotted spoon and fry in hot oil until lightly golden on all sides, 3 to 4 minutes. Serve hot.

SPINNERS

MAKES 4

These are Jamaican dumplings, often found in soups and stews. When making them, you spin the dough between the palms of your hands—thus the name. You will be able to tell when they are cooked, as they will become very dense and heavy in weight and texture.

2 cups (8 oz/250 g) all-purpose (plain) flour

1/4 teaspoon baking powder

1/4 teaspoon salt

water

Sift flour, baking powder, and salt into bowl. Add enough water to form a firm dough. Roll dough into sausage shapes 1 inch (2.5 cm) long and 1/4 inch (5 mm) thick. Drop spinners into soup or stew and cook, covered, 15 to 20 minutes before serving.

Or spinners can be prepared as an accompaniment. Roll into sausage shapes about 3 inches (8 cm) long and 1/2 inch (1 cm) thick. Drop into salted boiling water, cover, and cook for 15 to 20 minutes. Drain and serve hot.

Dumplings

DOUBLES

In the Caribbean, this Indian bread with curried chickpea filling is found only in Trinidad. Whenever I go over to Trinidad my uncle, Sankar, makes sure I taste the doubles before I leave. Roadside vendors in Port of Spain sell it wrapped up in paper with a little mango chutney or kuchilla, and it is delicious as a snack or for lunch. Serve with mango chutney (see page 270), kuchilla (see page 269), or hot pepper sauce (see page 274).

Dough:

1 teaspoon active dry yeast

1 cup (8 fl oz/250 ml) warm water

2 cups (8 oz/250 g) all-purpose (plain) flour

1/2 teaspoon salt

3/4 teaspoon turmeric

1/2 teaspoon ground cumin

4 cups (1 l) vegetable oil for deep frying

Filling:

8 oz (250 g) chickpeas, soaked overnight and drained

water

3 cloves garlic, minced

1 small onion, finely chopped

3 green onions, minced

1/2 teaspoon masala (see page 284), optional

1 tablespoon curry powder

1/4 teaspoon cumin seeds

1 hot red pepper, seeded and minced

2 tablespoons water

1/4 cup (2 fl oz/60 ml) vegetable oil

1/2 teaspoon ground cumin

salt

For dough: Sprinkle yeast over 1/2 cup (4 fl oz/125 ml) warm water in small bowl and let stand 5 minutes.

Sift flour, salt, turmeric, and cumin into large bowl. Gradually add yeast mixture and remaining 1/2 cup warm water and mix thoroughly, then knead to form a soft, smooth dough. Let rise in a warm place 2 hours.

Heat 4 cups oil in medium saucepan over medium high heat. Divide dough into small balls (about 2 tablespoons each) and knead into smooth balls on lightly floured surface. Gently roll out each on floured surface to 5 inches (12 cm) diameter. Fry in hot oil until lightly golden. Drain on paper towels.

For filling: Boil chickpeas in 8 cups (2 l) salted water until tender, about 45 to 60 minutes. Drain and set aside. Mix garlic, onions, masala, curry powder, cumin seeds, hot pepper, and 2 tablespoons water.

Heat oil in medium frying pan until hot. Add curry paste mixture and sauté 2 to 3 minutes. Stir in chickpeas and about 1/3 cup (3 fl oz/90 ml) water. Stir in ground cumin.

Put a tablespoon of filling in the middle of each bread circle. Fold in half, then in quarters. Serve immediately.

ALOO ROTI

SERVES 6

This Indian bread with spicy potato stuffing is eaten as a snack or a meal. Serve with a chutney or kuchilla (see page 269 to 272).

8 cups (2 lb/1 kg) all-purpose (plain) flour

1 tablespoon baking powder

1/2 teaspoon salt

2 to 3 cups (16 to 24 fl oz/ 500 to 750 ml) water

1 1/2 lb (750 g) baking potatoes, peeled and diced

1 green onion, green part only, minced, optional

2 cloves garlic, crushed

1 teaspoon cumin

1 hot pepper, seeded and minced

salt and freshly ground black pepper

1 tablespoon vegetable oil or melted ghee

about 1/2 cup (4 fl oz/125 ml) vegetable oil or melted ghee

Sift flour, baking powder, and salt into large mixing bowl. Gradually mix in enough water to form soft dough. Knead dough until smooth and elastic. Cover and let rest 1 hour.

Divide dough into eight equal parts and shape into smooth balls. Let rest 5 minutes.

Boil potatoes in water to cover until soft. Drain. Mash with green onion, garlic, cumin, hot pepper, and salt and pepper. Let cool slightly.

On floured surface, roll out one ball of dough into a circle 5 inches (12 cm) in diameter. Spread 1/2 teaspoon oil or ghee over surface with the back of a spoon. Spoon 1 to 2 heaping tablespoons of potato filling in the middle. Bring edges of dough to a central point and squeeze together. Flatten squeezed edges, maintaining ball shape. Place ball, edges down, on a lightly floured surface while preparing the remaining rotis.

Heat large shallow frying pan or tawa (a traditional flat iron griddle). Gently flatten one filled ball of dough on floured surface. Roll out carefully to 6 to 7 inches (15 to 18 cm) in diameter. Place on hot pan and reduce heat to medium. Turn roti after 1 minute and spread 1 to 2 teaspoons oil or ghee over the slightly cooked side. Repeat on second side. Cook on both sides until roti is lightly browned and begins to puff up. As each roti is cooked, place on large plate and cover with clean towel to keep hot. Serve immediately.

FOO FOO

This dish, also known as fufu, consists of pounded plantain that is formed into balls. It is thought to have originated in West Africa, where a similar dish is eaten and where the same method is used to prepare other vegetables. Eat the foo foo warm with soups and stews.

3 green plantains, unpeeled
1 tablespoon milk or water
2 tablespoons butter
salt

Boil whole plantains in large saucepan in plenty of water until soft, about 30 minutes. Let cool slightly, then peel. Chop plantains coarsely and mash with a fork, adding milk or water. Mix in butter and salt to taste. Form into balls and serve warm.

MOFONGO

This Puerto Rican dish is delicious served with stews or as accompaniment to any meat or fish dish. The pork crackling can be omitted if you prefer.

4 ripe yellow plantains
1/2 cup (4 fl oz/125 ml) water
salt
about 1 cup (8 fl oz/250 ml)
vegetable oil for deep frying
4 oz (125 g) chicharrones
(pork crackling) (see page 28)
freshly ground black pepper
2 cloves garlic, crushed

Peel plantains and cut diagonally into 1-inch (2.5 cm) pieces. Place in bowl with water and 1/2 teaspoon salt and let stand 10 minutes.

Heat oil in small saucepan until very hot. Drain plantains, reserving water. Fry until tender but not very crisp, about 8 minutes. Pat dry. Drain on paper towels.

Grind plantains in mixing bowl or large mortar, gradually adding chicharrones. Add 2 tablespoons of the reserved water and press gently into plantains. Season with salt and pepper and blend in garlic. Shape the mofongo into balls about the size of tennis balls and serve hot.

Mofongo

GREEN SALAD

SERVES 4

1/2 romaine (cos) lettuce, cleaned

2 firm tomatoes, sliced

1/2 large cucumber, thinly sliced

6 radishes, trimmed and quartered

1 firm ripe avocado,
peeled, pitted, and cubed

1 bunch watercress,
torn into small pieces

Vinaigrette:

3 tablespoons extra virgin olive oil

1 tablespoon white vinegar

1 clove garlic, pounded

salt and freshly ground
black pepper

Toss salad ingredients in bowl and chill. Mix vinaigrette ingredients and let stand 15 minutes. Discard garlic. Pour dressing over salad and serve.

COLESLAW

SERVES 6

1/2 white cabbage,
very finely grated

1 carrot, very finely grated

1/2 small onion, minced

1/4 green bell pepper (capiscum),
seeded, finely grated, and
drained on paper towel

3 tablespoons mayonnaise

salt and white pepper to taste

Combine all vegetables in bowl. Add mayonnaise, salt and pepper and mix well. Serve chilled.

AVOCADO SALAD

SERVES 6

1 tablespoon lemon juice

3 tablespoons extra virgin olive oil

2 teaspoons finely chopped
fresh parsley

1 clove garlic, pounded

salt and freshly ground
black pepper

2 large avocados,
peeled and pitted

Combine all ingredients except avocado and let stand 10 minutes.

Slice avocado and place in bowl. Discard garlic from dressing and pour over avocado. Serve immediately.

POTATO SALAD

SERVES 6

2 lb (1kg) boiling potatoes,
peeled and diced

1/2 teaspoon salt

1 small onion, sliced

1 green onion, chopped

1/3 green bell pepper (capsicum),
seeded and finely chopped

1/3 red bell pepper (capsicum),
seeded and finely chopped

3 hard-cooked eggs, sliced

salt and freshly ground
white pepper

1 teaspoon hot pepper sauce
(see page 274)

3/4 cup (6 fl oz/175 ml)
mayonnaise

1 teaspoon finely chopped
fresh parsley

Boil potatoes in water with salt until tender but not soft. Drain and cool.

Combine all vegetables and eggs in large bowl. Blend salt, pepper, and hot pepper sauce into mayonnaise. Add to salad and mix well. Garnish with parsley. Serve chilled.

TOMATO CHOKA

SERVES 4

A popular East Indian breakfast dish eaten with sada roti (see page 192). My aunt from Trinidad gave this recipe to me—it's virtually identical to the one found in Guyana. If possible, roast the tomatoes on a barbecue or over an open flame. Otherwise, roast them for about 30 minutes in a greased baking dish in an oven preheated to 400°F (200°C/Gas 6).

1 lb (500 g) ripe tomatoes
1/2 small onion, minced
salt
1 hot pepper, seeded and chopped
2 cloves garlic, minced
1 tablespoon vegetable oil

Roast tomatoes until soft and charred. Let cool slightly, then peel. Mash flesh to a pulp.

Stir in onion, salt, and hot pepper while tomatoes are still hot. Sprinkle garlic over; do not mix. Heat oil in very small pan until very hot. Pour over garlic, then stir into tomatoes. Serve hot.

SALADE DE TOMATES

SERVES 4

This side salad from Martinique is quick and easy to prepare. The combination of garlic and tomato makes an excellent accompaniment to virtually any meal.

2 ripe but firm tomatoes, sliced
2 cloves garlic, crushed slightly, then finely chopped
1 tablespoon wine vinegar
1/2 cup (4 fl oz/125 ml) olive or peanut oil
1/8 teaspoon salt or to taste

Place tomato slices in a shallow dish. Combine garlic, vinegar, oil, and salt and let stand 5 minutes. Pour over tomato slices and serve chilled or at room temperature.

Tomato Choka

BAIGAN CHOKA

This was much loved by my grandfather, who would often fill the house with the smell of roasting eggplant and tomatoes. Baigan means eggplant in Hindi, while choka refers to the method of roasting vegetables and blending them with spices. It is a superb accompaniment to a meal, or you can just eat it with a bread, such as bakes (see page 193).

1 large eggplant (aubergine)

2 cloves garlic, halved

1 medium tomato, cut into 6 segments

1 small onion, quartered

1/2 teaspoon cumin

salt and freshly ground black pepper

Preheat oven to 425° F (220 °C/Gas 7).

Make two lengthwise slits in eggplant. Insert garlic, tomato, and onion into slits. Wrap in foil, place on baking sheet, and bake until eggplant is soft, about 40 minutes.

Carefully unwrap eggplant. Peel back skin and scoop out flesh with a fork. Place eggplant flesh in bowl with garlic, tomato, and onion. Add cumin, salt and pepper and mash together until well blended. Serve hot.

SALADE D'AUBERGINES

Aubergines are also known as bélangère on the French-speaking islands. The dressing on this salad is very popular, and can be used on other vegetables such as christophenes or spinach.

2 eggplants (aubergines), peeled and cut into 1/4-inch (5 mm) rounds

1/2 teaspoon salt

1 tablespoon distilled white wine vinegar

3 tablespoons soy or extra virgin olive oil

1 clove garlic, crushed

2 green onions, finely chopped

1 small hot pepper, seeded and minced, optional

salt and freshly ground black pepper

1 teaspoon finely chopped parsley

Cook eggplant in medium saucepan with salt and enough water to cover until tender, about 10 to 15 minutes. Drain and place in shallow dish. Cut into smaller pieces.

Combine vinegar, oil, garlic, green onions, hot pepper, and salt and pepper to taste. Pour over eggplant and toss. Garnish with parsley and serve chilled.

MIXED BEAN SALAD

$^{1}/_{2}$ cup (3 oz/80 g)
cooked kidney beans

$^{1}/_{2}$ cup (3 oz/80 g)
cooked chickpeas

$^{1}/_{2}$ cup (3 oz/80 g)
cooked green beans

$^{1}/_{2}$ cup (3 oz/80 g)
cooked black-eyed peas

1 firm ripe avocado,
peeled, pitted, and cubed

1 small onion, sliced

$^{1}/_{2}$ red bell pepper (capsicum),
seeded and cut into strips

2 chives, finely chopped

Dressing:

2 cloves garlic, finely chopped

$^{1}/_{4}$ teaspoon ground allspice

$1^{1}/_{2}$ tablespoons white vinegar

$1^{1}/_{2}$ teaspoons lemon juice

$^{1}/_{2}$ cup (4 fl oz/125 ml)
extra virgin olive oil

1 small hot red pepper,
seeded and minced, optional

salt and freshly ground
black pepper

Combine all beans, avocado, onion, and bell pepper in bowl. Whisk together dressing ingredients, pour over beans, and toss. Refrigerate 2 hours. Serve garnished with chopped chives.

Following page: Mixed Bean Salad, Green Banana Salad, Serenata

167

GREEN BANANA SALAD

SERVES 4

2 green bananas, boiled
(see page 185) and cut into 1-inch
(2.5-cm) slices

1/2 bunch watercress,
torn into small pieces

1 celery stalk, finely chopped

1 avocado,
peeled, pitted, and cubed

1 small onion, sliced

1 romaine (cos) lettuce

1/2 cucumber, finely diced

1 carrot, grated

1 tomato, cubed

Dressing:

1/4 cup (2 fl oz/60 ml)
extra virgin olive oil

1/2 teaspoon dry mustard

1 clove garlic, crushed

1 tablespoon lemon juice

1 teaspoon finely chopped parsley

salt and freshly ground
black pepper

Combine bananas and all vegetables in large bowl. Whisk together dressing ingredients and pour over salad. Serve chilled.

SERENATA

SERVES 6

Serve this Puerto Rican salt cod salad with boiled yam, green bananas, or fried yellow plantain (see pages 170 and 185).

1 lb (500 g) salt cod

2 tomatoes, sliced

2 onions, sliced

1 cup (8 fl oz/250 ml) extra virgin olive oil

1/2 cup (4 ft oz/125 ml) white vinegar

salt and freshly ground black pepper

3 olives, pitted and sliced

Soak salt cod for at least 4 hours, preferrably overnight, in water to cover generously. Remove skin and bones, and flake fish.

Combine fish with tomatoes and onions in bowl. Whisk together oil, vinegar, and salt and pepper and pour over fish mixture. Garnish with sliced olives. Chill well before serving.

CONCH SALAD

SERVES 6

Abalone makes a good substitute for conch. The conch meat should be washed with lime juice and then pounded with a mallet before using to tenderize it.

1 lb (500 g) conch meat, pounded and cut into very small pieces

1/4 cup (2 fl oz/60 ml) lime juice

1/2 small onion, thinly sliced

1/4 cucumber, finely diced

1 tomato, peeled and finely chopped

1/2 celery stalk, finely chopped

1/2 hot red pepper, seeded and minced, optional

salt and freshly ground black pepper

1/2 romaine (cos) lettuce

1 tablespoon finely chopped parsley

Combine conch meat with lime juice in bowl. Add remaining ingredients, except lettuce and parsley, and mix well. Refrigerate for 1 hour. Serve on lettuce leaves and garnish with parsley.

FRIED CARAILLA

SERVES 4 TO 6

This bitter melon dish is often eaten with dhal (see page 153) or boiled white rice (see page 174). See glossary for more information.

2 lb (1 kg) carailla, seeded, cored, and very thinly sliced

2 teaspoons salt

4 to 6 tablespoons vegetable oil

2 cloves garlic, crushed

1/2 small onion, chopped

Place carailla slices in shallow dish and sprinkle with salt. Let stand 1 hour to extract bitter juices. Squeeze more juice out of carailla using paper towels.

Heat oil in shallow saucepan over high heat. Add garlic and onion and sauté 1 minute. Add carailla, reduce heat to medium high, and cook until brown and crisp. Serve hot.

FRIED PLANTAINS

SERVES 6

This was a family favorite when we were growing up in London, where plantain was an occasional treat. Plantain can be cut into larger sections, and parboiled for 10 to 12 minutes before frying. Serve as an accompaniment to any meal, or on their own as a quick snack.

2 ripe yellow plantains, peeled

6 tablespoons vegetable or corn oil

Cut each plantain into 3 equal sections. Cut each section lengthwise into slices about 1/4 inch (5 mm) thick.

Heat oil in large frying pan over medium heat. Fry plantains on both sides until golden brown, about 2 to 3 minutes. Drain on paper towels and serve hot.

Fried Plantains

FRIED CASSAVA

SERVES 4 TO 6

salt

8 cups (2 l) water

2 lb (1 kg) cassava, peeled and
cut into 2-inch (5 cm) cubes

1/2 cup (4 fl oz/125 ml)
vegetable oil

Bring salted water to boil. Add cassava pieces and boil until tender but not mushy, 10 to 12 minutes. Drain and remove any stringy parts from cassava.

Heat oil in frying pan until hot. Add cassava and fry over medium heat until very lightly golden, turning to brown evenly. Drain on paper towels and serve hot.

SAUTÉED BORA

SERVES 6 TO 8

Bora are also known as yard-long beans or snake beans. Serve this with roti (see page 196) or as a side dish.

3 tablespoons vegetable oil

1 medium onion, sliced

2 cloves garlic, minced

2 medium tomatoes, chopped

1 hot red pepper, seeded and
finely chopped, optional

1 lb (500 g) bora, washed,
stringed, and cut into
1-inch (2.5 cm) pieces

3 tablespoons water

1/4 teaspoon cumin

salt and freshly ground
black pepper

Heat oil in frying pan over medium high heat. Add onion and garlic and sauté 1 minute. Add tomatoes and hot pepper and sauté 3 more minutes. Add bora and water and stir well. Add cumin and salt and pepper. Reduce heat to low, cover, and cook until bora are tender, about 8 to 10 minutes, stirring regularly. Serve hot.

PUMPKIN CURRY

SERVES 4

Serve with boiled rice (see page 174) or roti (see pages 192 and 196) and dahl (see page 153).

3 tablespoons vegetable oil

1 medium onion, chopped

2 green onions, chopped

2 cloves garlic, crushed

1/4 red bell pepper (capsicum), seeded and chopped

1 hot pepper, seeded and chopped, optional

2 teaspoons curry powder

1/4 teaspoon turmeric

1/4 teaspoon cumin

1/2 teaspoon garam masala

1/4 teaspoon mixed dried herbs (thyme, marjoram, basil, oregano, sage)

freshly ground black pepper

1/2 cup (4 fl oz/125 ml) water

1 lb (500 g) pumpkin, peeled, cleaned, and cubed

salt

Heat oil in medium saucepan over high heat. Add onions, garlic, bell pepper, and hot pepper and fry until onion is golden brown and tender. Increase heat to high, add curry powder, turmeric, cumin, garam masala, mixed herbs, and black pepper and fry 2 to 3 minutes, stirring frequently to keep spices from sticking. Add half the water, stirring constantly. Add pumpkin, salt, and remaining water and mix well. Reduce heat to medium low, cover, and cook until pumpkin is very soft, about 30 minutes, stirring occasionally. Serve hot.

BOILED WHITE RICE

SERVES 4

2 cups (12 oz/350 g) long-grain rice, rinsed until water runs almost clear

2 cups (16 fl oz/500 ml) cold water

1 teaspoon butter

1/4 teaspoon salt, optional

Combine rice and water in medium saucepan and bring to boil over medium high heat. Boil 4 to 5 minutes. Add butter and salt and cook until most (but not all) water is evaporated, about 3 to 4 minutes. Reduce heat to very low, cover tightly, and cook 18 minutes, without lifting lid. Lift lid and check to see if all water has been absorbed. If not, cover and cook for another few minutes.

FRIED RICE

SERVES 4

Vary this dish by using corn or peas instead of carrots and beans. Or stir in a beaten egg after adding rice.

3 tablespoons peanut or corn oil

1 lb (500 g) chicken breast, chopped into 1 inch (2.5 cm) pieces

1 onion, chopped

1 green onion, chopped

1 clove garlic, finely chopped

1 sprig thyme, finely chopped

1 hot pepper, seeded and minced

1/3 green bell pepper (capsicum), finely chopped

1/3 red bell pepper (capsicum), finely chopped

6 celery leaves, finely chopped

1/2 teaspoon tomato puree (paste)

1/2 cup (2 oz/60 g) cooked green beans, sliced into 1/2-inch (1-cm) pieces

2 carrots, cooked and diced

1 tablespoon soy sauce (optional)

4 cups (1 lb/500 g) cooked rice

Heat oil in large saucepan or wok and fry chicken until browned. Add onions, garlic, thyme, hot pepper, peppers, and celery leaves and cook until onions are soft. Add tomato puree, beans, carrots, and cook 3 to 4 minutes over low heat. Add soy sauce. Add rice. Stir well until all ingredients are combined and heated through. Serve hot.

Fried Rice

ALOO CURRY

SERVES 4

This potato curry should be served with sada roti (see page 192) or roti (page 196).

3 tablespoons vegetable oil

1/4 teaspoon cumin seeds

2 cloves garlic, minced

1 small onion, finely chopped

1 green onion, finely chopped

3 celery leaves, finely chopped

1 hot green or red pepper,
seeded and minced

1 tablespoon curry powder

1/4 cup (2 fl oz/60 ml) water

2 lb (1 kg) potatoes,
peeled and cubed

2 cups (16 fl oz/500 ml) hot water

Heat oil in medium saucepan over medium high heat. Add cumin seeds and fry 1 minute. Add garlic, onions, celery leaves, and hot pepper and fry 2 minutes.

Combine curry powder and 1/4 cup water in small bowl to form a paste. Add to pan and sauté 3 minutes. Add potatoes and stir well. Add hot water and cook over medium low heat until potatoes are very tender, about 10 minutes. Serve hot.

JACKFRUIT CURRY

SERVES 4 TO 6

Jackfruit is very closely related to breadfruit. Both produce very large seeds which are edible when boiled and salted. Serve this curry with roti (see page 196) or boiled rice (see page 174).

1 jackfruit, peeled, halved and seeded

1/4 cup (2 fl oz/60 ml) vegetable oil

2 cloves garlic, minced

1 small onion, finely chopped

3 green onions, finely chopped

1 hot red pepper, seeded and minced

1/2 teaspoon cumin seeds

1 teaspoon ground cumin

1 tablespoon curry powder

2 tablespoons water

2 cups (16 fl oz/500 ml) coconut milk (see page 289) or water

salt

Remove core from jackfruit and cut flesh into small pieces. Wash, drain, and set aside.

Heat oil in large, heavy saucepan over medium high heat. Add garlic, onions, hot pepper and cumin seeds and fry 1 minute. Combine ground cumin and curry powder with water to form a paste, add to pan, and fry 3 minutes. Stir in jackfruit. Add coconut milk and salt, reduce heat to low, and cook until soft, about 30 minutes, stirring occasionally. Serve hot.

FRIED OKRA

SERVES 4

Okras are eaten all over the Caribbean and are very much part of the everyday cuisine. Serve as an accompaniment to dhal (see page 153), curries, and stews.

1/4 cup (2 fl oz/60 ml) vegetable oil

2 cloves garlic, chopped

1 medium onion, chopped

1 lb (500 g) okra, trimmed and sliced

1 teaspoon cumin

salt and freshly ground black pepper

Heat oil in medium saucepan over medium heat and sauté garlic and onion until soft. Add okra and cook over medium heat 10 minutes, stirring frequently. Add cumin and salt and pepper and cook 10 minutes longer. Serve hot.

SAUTÉED OKRA WITH SHRIMP

SERVES 4

Serve with boiled rice (see page 174) or dhal and roti (see pages 153 and 196).

1 lb (500 g) shrimp (prawns), peeled

juice of 1/2 lime

1/4 cup (2 fl oz/60 ml) vegetable oil

2 cloves garlic, minced

2 green onions, finely chopped

1 small onion, finely chopped

1 lb (500 g) okra, trimmed and cut into 1/4-inch (5 mm) pieces

1 small hot red pepper, seeded and finely chopped, optional

1 teaspoon cumin

salt

Sprinkle shrimp with lime juice.

Heat oil in frying pan over medium high heat. Add garlic and onions and sauté 1 minute. Add okra, hot pepper, cumin, and salt to taste and sauté 4 more minutes. Add shrimp and sauté until okra is soft, about 10 to 12 minutes. Serve hot.

Fried Okra

CHRISTOPHENE SALAD

SERVES 4 TO 6

This squash, originating in Mexico, is very versatile; it can be stuffed or used in soups, stews, or salads. The salad, which is eaten on the French-speaking islands of Martinique and Guadeloupe, makes a good accompaniment to any meal.

2 lb (1 kg) christophenes
(chayote squash/chokos)

salt

3 tablespoons corn or soy oil

1 tablespoon white wine vinegar
or distilled white vinegar

1 clove garlic, crushed

2 green onions, chopped, optional

2 shallots, chopped

1/4 teaspoon minced seeded
hot pepper

freshly ground black pepper

Bring large saucepan of salted water to boil. Add christophenes and boil until tender, about 20 minutes. Let cool.

Peel and halve christophenes, discarding the seed and tough surrounding flesh. Cut into cubes.

Combine oil, vinegar, garlic, green onions, shallots, hot pepper, and salt and pepper to taste and mix well. Pour over christophenes and chill before serving.

ROAST BREADFRUIT

SERVES 6–8

The best breadfruit is yellow-heart. It's good as an accompaniment to ackee (see page 124) or roast fish (see page 116) as well as meat dishes.

1 breadfruit
(preferably yellow-heart)

2 tablespoons butter
or to taste

Preheat oven to 350°F (180°C/Gas 4). Place breadfruit on baking sheet or in ovenproof dish and roast until soft to touch, about 30 to 40 minutes. (To test, insert a skewer into breadfruit; if it comes out clean, breadfruit is cooked.) Slice top off breadfruit. Using a sharp knife, cut out the core; use a large spoon to scoop it out. Peel the breadfruit, protecting your hands from the heat with a towel. Halve, then cut into slices. Dot generously with butter and serve hot.

STUFFED BREADFRUIT

SERVES 6

This makes an excellent and impressive meal. Serve on a platter surrounded by salad.

1 medium breadfruit
(preferably yellow-heart)

1 tablespoon butter

1/2 teaspoon salt or to taste

3 tablespoons milk

3 tablespoons vegetable oil

1 onion, finely chopped

1 clove garlic, finely chopped

1 hot pepper, seeded and chopped

8 oz (250 g) salt pork or bacon,
cut into 1/2-inch (1 cm) pieces

2 oz (60 g) bacon, chopped

1 medium tomato, chopped

1/4 teaspoon ground allspice

Prepare breadfruit as instructed in recipe for roast breadfruit (see page 180) up through removal of core. Reserve cut-off top. Scoop out roasted breadfruit, taking care not to pierce the skin, and reserve shell. Place breadfruit flesh in large bowl with butter, salt, and milk and mash together.

Heat oil in frying pan over high heat. Add onion, garlic, and hot pepper and cook 2 minutes. Add meat and cook until lightly browned, about 5 minutes. Add tomato, reduce heat to medium, and cook until liquid evaporates.

Preheat oven to 300°F (150°C/Gas 2). Combine meat mixture with breadfruit and spoon back into empty breadfruit shell. Replace top and secure with toothpicks. Wrap breadfruit in foil and place in baking dish. Bake until warmed through, about 10 to 15 minutes. Unwrap breadfruit and serve.

MACARONI PIE

SERVES 6 TO 8

Interestingly, this dish turns up in Barbados as a frequently served accompaniment to stews and meals.

8 oz (250 g) macaroni

1/4 cup (2 oz/60 g) margarine or butter

8 oz (250 g) cheddar cheese, grated

1 onion, minced

1/2 teaspoon dry mustard

salt and freshly ground black pepper

1 cup (8 fl oz/250 ml) milk

2 eggs, beaten

paprika

Preheat oven to 350°F (180°C/Gas 4). Grease 9 x 5-inch (23 x 13 cm) baking dish. Boil macaroni in salted water until just cooked. Drain thoroughly.

Return drained macaroni to saucepan. Add margarine, cheese, onion, mustard, and salt and pepper and mix well. Blend milk and eggs and quickly stir into macaroni.

Pour mixture into prepared baking dish and sprinkle with paprika. Bake until firm and golden brown, about 20 minutes. Slice and serve hot.

YAM FRITTERS

SERVES 4

1 lb (500 g) yam, peeled and finely grated

1 tablespoon softened butter

2 green onions, finely chopped

1 tablespoon all-purpose (plain) flour

1/2 teaspoon baking powder

salt and freshly ground black pepper

1 oz (30 g) bacon, chopped, optional

2 tablespoons vegetable oil, optional

1 egg, beaten

1/2 cup (4 fl oz/125 ml) vegetable oil

Combine yam, butter, green onions, flour, baking powder, and salt and pepper in mixing bowl.

Fry bacon in 2 tablespoons vegetable oil or broil (grill) until crisp. Add to yam mixture. Blend in egg.

Heat oil in saucepan over medium high heat. Drop in mixture by tablespoons and fry until golden brown. Drain on paper towels and serve immediately.

Macaroni Pie

ENSALADA MIXTA

A mixed salad typical of the Spanish-speaking islands.

2 hard-cooked eggs, sliced

2 large boiling potatoes, cooked and sliced

1 small onion, thinly sliced

4 oz (125 g) carrots, thinly sliced

8 olives

10 cooked asparagus tips

2 sweet gherkins, optional

1 cup (4 oz/125 g) cooked peas

1/4 cup (2 fl oz/60 ml) extra virgin olive oil

2 teaspoons white vinegar

1/2 teaspoon salt

1/8 teaspoon white pepper

1/4 cup (2 fl oz/60 ml) mayonnaise

Place 1 1/2 eggs and potatoes in bowl. Add onion, carrots, olives, asparagus tips, gherkins, and peas.

Combine olive oil, vinegar, salt, and pepper. Pour over salad. Add mayonnaise and mix well.

Garnish salad with remaining sliced egg. Chill before serving.

GROUND PROVISIONS

The term ground provisions refers to the numerous starchy root vegetables that seem to accompany almost any and every meal in the Caribbean. Here is a guide of how to prepare and cook some of the most commonly used ones. The Spanish-speaking islands often serve ground provisions boiled and/or fried with either mojo criollo (see page 277) or just a little olive oil or butter. If any of these vegetables are unavailable for use in recipes, substitute with potatoes. Store all root vegetables in a cool, dark place. See glossary for more information.

VEGETABLE	USES	PREPARATION
Cassava *(also known as gari, manioc, yucca)* has a subtle yet distinctive taste	Can be boiled then fried, or roasted or added to soups and stews. Can also be dried and ground to form cassava meal which is used to make bammies. Can be thinly sliced then deep fried and salted to make cassava chips.	Peel, wash, and cut into large cubes. Place in saucepan in water to cover, add salt and bring to the boil. Cook until tender, about 15 to 20 minutes. Drain and remove fibrous bits. If frying, parboil for only 10 to 15 minutes. Drain well then fry lightly in oil. Drain on paper towels. If roasting, place in pan with about 4 tablespoons oil and bake at 375°F (190°C/Gas 5) for 25 to 30 minutes.
Dasheen, Eddo *(also known as taro, coco, malanga, yautía)* has a slightly nutty taste	Can be boiled or steamed then served or mashed with butter, salt, milk, and pepper. Can be baked in their skins. Can be parboiled then fried. Can be added to soups and stews. Can be made into fritters.	Prepare and boil as instructions for cassava. If baking in their skins, wash well then cut into smaller pieces if necessary. Place in roasting dish, cover with foil and bake at 375°F (190°C/Gas 5) for 25 to 30 minutes; unwrap for the last 5 minutes to crisp skins.
Tannia	Can be used in the same manner as dasheen and eddo but more often used in soups as it is more robust and hardy.	As for dasheen and eddo but boil for 20 to 25 minutes.
Yam *(also known as igname)*	Can be boiled or steamed then served or mashed with butter, salt, milk, and pepper. Can be roasted or made into fritters.	Peel, wash, and cut into large cubes. Place in saucepan in water to cover, add salt and bring to the boil. Cook until tender, about 15 to 20 minutes. Drain. See recipe for yam fritters on page 182.
Sweet potatoes *(sometimes referred to as yam in the USA, also known as patates douces or patatas dulces)*	Can be boiled, parboiled and then either fried, roasted, or mashed. Can be added to soups and stews. Used often in desserts and puddings.	As for yam. See dessert recipes on pages 209 and 229.

BREADS, BUNS, AND CAKES

B reads and cakes were made in the Caribbean well before the Spanish first spotted the islands on the horizon. The Arawaks and Caribs used to make bread with grated cassava—a tradition from which Jamaica gets its bammie. Today in Dominica, the few Caribs who live there still make the bread in the traditional way.

Many of the other savory breads in this section—such as roti, dhal puri, and sada roti—originate from India. Roti, in particular, appears on dinner tables around the region, with the notable exception of the Spanish-speaking islands.

The Europeans had a major impact on baking in the West Indies. Hojaldre and sopa borracha, for example, have their roots in Spain. West Indian rock cakes and cakes such as orange tea cake have their origins in English cookery. The French-speaking islands have adapted many French tarts and pastries—you can find many a coconut and banana tart in their patisseries.

The West Indies have turned the calm, English version of a Christmas cake into a rum, sherry, and fruit frenzy. Topped with a special mixed essence, this cake involves soaking the fruit in alcohol for months. So, for a merry Christmas, you'd better get started well in advance.

Sopa Boracha, page 201

SALARA BUNS

MAKES 12 BUNS

Well loved by my mother, who has recounted her childhood memories of eating these Guyanese buns more times than I can remember! There are many variations on these buns throughout the Caribbean—all are scrumptious. Serve warm or at room temperature.

Dough:

1 envelope (1/4 oz/7 g) dry yeast

1 teaspoon sugar

1/4 cup (2 fl oz/60 ml) warm water

3 cups (12 oz/375 g) flour

1 teaspoon mixed spice or pumpkin pie spice

3/4 cup (6 fl oz/180 ml) milk

1 tablespoon shortening

1 egg, beaten

1/2 cup (4 oz/125 g) sugar

1 egg white, lightly beaten

sugar for sprinkling

Filling:

1 1/2 cups (6 oz/175 g) finely grated fresh coconut

3/4 cup (6 oz/175 g) sugar

3/4 teaspoon cinnamon

1 teaspoon vanilla extract

few drops red food coloring

For dough: Dissolve yeast and 1 teaspoon sugar in warm water in small bowl and let stand about 10 minutes. Sift flour and spice into large bowl. Warm milk, mix in shortening, and leave to cool a little. Add beaten egg and sugar. Add milk mixture and yeast mixture to dry ingredients and knead lightly to form a smooth dough. Place in very large greased bowl and let rise in a warm place until doubled in size, about 1 hour.

For filling: Combine all filling ingredients in bowl and mix well. Let stand 45 to 60 minutes, then stir.

Preheat oven to 375°F (190°C/Gas 5). Grease baking sheet. Transfer dough to floured surface and divide into 12 equal parts. Gently roll out each piece into a 4-inch (10 cm) square and spoon 3 to 4 teaspoons filling in middle. Fold in half, moisten edges with a little water, and seal. Arrange on prepared baking sheet, spacing buns at least 2 inches (5 cm) apart. Cover loosely with towel and let rise until doubled.

Brush buns with egg white. Sprinkle with sugar. Bake until golden, 20 to 30 minutes.

HOJALDRE

SERVES 8

This spice cake comes from the Spanish-speaking Caribbean but is reflective of the way spices are used in cakes throughout the region.

3/4 cup (6 oz/185 g) butter

2/3 cup (6 oz/185 g) packed dark brown sugar

4 eggs

2 cups (8 oz/250 g) all-purpose (plain) flour

1 1/2 teaspoons baking powder

1 1/2 teaspoons cinnamon

1/2 teaspoon ground cloves

1 1/4 teaspoons ground or freshly grated nutmeg

1/3 cup (3 fl oz/80 ml) sweet red wine

about 1/3 cup (3 fl oz/80 ml) milk

confectioners' (icing) sugar

Preheat oven to 325°F (170°C/Gas 3). Grease 8-inch (20 cm) tube pan. Cream butter and sugar. Beat in eggs one at a time. Sift flour, baking powder, cinnamon, cloves, and nutmeg together and add to creamed mixture alternately with wine, mixing with wooden spoon until well combined. Stir in enough milk so that the mixture is light and smooth.

Pour into prepared pan and bake until a skewer inserted in middle comes out clean, about 45 to 50 minutes. Turn out onto rack to cool, then sprinkle with sugar.

WEST INDIAN ROCK CAKES

MAKES 10

These cakes are a memento of British settlement. The currants and mixed peel can be replaced with 4 oz (125 g) grated coconut.

2 cups (8 oz/250 g) all-purpose (plain) flour

2 teaspoons baking powder

1/2 teaspoon mixed spice or pumpkin pie spice

pinch of salt

6 tablespoons margarine or shortening

1/2 cup (4 oz/125 g) raw sugar

1 tablespoon dried currants

1 tablespoon mixed candied peel

1 egg, beaten

3 tablespoons milk

Preheat oven to 400°F (200°C/Gas 6). Grease baking sheet. Sift flour, baking powder, spice, and salt into mixing bowl. Cut in margarine until mixture resembles breadcrumbs, lifting flour to trap air in the mixture. Stir in sugar, currants, and mixed peel. Blend in egg, then milk 1 tablespoon at a time until mixture forms a very soft dough.

Drop by tablespoons onto prepared baking sheet and bake until golden brown, 15 to 20 minutes. Serve warm.

BAMMIES

SERVES 6 TO 8

This is an old Amerindian recipe for cassava bread. You can reserve the juice to make cassareep (see page 282). To serve, toast bammies under broiler (grill), fry in a shallow frying pan in oil or butter, or eat them just as they are.

4 cups (2 lb/1 kg) grated sweet cassava

2 teaspoons salt

vegetable oil or butter, optional

Place half the cassava in a piece of cheesecloth (muslin) and squeeze out as much juice as possible. Repeat with remaining cassava. Add salt to cassava.

Place 1/2 cup (4 oz/125 g) cassava in a lightly greased frying pan and press down firmly. Place over medium heat and cook until firm, 3 to 4 minutes, flattening the bread with a wide spatula. Turn and cook the other side. Continue turning and cooking until dry, about 10 minutes. Repeat until you have a stack of bammies.

WEST INDIAN BUN

MAKES TWO 6-INCH (15 CM) LOAVES

This makes a great snack, with butter and/or slices of mild cheese. It's a popular Easter bread in Jamaica.

1 envelope (1/4 oz/7 g) dry yeast

about 1 1/2 cups (12 fl oz/375 ml) warm water

4 cups (1 1/4 lb/500 g) all-purpose (plain) flour

1/2 teaspoon salt

1 nutmeg, freshly grated, or 1 tablespoon ground

1 teaspoon cinnamon

1/4 teaspoon ground allspice

4 oz (125 g) mixed candied peel

1 tablespoon seedless raisins

1 cup (8 oz/250 g) dark brown sugar

3/4 cup (6 oz/175 g) butter, softened

1 egg, beaten

1/2 cup (4 fl oz/125 ml) warm milk

1/4 cup (2 oz/60 g) sugar

Grease 2 x 6-inch (15 cm) loaf pans. Dissolve yeast in 1/4 cup warm water in a bowl; let stand 10 minutes.

Sift flour, salt, and spices into large bowl. Stir in mixed peel and raisins. Add brown sugar, butter, egg, milk, and yeast mixture and blend well. Add enough water to make a stiff dough, kneading until smooth and elastic. Place dough in lightly greased large bowl, cover, and let rise in a warm place until doubled in size.

Punch dough down, shape into loaf, and place in prepared pan. Let rise again until almost doubled. Preheat oven to 350°F (180°C/Gas 4). Bake bun until golden and springy to touch and a skewer inserted in the middle comes out clean, 30 to 45 minutes.

Dissolve sugar in 1/4 cup water in small saucepan over medium heat and stir until syrup forms. When bun has browned, brush with sugar syrup and return briefly to oven to glaze. Turn out on rack to cool.

West Indian Bun

SADA ROTI

SERVES 4

This is one of the many breads brought to the West Indies by the East Indian community. It is typically eaten for breakfast with choka (see pages 162 and 164). To cook the bread you should use either a frying pan with a surface at least 8 inches (20 cm) in diameter, or a tawa (a traditional flat iron griddle).

4 cups (1 lb/500 g) all-purpose (plain) flour

4 teaspoons baking powder

1/2 teaspoon salt

about 1 2/3 cups (13 fl oz/400 ml) water

Sift flour, baking powder, and salt into mixing bowl. Add water and mix to form a soft dough, adding a little extra water if necessary. Knead dough until smooth and elastic. Cover and let rest 15 minutes.

Divide dough into 8 equal parts and shape into smooth balls. Let rest another 10 minutes.

Flour work surface. Heat frying pan or tawa over medium heat. Roll out each ball of dough to a thickness of about 1/4 inch (5 mm), making sure to roll right over the edges. Cook on both sides until lightly golden. If you are using a frying pan, move the pan halfway off the heat, lift the roti out of the pan with a spatula (resting the roti on part of the pan), and toast the edges of the roti over medium low heat, turning regularly so it does not burn. Each roti should puff up slightly. Stack rotis on a plate, covering the stack as each one is cooked. Serve warm.

JOHNNY CAKES

MAKES 14

The perfect accompaniment to any meal, these breads are similar to Guyanese bakes (see below) and Trinidadian floats. They are usually served warm but are also delicious cold.

4 cups (1 lb/500 g) all-purpose (plain) flour

½ teaspoon salt

1 teaspoon baking powder

1 tablespoon margarine

about 1½ cups (12 fl oz/350 ml) water

about 4 cups (32 fl oz/1 l) vegetable oil for deep frying

Sift flour, salt, and baking powder into large mixing bowl. Add margarine and enough of the water to make a firm dough. Knead until smooth and elastic.

On a lightly floured surface divide dough into 14 pieces and shape each into a circle ½ inch (1 cm) thick. Heat oil in deep frying pan until hot. (To test, add a pinch of dough: if it rises to the top immediately, oil is hot enough.) Add johnny cakes a few at a time and fry until golden brown on both sides. Drain on paper towels and serve warm.

BAKES

SERVES 4

These light Guyanese breads are variations on johnny cakes (see above). Although deep-fried, they are not greasy when cooked properly, as the quick cooking process does not allow them to soak up much oil.

2 cups (8 oz/250 g) self-rising flour

½ teaspoon salt

1 egg, optional

1 teaspoon brown sugar

about 1 cup (8 fl oz/250 ml) tepid water

about 2 cups (16 fl oz/500 ml) vegetable oil for deep frying

Sift flour and salt into large mixing bowl. Add egg and sugar. Gradually add water, mixing to form a medium firm dough. Knead dough until it forms a smooth ball, 5 to 10 minutes.

On a floured surface, roll dough into a sausage shape 1½ inches (4 cm) in diameter. Cut into 1½-inch (4 cm) pieces. Knead each piece in the palm of your hand for 1 minute to form a smooth ball. Roll out each bake to ¼-inch (5 mm) thickness.

Heat oil until very hot in deep pan or wok. (To test, add a pinch of dough: if it rises to the top immediately, oil is hot enough.) Gently lower two bakes into hot oil and cook until puffed and lighter golden brown, 1 to 2 minutes on each side, basting the top with oil to ensure even cooking. Repeat with remaining dough, cooking two bakes at a time. Drain on paper towels and serve.

Following page: Bakes, Roti, Dhal Puri

ROTI

Though correctly called paratha roti, this bread is commonly referred to as roti in Trinidad, Guyana, and Barbados. It is widespread in Trinidadian fast-food outlets and throughout the Caribbean. Serve with curry or dhal (see page 153), or as an accompaniment to a meal. The larger the proportion of ghee you use, the richer the taste—I suggest a blend of oil and ghee (half and half).

8 cups (2 lb/1 kg) all-purpose (plain) flour

1 tablespoon baking powder

1/2 teaspoon salt

2 to 2 1/2 cups (16 to 20 fl oz/ 500 to 625 ml) water

about 1 cup (8 fl oz/250 ml) vegetable oil and/or melted ghee

Sift flour, baking powder, and salt into large mixing bowl. Add water and mix to form a soft dough, adding a little extra water if necessary. Knead dough until smooth and elastic. Cover and let rest 1 hour.

Divide dough into 8 equal parts and shape into smooth balls. On a floured surface, roll out one piece of dough into a circle 5 to 6 inches (12.5 to 15 cm) in diameter. Place a teaspoon of oil/ghee in the middle and spread almost to the edges using the back of a spoon. Cut a line from middle point to edge. Lift the cut edge and begin to roll it clockwise into a cone shape. When you have nearly reached the end, lift the cone, stretch remaining piece of dough under the base of the cone, and firmly press into the base. Place cone back on work surface, press down, and reshape into a ball. Continue with remaining dough, then let rest 20 minute.

Flour work surface. Heat a large frying pan or tawa (a traditional flat iron griddle) over medium heat. Flatten a ball of oiled dough and roll out to form a circle about 1/8 inch (3 mm) thick and 6 to 7 inches (15 to 17.5 cm) in diameter. Cook 2 to 3 minutes. Turn the roti and spread a teaspoon of oil over the entire surface. Turn over and repeat. Cook both sides until lightly golden.

After each roti cooks, turn it onto plate. Hold the cooked roti in one hand and let go, catching it using a clapping motion with both hands. Do this two or three times to separate the layers.

Keep warm on a plate lined and covered with cloth.

DHAL PURI

MAKES 15

The meal I love most is dhal puri and chicken curry, served at Christmastime. The bread is cooked on special occasions and, although the recipe is tricky, it's worth it! My cousins in Guyana grind all the filling ingredients by hand, and I'm convinced they taste the better for it. But if you find this too much of a challenge, use a blender. This is another of my grandmother's specialities; serve it with your choice of curry.

Filling:

1 lb (500 g) dried yellow split peas, rinsed

8 cups (2 l) water

1 green onion, green part only, finely chopped

4 cloves garlic, minced

2 teaspoons cumin

1 teaspoon turmeric

2 small hot peppers, seeded and minced

salt

Dough:

8 cups (2 lb/1 kg) all-purpose (plain) flour

4 teaspoons baking powder

1 teaspoon salt

about 4 cups (32 fl oz/1 l) water

about 1 cup (8 fl oz/250 ml) vegetable oil

For filling: Place peas in large saucepan with 8 cups water and bring to boil. Cover partially and cook over medium heat until peas are tender, about 20 to 25 minutes. Drain and spread peas on clean kitchen towels to dry, about 20 to 30 minutes.

Meanwhile, prepare dough: Sift flour, baking powder, and salt into large mixing bowl. Gradually mix in enough water to make a soft dough. Knead dough until smooth and elastic. Cover and let rest 30 minutes.

Grind peas in processor or blender until they resemble very fine breadcrumbs. Transfer to large bowl. Add green onion, garlic, cumin, turmeric, hot peppers, and salt to taste and mix well. Set aside.

Place dough on floured surface and divide into 15 equal pieces. Take one piece and knead 30 seconds, then flatten to a diameter of about 4 inches (10 cm). Holding dough in the palm of your hand, spoon a heaping tablespoon of filling into the middle. Carefully fold edges of dough toward the middle, forming a ball. Firmly press edges together to seal. Repeat with remaining dough and filling, placing each ball sealed edge down on a lightly floured surface.

Heat large frying pan or tawa (a traditional flat iron griddle) over medium heat. Working on a floured surface, flatten one dough piece, then roll out to a diameter of 7 to 8 inches (17.5 to 20 cm), turning it over while rolling. Cook the dhal puri until lightly brown on one side, then turn and brush cooked side and edges with oil. Continue to cook until underside is browned; the dhal puri should puff like a balloon.

Place cooked dhal puri on plate lined with clean kitchen towel. Fold the dhal puri in half and cover with another towel while cooking the remainder. Serve warm. To reheat, place dhal puri under a broiler (grill), preheated to low, for 1 minute on each side.

BULLAS

MAKES ABOUT 20

These flat, round Jamaican cakes look like large cookies, only thicker, and they are soft on the inside. Serve warm or cold.

1 cup (8 oz/250 g) packed dark brown sugar

1/2 cup (4 fl oz/125 ml) water

3 cups (12 oz/350 g) all-purpose (plain) flour

1 teaspoon baking powder

1/4 teaspoon salt

3/4 teaspoon cinnamon

1/2 teaspoon freshly grated nutmeg

1/2 teaspoon ground ginger

1/4 teaspoon ground allspice

2 tablespoons butter, melted

Preheat oven to 400°F (200°C/Gas 6). Lightly grease baking sheet. Combine sugar and water in small saucepan and stir to dissolve sugar. Bring to boil, then reduce heat and simmer until a thick syrup forms, about 25 minutes.

Sift flour, baking powder, salt, and spices into mixing bowl. Add melted butter and sugar syrup and mix to form a firm dough. Turn out onto floured surface and pat to thickness of 1/3 inch (1 cm). Cut out 5-inch (12 cm) circles from dough. Transfer to prepared baking sheet and bake until golden, about 20 minutes. Remove cakes from baking sheet and cool on rack.

CARROT CAKE

MAKES TWO 9 X 5-INCH (23 X 13 CM) LOAVES

2 cups (8 oz/250 g) all-purpose (plain) flour

2 teaspoons baking powder

2 cups (1 lb/500 g) raw sugar

1/2 teaspoon cinnamon

1/2 teaspoon ground allspice

1/2 teaspoon ground or freshly grated nutmeg

1/2 teaspoon salt

1/4 cup (2 oz/60 g) unsalted butter

3 eggs, beaten

2 cups (6 oz/175 g) grated carrots

1 cup (8 fl oz/250 ml) milk

1/2 cup (2 oz/60 g) chopped nuts

2 tablespoons dark rum, optional

2 tablespoons seedless raisins

Preheat oven to 350°F (180°C/Gas 4). Grease two 9 x 5-inch (23 x 13 cm) loaf pans. Sift dry ingredients into large mixing bowl. Rub in butter. Blend in eggs, carrots, milk, nuts, rum, and raisins. Divide between prepared pans. Bake until a skewer inserted in middle comes out clean, 45 to 60 minutes. Turn out onto racks to cool.

Bullas

ORANGE CAKE

MAKES ONE 9 X 5-INCH (22.5 X 12.5 CM) LOAF

Most of the English-speaking West Indies has a version of this cake. This one is from Antigua.

3/4 cup (6 oz/180 g)
unsalted butter

2/3 cup (5 oz/155 g) sugar

3 eggs, beaten

2 teaspoons finely grated
orange peel

2 cups (8 oz/250 g) all-purpose
(plain) flour

1 tablespoon baking powder

1/2 teaspoon salt

1/2 cup (4 fl oz/125 ml)
fresh orange juice

Preheat oven to 350°F (180°C/Gas 4). Grease 9 x 5-inch (22.5 x 12.5 cm) loaf pan. Cream butter and sugar until fluffy. Beat in eggs one at a time. Mix in orange peel. Sift together flour, baking powder, and salt. Beat in dry ingredients alternately with orange juice. Spread batter in prepared pan. Bake until a skewer inserted in middle comes out clean, 45 to 60 minutes. Turn out on rack to cool.

RUM CAKE

MAKES ONE 8-INCH (20 CM) ROUND CAKE

1/2 cup (4 oz/125 g) butter

1/2 cup (4 oz/125 g) sugar

4 eggs

1 1/2 cups (6 oz/175 g) all-purpose
(plain) flour

2 teaspoons baking powder

1/4 teaspoon cinnamon

3/4 cup (3 oz/85 g) cornstarch

1/3 cup (3 fl oz/80 ml) dark rum

1 tablespoon lime juice

1/2 teaspoon finely grated
orange peel

1/4 teaspoon finely grated
lime peel

Preheat oven to 350°F (180°C/Gas 4). Grease 8-inch (20-cm) round cake pan. Cream butter and sugar until light and fluffy. Beat in eggs one at a time. Sift in flour, baking powder, cinnamon, and cornstarch and blend well. Stir in rum, lime juice, orange peel, and lime peel. Spread batter in prepared pan and bake until a skewer inserted in middle comes out clean, about 1 hour. Turn out on rack to cool.

SOPA BORRACHA

SERVES 12

This translates from Spanish as "drunken soup," possibly because of the quantity of wine used in its making. This Puerto Rican cake can also be made in individual portions. Cut the sponge into 10 to 12 pieces. Pour the syrup on top and cover each piece with meringue.

Sponge cake:

1 cup (4 oz/125 g) all-purpose (plain) flour

1 teaspoon baking powder

pinch of salt

5 eggs, separated

1 cup (8 oz/250 g) sugar

1/2 teaspoon finely grated lime peel

2 tablespoons cold water

1 tablespoon lemon juice

Syrup:

1 1/2 cups (12 oz/375 g) sugar

1/2 cup (4 fl oz/125 ml) water

1 cup (8 fl oz/250 ml) sweet wine

Meringue:

2 egg whites

2 tablespoons superfine (caster) sugar

1 tablespoon candied peel for garnish

Preheat oven to 325°F (170°C/Gas 3). Lightly grease 9-inch (23-cm) square pan. Sift flour, baking powder, and salt; set aside. Beat egg yolks with sugar and lime peel until fluffy. Blend in water and lemon juice. Using clean beaters, beat egg whites until they form soft peaks. Fold half the egg whites into yolk mixture. Gently fold in dry ingredients. Fold in remaining egg whites. Spread batter in prepared pan. Bake until cake springs back when pressed gently, 40 to 45 minutes.

Let cool 5 minutes in pan, then loosen edges and turn out on rack. When cool, place on large platter.

For syrup: Combine sugar and water in saucepan and bring to boil over medium high heat. Reduce heat to medium and simmer until mixture forms a syrup, about 30 minutes. Let cool. Stir in wine. Spoon syrup over cake evenly.

For meringue: Beat egg whites in clean bowl until they form peaks. Beat in sugar. Spread evenly over cake. Garnish with candied peel and chill before serving.

BANANA BREAD

MAKES ONE 9 X 5-INCH (22.5 X 12.5 CM) LOAF

1 cup (8 oz/250 g) butter

1 cup (8 oz/250 g) packed raw sugar

3 very ripe medium bananas, mashed

1 egg, beaten

4 cups (1 lb/500 g) all-purpose (plain) flour

1 tablespoon baking powder

1/2 teaspoon cinnamon

1/2 teaspoon freshly grated nutmeg

1/2 teaspoon ground allspice

1/2 cup (4 fl oz/125 ml) milk

1 teaspoon vanilla extract

1 tablespoon seedless raisins

Preheat oven to 350°F (180°C/Gas 4). Butter 9 x 5-inch (22.5 x 12.5 cm) loaf pan. Cream butter and sugar until light. Add bananas and egg and mix well. Sift in flour, baking powder, cinnamon, nutmeg, and allspice and stir well. Gradually beat in milk. Stir in vanilla and raisins.

Pour batter into prepared pan and bake until a skewer inserted in the middle comes out clean, about 1 hour. Let cool in pan 10 minutes, then turn bread out onto rack to cool completely.

COCONUT BREAD

MAKES TWO 9 X 5-INCH (22.5 X 12.5 CM) LOAVES

This is great served sliced on its own or with butter. It's well worth using fresh coconut, but dried is good too!

4 cups (1 lb/500 g) all-purpose (plain) flour

3 1/2 teaspoons baking powder

1/4 teaspoon cinnamon

1/2 teaspoon ground or freshly grated nutmeg

pinch of salt

2 cups (12 oz/375 g) raw sugar

2 tablespoons seedless raisins, optional

2 3/4 cups (10 oz/300 g) finely grated coconut

2 eggs, beaten until fluffy

1/2 cup (4 fl oz/125 ml) evaporated milk

1/2 cup (4 oz/125 g) unsalted butter, melted

1 tablespoon water

Preheat oven to 325°F (170°C/Gas 3). Grease two 9 x 5-inch (22.5 x 12.5 cm) loaf pans. Sift flour, baking powder, cinnamon, nutmeg, and salt into large mixing bowl. Stir in sugar, raisins, and coconut. Blend in eggs, milk, and butter. Rinse out milk container with 1 tablespoon water and add to mixture. Divide dough between prepared pans. Bake until a skewer inserted in middle comes out clean, about 1 hour. Turn out on racks to cool.

Banana Bread

PINEAPPLE UPSIDE-DOWN CAKE

SERVES 6

There is many a sponge cake in the English-speaking Caribbean, no doubt an import from the British, but they all have a special Caribbean touch. Here's one example, from Jamaica. Serve warm with fresh whipped cream.

2 tablespoons butter

1 tablespoon raw sugar

6 pineapple slices
(if canned, drained)

sprinkle of freshly grated nutmeg

6 maraschino cherries

1/2 cup (4 oz/125 g) butter

3/4 cup (6 oz/175 g) sugar

1 teaspoon vanilla extract

2 eggs, beaten until fluffy

2 cups (8 oz/250 g) all-purpose
(plain) flour

1 teaspoon baking powder

1/4 cup (2 fl oz/60 ml) milk

1/2 teaspoon finely grated
orange peel

Preheat oven to 350°F (180°C/Gas 4). Grease 8-inch (20 cm) square baking pan. Melt 2 tablespoons butter in frying pan over low heat until it begins to foam. Add raw sugar and cook 2 minutes without stirring. Add pineapple slices and cook 3 minutes. Add nutmeg and remove from heat.

Arrange pineapple in prepared pan and place a cherry in the middle of each slice. Pour sugary syrup from pan over pineapple and set aside.

Cream butter and sugar until light and fluffy. Beat vanilla into eggs. Sift flour and baking powder together. Fold half of egg mixture and half of flour into butter mixture; repeat with remaining egg mixture and flour. Fold in milk and orange peel. Spread over pineapple. Bake until golden and springy when pressed, about 40 minutes. Remove from oven and let stand 5 minutes. Loosen edges and turn out onto a serving plate.

GUYANESE CHRISTMAS CAKE

SERVES 12

My grandmother's treat at Christmastime. When we were younger and helped my grandmother prepare this cake, there would always be a fight over who could lick the spoon (I still find it hard to resist now). Making the cake has always been a fun event when the women of the family get together. The cake is always made big enough for guests and family who visit over the holiday.

8 oz (250 g) seedless raisins

8 oz (250 g) dried currants

6 oz (175 g) prunes, pitted

4 oz (125 g) mixed candied peel

1 cup (8 fl oz/250 ml) sweet sherry or red wine

1/3 cup (3 fl oz/80 ml) dark rum or brandy

2 cups (1 lb/500 g) butter or margarine, melted

2³/4 cups (22 oz/875 g) raw sugar or packed dark brown sugar

12 eggs, beaten until fluffy

4 cups (1 lb /500 g) self-rising flour

1 teaspoon baking powder

1 tablespoon vanilla extract

1¹/2 teaspoons mixed spice or pumpkin pie spice

1 cup (5 oz/150 g) finely chopped nuts

Mince fruit in grinder or food processor. Transfer to bowl, add sherry and rum, cover, and let soak 2 to 8 weeks (the longer the better).

Preheat oven to 350°F (180°C/Gas 4). Grease two 9-inch (22.5 cm) round cake pans. Blend butter and sugar. Beat in eggs two at a time. Add fruit and liquor and mix well.

Sift flour and baking powder; add to fruit mixture with vanilla and spice. Stir in nuts. Divide batter between prepared pans and bake in middle of oven until a skewer inserted comes out clean, 45 to 60 minutes. Let cakes cool in pans before turning out.

DESSERTS AND SWEET TREATS

In the West Indies you can enjoy luscious fresh fruit the whole year round as each season brings its different crop. You will find genips (a small, green fruit with a sweet cream-colored flesh), mangoes, bananas, pineapples, tangerines, passionfruit, tamarind, guavas, plums, cherries, papayas (kind of makes you want to immigrate, doesn't it), soursop, starfruit, grapefruit, cashewfruit, not to mention the ever-available green coconuts. Let me tell you about the joy, the sheer delight of a green coconut! First there is the coconut water—refreshing, thirst-quenching, and delicious. Then, when the coconut is cracked open, it reveals the coconut jelly which can be eaten straight out of the shell. The West Indies is truly a paradise of fruit!

Coconut candies can be found everywhere in the Caribbean. In fact, coconut has proved itself to be quite versatile, featuring in both simple treats like grater cake or coconut drops, and more complex desserts like tembleque and conkies. Like papaya and tamarind, it can be found in both sweet and savory dishes.

When going through these recipes, you will notice that many of the desserts contain not only fruit but sweetened condensed milk or evaporated milk, traditionally used in Caribbean cuisine due to a lack of refrigeration.

You may also be struck by the frequent use of different brown sugars (including demerara sugar) and, to a lesser extent, molasses. If you can obtain these sugars, do use them. They'll give your candies, sweet treats, and cakes a peculiarly Caribbean flavor.

Tropical Fruit Salad, page 233

CONKIES

MAKES ABOUT 30

These parcels filled with sweet potato, pumpkin, and coconut pudding are similar to Jamaica's tie-a-leaf and Antigua's ducana (see page 30). Serve with cream or ice cream.

1/2 cup (4 oz/125 g) seedless raisins

about 1 cup (8 fl oz/250 ml) boiling water

1 1/4 cups (5 oz/150 g) finely grated coconut

12 oz (350 g) pumpkin, peeled, cleaned, and finely grated

8 oz (250 g) sweet potato, peeled and finely grated

2 cups (8 oz/250 g) cornmeal

3/4 cup (3 oz/85 g) all-purpose (plain) flour

1 1/2 cups (12 oz/350 g) packed brown sugar

1/2 cup (4 fl oz/125 ml) milk

1/2 cup (4 oz/125 g) butter or margarine, melted

1/4 cup (2 oz/60 g) lard or shortening, melted

1/4 teaspoon vanilla extract

1 teaspoon mixed spice or pumpkin spice

1/2 teaspoon ground or freshly grated nutmeg

1 teaspoon salt

plantain or banana leaves, or 6-inch (15 cm) square foil pieces

In small bowl steep raisins in boiling water and set aside.

Meanwhile, mix coconut, pumpkin, sweet potato, cornmeal, and flour in large mixing bowl. Add sugar, milk, melted butter, lard, vanilla, spices, and salt.

Drain raisins. Add to mixture and blend well. Drop 2 tablespoons of mixture into each leaf or lightly greased square of foil. If using leaves, fold up edges towards the middle and tie parcel with string. If using foil, fold up edges tightly to seal.

Fill large saucepan two-thirds full of water and bring to boil. Drop wrapped conkies into water and cook until firm, 40 to 45 minutes. Drain. Unwrap parcels and serve.

BUÑUELOS DE VIENTO

SERVES 4 TO 6

Known also as "air crullers," these are eaten from Cuba to the Dominican Republic to Puerto Rico. Serve sprinkled with confectioners' (icing) sugar or a syrup of your choice—the lime syrup below or one from pages 280 to 282.

1/2 cup (4 fl oz/125 ml) water

1 tablespoon butter

1/2 teaspoon salt

1/2 teaspoon cinnamon, ground aniseed, or grated lemon or orange peel

1/2 cup (2 oz/60 g) all-purpose (plain) flour

2 eggs

about 3 cups (24 fl oz/750 ml) vegetable oil for deep frying

Syrup:

2 cups (16 fl oz/500 ml) water

1 1/3 cups (11 oz/340 g) sugar

1/4 teaspoon grated lime peel

Combine water, butter, salt, and flavoring in saucepan and bring to boil over medium heat. Reduce heat to low, add flour, and stir well until mixture forms a mass. Reduce heat to very low and beat in eggs one at a time. Remove from heat.

Heat oil in deep saucepan until very hot. Drop dough into the oil by the tablespoonful and fry over medium heat until puffed and golden brown. Drain on paper towels and serve warm.

For lime syrup: Combine water and sugar in saucepan and bring to boil over high heat. Immediately reduce heat to medium, add grated peel, and cook until a syrup forms, about 20 minutes. Drizzle over buñuelos.

NÍSPEROS DE BATATA

MAKES 12 TO 15

The Spanish name for naseberry or sapodilla is níspero. There are no nísperos in this dessert, but the sweet potato paste resembles their flesh and the cinnamon coating looks like their reddish-brown skin.

1 lb (500 g) white sweet potato (see glossary), peeled and cut into 2-inch (5 cm) pieces

1 1/4 cups (10 oz/300 g) sugar

1/3 cup (3 fl oz/80 ml) coconut cream (see page 289)

1 egg yolk

1 tablespoon cinnamon

whole cloves

Boil sweet potato until soft in salted water to cover, about 30 minutes. Drain and remove any fibrous bits.

Mash potato in saucepan to a smooth puree. Blend in sugar, coconut cream, and egg yolk and cook over low heat, stirring frequently with wooden spoon in a zigzag motion, until mixture thickens and begins to leave bottom and sides of pan, about 35 to 40 minutes. Let cool. Dust your hands with cinnamon to prevent sticking. Form tablespoonsful of mixture into smooth balls Roll each in cinnamon to coat lightly. Insert a clove in the middle of each ball.

FLAN DE PIÑA

SERVES 6

This is a very popular dessert in Puerto Rico.

2 cups (16 fl oz/500 ml) fresh or
canned pineapple juice

1 cup (8 oz/250 g) sugar

1 tablespoon brandy, optional

8 eggs, beaten

Preheat oven to 350°F (180°C/Gas 4). Lightly grease 1-quart (1 l) baking dish. Combine pineapple juice and sugar in saucepan and bring to boil. Reduce heat and simmer until mixture forms a thick syrup consistency. Let cool. Beat pineapple syrup and brandy into beaten eggs. Pour into prepared baking dish and set dish in a roasting pan. Add enough hot water to pan to come halfway up sides of baking dish. Bake until a knife inserted in middle of custard comes out clean, about 1 hour. Remove from water bath and let cool, then chill well before serving.

PASTELES

MAKES 9

These guava tarts can be found in the Spanish-speaking countries. This particular recipe is from Cuba.

3 cups (12 oz/375 g) all-purpose
(plain) flour

1/4 teaspoon baking
soda (bicarbonate)

1 1/4 teaspoons salt

1 cup (8 oz/250 g) cold shortening
or margarine, cut into small cubes

1/2 cup (4 fl oz/125 ml) cold milk

6 pink guavas,
peeled, seeded, and sliced

1 cup (8 fl oz/250 ml) water

2/3 cup (5 oz/150 g) sugar

1 tablespoon butter

1/2 teaspoon cinnamon

1 tablespoon milk

Sift flour, baking soda, and salt into bowl. Cut in shortening until mixture begins to resemble breadcrumbs. Slowly add 1/2 cup milk and combine until dough binds together. (If more liquid is required, add water by the tablespoon.) Knead gently 1 minute. Refrigerate.

Combine guavas, water, sugar, butter, and cinnamon in saucepan and boil over high heat until only a small amount of liquid remains; be careful not to let guavas become mushy. Let cool.

Roll out pastry into a 9-inch (21 cm) square. Cut into 3-inch (7 cm) square pieces. Place 1 to 2 tablespoons guava mixture on each, then fold over pastry to form rectangles. Moisten edges and seal. Brush with milk.

Preheat oven to 350°F (180°C/Gas 4). Bake pasteles until golden brown, 25 to 35 minutes. Let cool before serving.

Flan de Piña

ARROWROOT DROPS

MAKES 10

As one of the world's largest exporters of arrowroot, St Vincent makes use of the fine-grained starch in numerous recipes. This one was given to me by Julia from Vee Jays Rooftop in Kingstown.

1/2 cup (4 oz/125 g) butter, softened

1/2 cup (4 oz/125 g) sugar

2 eggs, beaten

1 1/2 cups (7 1/2 oz/225 g) arrowroot

maraschino cherries

1/4 cup (2 fl oz/60 ml) milk

Preheat oven to 350°F (180°C/Gas 4). Cream butter and sugar until light. Blend in eggs, then arrowroot. Spoon 2 to 3 teaspoons of the mixture into small cupcake tins lined with paper liners. Place a cherry on top of each. Bake until cakes spring back when gently pressed, about 20 minutes. Let cool on rack before serving.

COCONUT DROPS

MAKES 12 TO 15

This Jamaican treat is the coconut sweet I love the most. My mother used to buy it from a West Indian grocery in London on her way home from work, or on Saturdays as a treat. They will keep in an airtight container for up to 2 weeks and are a must for a sweet tooth!

1 small coconut

2 cups (16 fl oz/500 ml) water

1 tablespoon finely chopped fresh ginger

2 cups (16 oz/500 g) packed brown sugar

Grease baking sheet. Break open coconut (see page 289) and peel off brown skin. Cut coconut into small pieces, or grate using the large holes of a grater. Bring water to boil in heavy saucepan. Add coconut. Reduce heat to medium and cook coconut 15 minutes. Add ginger and cook 5 minutes.

Gradually add sugar, stirring constantly until dissolved. Cook mixture over medium high heat until it is very thick and sticky. (To test, drop a small amount into a glass of cold water; if it forms a ball, the mixture is ready.) Drop mixture by teaspoons onto prepared baking sheet and let cool.

GRATER CAKES

MAKES 12 TO 15

1 small coconut,
peeled and grated, or 2 cups
(8 oz/250 g) grated coconut

1½ cups (12 oz/375 g) sugar

¼ cup (2 fl oz/60 ml) water

2 drops red food coloring

Remove meat from coconut and grate following the instructions on page 289.

Combine grated coconut, sugar, and water in saucepan over medium heat. Cook, stirring constantly, until mixture thickens and pulls away from sides of pan. Stir in food coloring.

Drop tablespoons of mixture onto greased baking sheet or waxed paper and let cool.

Store in an airtight container, in a cool place for up to 2 weeks.

JALEBI

MAKES 12 TO 14

When my grandmother was a young girl in Guyana, they would pierce holes in the eyes of a coconut shell and use it as a funnel for the jalebi mixture.

2 cups (8 oz/250 g) all-purpose
(plain) flour, sifted

¼ cup (2 fl oz/60 ml) plain yogurt

1¼ cups (10 fl oz/300 ml)
warm water

1 teaspoon powdered saffron or
⅛ teaspoon saffron strands or
3 drops yellow food coloring

1⅔ cups (13 fl oz/350 ml) water

1¼ cups (10 oz/300 g) sugar

1 teaspoon cardamom seeds or
¼ teaspoon ground cardamom

vegetable oil or ghee
for deep frying

Combine flour, yogurt, and warm water to form a batter. Blend in saffron. Cover with clean cloth and let stand overnight.

Bring water, sugar, and cardamom to boil in medium saucepan. Reduce heat to medium and cook until mixture forms a thick syrup.

Beat flour/yogurt batter until smooth. Heat oil in deep frying pan over medium high heat. Pour a stream of batter through a pastry bag or funnel into hot oil using a circular motion, forming coils about 4 to 5 inches (10 to 12.5 cm) in diameter; when coil is large enough, put your finger over the hole to stop the flow of batter. Cook until golden on both sides. Drain on paper towels. Immerse jalebis briefly in hot cardamom syrup. Stack and serve warm.

Following page: Grater Cakes, Jalebi, Tooloom, Tamarind Balls

TOOLOOM

MAKES ABOUT 16

1 cup (8 fl oz/250 ml) molasses

1/2 cup (4 oz/125 g) sugar

1 teaspoon grated fresh ginger

2 cups (8 oz/250 g) grated coconut

2 inches (5 cm) dried orange peel, broken into small pieces

Grease baking sheet. Heat molasses in saucepan over medium heat and add sugar, ginger, coconut, and orange peel. Stir until mixture is stiff. Shape into balls with a spoon, arrange on prepared baking sheet, and let cool. Store in an airtight container in a cool place for up to 2 weeks.

TAMARIND BALLS

MAKES 25 TO 30

1/2 cup (4 oz/125 g) tamarind flesh

1 cup (8 oz/250 g) packed brown sugar or superfine (caster) sugar

additional superfine (caster) sugar

Combine tamarind flesh and sugar and mix well. Knead until sugar is well incorporated. Roll into smooth balls about 1/2 inch (1 cm) in diameter. Roll in extra sugar and store in an airtight container.

CANDIED PAPAYA

MAKES ABOUT 3 CUPS

In this recipe I have used a very quick candying method. The longer method spans over days and involves leaving the fruit to stand in the syrup which is topped up with more sugar each day.

2 green papayas (pawpaws), peeled, seeded, and cut into thin strips

water

2 teaspoons salt

sugar

Place papaya in bowl with 4 cups (1 l) water and salt. Let soak 30 minutes, then drain and rinse.

For each cup of papaya, combine 2 cups (16 fl oz/500 ml) water and 3 cups (24 oz/750 g) sugar in saucepan and heat over medium heat until sugar is dissolved. Add papaya strips and bring to boil. Reduce heat and cook until the papaya is tender but not too soft.

Drain fruit and roll in sugar. Store in airtight container in refrigerator for up to 1 week.

PRESERVED MANGOES

MAKES ABOUT 2 LB (1 KG)

The mangoes should firm and just ripe or even underripe. The preserved fruit will keep for weeks.

12 cups (3 l) water

1 1/2 cups (12 oz/375 g) sugar

2 lb (1 kg) mangoes, peeled and cut into strips

1 tablespoon lime juice

1/4-inch (5 mm) cinnamon stick

Bring water to boil and gradually stir in sugar until dissolved. Boil 5 minutes.

Add mangoes, lime juice, and cinnamon and boil 5 more minutes, stirring occasionally.

Remove from heat. Drain mangoes, reserving syrup and cinnamon stick. Return syrup with cinnamon to heat and cook until syrup thickens slightly, about 10 to 15 minutes. Add mangoes and cook 5 more minutes. Discard cinnamon stick. Remove fruit and cool thoroughly. Pack fruit into sterilized jars, cover with syrup, and seal. Cool, then store in a cool place.

STEWED GUAVAS

SERVES 4 TO 6

Soaked with grenadine, the guavas in this dessert are a wonderful rich red that makes them look appealing on any dinner table. They are best served with coconut or vanilla ice cream (see page 222), or just on their own.

3 tablespoons sugar

2 cups (16 fl oz/500 ml) water

2 white or pink guavas, peeled, halved, and seeded

2 tablespoons grenadine

Heat sugar and water in saucepan over low heat while preparing guavas. Slice guava halves into slices about 1/8 inch (3 mm) thick and add to saucepan. Simmer gently until guavas are tender but not mushy, about 10 minutes. Transfer guavas and syrup to bowl. Stir in grenadine, taking care not to break or mash the guavas. Let stand 3 to 5 hours, preferably overnight, before serving. Serve chilled.

GUAVA JELLY

MAKES ABOUT 15 OZ/450 G

In Barbados, this fragrant jelly is sometimes served as an accompaniment to roast lamb. Usually it is served with toast or on fresh bread. The guavas themselves are not used in this recipe and can be reserved for another recipe, such as guava cheese (see page 228).

4 cups (32 fl oz/1 l) water

2 lb (1 kg) ripe but firm pink guavas, halved

1-inch (2.5 cm) cinnamon stick

about 3 cups (24 oz/750 g) sugar

2 tablespoons lime juice

Combine water, guavas, and cinnamon stick in saucepan and bring to boil. Simmer 30 minutes. Strain liquid and reserve guavas for another use.

Measure liquid and pour into medium saucepan. Add the same quantity of sugar as there is liquid. Add lime juice. Cook over medium heat, stirring almost constantly, until mixture is very thick, about 20 to 30 minutes. To test, drop a tiny amount of mixture into cold water; if it forms a ball, it is ready. Pour into sterilized jars and seal.

Stewed Guavas

COCONUT ICES

SERVES 4 TO 6

This is similar to snowcones (see page 248) and can be served with a syrup of your choice, including those found on pages 280 to 282. Another variation to this are mango ices where 3 cups (24 fl oz/375 ml) mango pulp is substituted for the coconut milk.

3/4 cup (6 oz/175 g) sugar

3 1/2 cups (28 fl oz/875 ml) coconut milk (see page 289)

3/4 cup (6 fl oz/180 ml) heavy (double) cream

1/4 teaspoon vanilla extract

Combine sugar and coconut milk in saucepan and stir over medium heat until sugar is dissolved. Allow to cool a little. Stir in cream and vanilla. Pour into bowl and let cool, then cover and freeze until solid.

When ready to serve, shave frozen coconut ice into a cup and top with syrup.

TABLETTES DE COCO

MAKES ABOUT 24

Although these coconut treats come from the French West Indies, similar candies can be found through-out the region. Use the water from inside the coconut for this recipe and make up the quantity to 1 cup with water.

1 small coconut, peeled and finely grated

1 cup (8 fl oz/250ml) coconut water with water

1/2 teaspoon cinnamon

2 cups (16 oz/500 g) raw sugar

few drops vanilla extract

Combine coconut, water, and cinnamon in saucepan and simmer 20 minutes. Add sugar and vanilla and cook until mixture is very thick and pulls away from sides of saucepan, about 10 to 15 minutes, stirring frequently. Allow to cool slightly, then form into small balls onto marble surface or a lightly greased baking sheet. Let cool completely. Store in an airtight container. Will keep for up to 2 weeks.

PEANUT BRITTLE

MAKES ABOUT 14 OZ/400 G

2 cups (1 lb/500 g) sugar

1 cup (6 oz/175 g) unsalted peanuts

1/4 teaspoon cream of tartar

1/2 cup (4 fl oz/125 ml) water

1/4 teaspoon salt

1/4 teaspoon baking soda (bicarbonate)

1/4 cup (2 oz/60 g) butter

Grease a baking sheet.

Combine sugar, nuts, cream of tartar, and water in heavy saucepan and bring to boil. Cook until syrup is thick and light brown and measures 320°F (170°C) on candy thermometer. Remove from heat and immediately stir in salt, baking soda, and butter. Spread in prepared pan and let cool. Break into pieces when cold. Store in an airtight container.

RUM AND RAISIN FUDGE

MAKES ABOUT 20 PIECES

This fudge incorporates all things wonderful: rum, sugar, and raisins. Even if you're not fond of rum, you'll enjoy this.

1/2 cup (4 fl oz/125 ml) water

2 cups (10 oz/315 g) packed dark brown sugar

1 cup (8 fl oz/250 ml) sweetened condensed milk

1/4 cup (2 oz/60 g) butter

1 tablespoon light or dark rum

1/2 cup (3 oz/90 g) seedless raisins, finely chopped

1 teaspoon vanilla extract

Butter 6-inch (15 cm) square pan and set aside. Bring water to boil. Add sugar and cook over medium heat until sugar is dissolved. Continue to cook until syrup thickens. Remove from heat. Stir in condensed milk, then cook over medium low heat, stirring occasionally, until mixture reaches 245°F (130°C) on candy thermometer and a small amount dropped into cold water forms a soft ball.

Remove from heat and beat in butter, rum, raisins, and vanilla. Beat mixture until very thick, 3 to 4 minutes. Pour into prepared pan and let cool, then cut into squares.

COCONUT ICE CREAM

SERVES 4

Havana's ice cream parlor, Coppelia, serves some of the finest ice creams in the region. Coconut ice cream, I think, is one of the best.

1 cup (8 fl oz/250 ml) coconut milk (see page 289)

1 cup (8 fl oz/250 ml) milk

3 tablespoons cornstarch

1 cup (8oz/250 g) sugar

1/4 teaspoon salt

2 tablespoons grated coconut

2 egg whites, beaten to soft peaks

Combine coconut milk and half the milk in medium saucepan. Combine remaining milk and cornstarch and add to saucepan with sugar and salt. Cook over medium low heat, stirring constantly, until mixture forms a thick custard. Stir in coconut. Let cool. Pour custard into lidded container, cover, and place in freezer until partially frozen.

Transfer mixture to bowl, add egg whites, and beat until smooth. Return ice cream to container and freeze 3 hours, then beat again until smooth and creamy. (Alternatively, freeze in ice cream maker following manufacturer's instructions.) Return to freezer until frozen.

Coconut Ice Cream

SOURSOP ICE CREAM

SERVES 6

3 cups (24 fl oz/750 ml)
soursop pulp

1/2 cup (4oz/125 g) sugar

1 cup (8 fl oz/250 ml) sweetened
condensed milk

1 cup (8 fl oz/250 ml)
evaporated milk, chilled

Mix soursop pulp with sugar and condensed milk. Chill in freezer container until mixture begins to crystallize, then beat until creamy. Add evaporated milk and freeze almost solid, then beat again until smooth and creamy. Freeze again until solid. Alternatively, process in ice cream maker following manufacturer's instructions.

PAPAYA ICE CREAM

SERVES 6

2 cups (16 fl oz/500 ml) ripe
papaya (pawpaw) pulp

1/2 cup (4 fl oz/125 ml) sweetened
condensed milk

2 teaspoons lemon or lime
juice

1/4 teaspoon salt

2 egg whites

1/4 cup (2 oz/60 g) superfine
(caster) sugar

Mix pulp with condensed milk, juice, and salt. Pour into freezer container and freeze until mixture starts to crystallize, then beat until creamy.

Beat egg whites until they form soft peaks. Beat in sugar. Fold into ice cream mixture and refreeze. Alternatively, process in ice cream maker following manufacturer's instructions.

GUAVA SORBET

SERVES 4

Serve in glasses garnished with thin slices of fresh pink guava or stewed guavas (page 218).

2 teaspoons unflavored gelatin

1/4 cup (2 fl oz/60 ml) water

2 cups (16 fl oz/500 ml) pureed pink guava

1/4 cup (2 oz/60 g) superfine (caster) sugar

3 tablespoons white rum

Sprinkle gelatin over water in small heatproof bowl. Place in small saucepan of water and set over low heat until gelatin dissolves. Let cool.

Add gelatin mixture to guava puree. Stir in sugar and rum. Pour into freezer container, cover, and freeze until sides and bottom of sorbet are almost frozen. Beat sorbet vigorously, then return to freezer and freeze until solid. Let soften in refrigerator about 20 minutes before serving.

MANGO ICE CREAM

SERVES 6

2 large ripe mangoes, peeled

1 tablespoon lime juice

2 egg whites

1/4 cup (2 oz/50 g) superfine (caster) sugar

1 cup (8 fl oz/250 ml) heavy (double) cream

Puree mango flesh with lime juice in food processor, or force through sieve. Beat egg whites in clean bowl until they form soft peaks. Beat in sugar.

In separate bowl, whip cream until it forms soft peaks, then gently whisk in mango puree. Fold in egg whites.

Pour into freezer container and freeze until mixture begins to crystallize. Beat until creamy, then freeze again. Alternatively, process in ice cream maker following manufacturer's instructions.

MANGO MOUSSE

SERVES 4

2 teaspoons unflavored gelatin

1/4 cup (2 fl oz/60 ml) cold water

4 ripe mangoes, peeled

2 tablespoons lime juice

3 tablespoons raw sugar

1 cup (8 fl oz/250 ml) heavy (double) cream

2 egg whites

ground or freshly grated nutmeg, optional

Sprinkle gelatin over water in small heatproof bowl and set aside. Puree mango in blender or by forcing flesh through a sieve. Mix in lime juice and sugar.

Place bowl of gelatin in saucepan of simmering water and stir until gelatin is dissolved completely—do not allow water to boil. Remove from heat, let cool a little, then stir into mango mixture. Beat cream until it forms soft peaks; fold into mango puree. Using clean beaters, beat egg whites until they form peaks; fold into mango mixture.

Pour mousse into individual serving dishes and chill thoroughly. Sprinkle with a little nutmeg just before serving.

Mango Ice Cream

CASSAVA PONE

SERVES 6 TO 8

One of my mother's favorites, I wish she would make it as much as she talks about it!

2 cups (10 oz/300 g) sweet cassava, peeled and finely grated, or 1 cup (4 oz/125 g) cassava meal

1 cup (4 oz/125 g) grated coconut

1 cup (8 oz/250 g) sugar

1/2 teaspoon ground or freshly grated nutmeg

1/2 teaspoon cinnamon

1/2 teaspoon freshly grated ginger

1 teaspoon vanilla extract

3 tablespoons butter or margarine, melted

about 1 cup (8 fl oz/250 ml) milk or evaporated milk

Preheat oven to 350°F (180°C/Gas 4). Grease 8-inch (20 cm) square baking dish. Combine cassava and coconut in large mixing bowl. Add sugar, nutmeg, cinnamon, ginger, vanilla, and butter and mix well. Gradually mix in enough milk to form a thick batter.

Turn mixture into prepared baking dish. Bake until set and top is browned, about 1 1/4 hours. Let cool, then cut into slices to serve.

GUAVA CHEESE

MAKES ABOUT 32 SQUARES

In Puerto Rico this is eaten with white, slightly salty cream cheese on top of each square of guava "cheese." The two flavors, sweet and salty, compliment one another well.

2 lb (1 kg) guavas (half should be not quite ripe and the other half, fully ripe)

2 cups (16 fl oz/500 ml) water

1 tablespoon lime juice

about 3 cups (24 oz/750 g) sugar

confectioners' (icing) sugar

Peel and quarter guavas. Bring the water to boil in a large saucepan, then add guavas and lime juice. Cover and cook over medium heat until guavas are tender, about 5 minutes. Drain. Mash guavas in large bowl, then force through a sieve using the back of a spoon, discarding seeds. Measure pulp and transfer to medium saucepan. Add the same quantity of sugar as there is guava pulp.

Wet the bottom and sides of a shallow pan, about 8 x 8 inches (20 x 20 cm), and set aside. Cook guava paste over low heat, stirring constantly in a zigzag (not circular) motion, until mixture thickens and begins to pull away from sides and bottom of pan; a bit of the mixture dropped into a glass of cold water should form a ball. Pour mixture into prepared pan and let cool. To serve, sift a little confectioners' sugar over the top and cut into squares.

BONIATILLO CON MANGO

SERVES 6

This sweet potato paste is from Cuba. It can have many different flavors: eat it on its own and lightly buttered, sprinkle it with cinnamon, or top it with meringue and bake it at 325°F (170°C/Gas 3) for about 15 minutes or until golden.

1 lb (500 g) sweet potatoes,
peeled and diced

1/4 teaspoon cinnamon

2 cups (1 lb/500 g) sugar

pinch of salt

1 cup (8 fl oz/250 ml) water

1 cup (8 fl oz/250 ml) mango pulp

Cover potatoes with water in medium saucepan and boil until tender, about 20 to 25 minutes. Drain. Mash until smooth, or puree in food processor. Return potatoes to saucepan and add cinnamon.

Combine sugar, salt, water, and mango pulp in another saucepan and bring to boil. Reduce heat to medium low and simmer until thick. Add this syrup to sweet potato mixture and cook over medium heat until mixture thickens and pulls away from sides and bottom of pan. Pour into shallow dish, let cool, and cut into 2-inch (5 cm) squares.

SWEET POTATO PUDDING

SERVES 6 TO 8

This Jamaican dessert is great served with ice cream.

2 cups (16 fl oz/500 ml) coconut
milk (see page 289)

1/2 cup (4 oz/125 g) raw sugar

1 tablespoon butter, melted

1 3/4 lb (875 g) sweet potato,
peeled and finely grated

4 oz (125 g) yam,
peeled and finely grated

1/2 cup (4 oz/125 g) raisins

1/2 teaspoon freshly grated
nutmeg

1/2 teaspoon cinnamon

1 teaspoon ground ginger

1 teaspoon vanilla extract

Preheat oven to 350°F (180°C/Gas 4). Grease 80 fl oz (2.5 l) baking dish. Mix coconut milk, sugar, and melted butter. Add remaining ingredients. Pour into prepared baking dish and bake in middle of oven until top is firm and a skewer inserted in middle of pudding comes out clean, about 1 hour. Let cool before serving.

TARTE À LA BANANE

SERVES 4 TO 6

The French-speaking islands offer an extensive array of pastries, breads, and cakes that are French in origin but distinctly Caribbean in style and flavor. This one is from Guadeloupe.

Pastry:

1/2 cup (4 oz /125 g) butter

2 cups (8 oz/250 g) all-purpose (plain) flour

1 egg

2 to 3 tablespoons cold water

Filling:

3 ripe bananas, peeled and thinly sliced

2 eggs, beaten

1/4 cup (2 fl oz/60 ml) heavy (double) cream

1 tablespoon sugar

1 teaspoon vanilla extract

1/4 teaspoon cinnamon

For pastry: Preheat oven to 400°F (200°C/Gas 6). Cut butter into flour until mixture resembles breadcrumbs. Blend in egg and just enough water to form a dough. Roll out pastry on floured surface into 10-inch (25 cm) circle. Transfer to buttered 8-inch (20 cm) pie plate, gently pressing into bottom and sides. Bake blind for 15 minutes. Let cool while preparing the filling.

For filling: Arrange banana slices over pastry. Blend eggs, cream, sugar, and vanilla in bowl and pour over bananas. Sprinkle with cinnamon. Bake until custard has set and pastry is golden, 15 to 20 minutes. Let cool before serving.

Tarte à la Banane

BOJO

A cassava pudding from Suriname that can be served warm or cold.

4 eggs

1/2 cup (4 oz/125 g) raw sugar

1/2 teaspoon vanilla extract

1/4 teaspoon almond extract

3/4 cup (6 fl oz/175 ml) milk

3 tablespoons butter, melted

2 lb (1 kg) sweet cassava,
peeled and finely grated

3 cups (12 oz/350 g)
finely grated coconut

1/2 cup (3 oz/90 g) seedless raisins

1 teaspoon cinnamon

1/8 teaspoon salt

Preheat oven to 375°F (190°C/Gas 5). Grease 8-inch (20 cm) baking dish. Beat eggs, sugar, and extracts in mixing bowl. Stir in milk and melted butter. Add cassava, coconut, raisins, cinnamon, and salt. Turn into prepared dish and bake until golden, 1 to 1 1/2 hours.

BEIGNETS DE BANANES

These delicious banana fritters from the French-speaking countries of the Caribbean are best served hot.

1 1/2 cups (6 oz/150 g) all-purpose
(plain) flour

1/4 teaspoon salt

1/2 tablespoon butter, softened

1 egg

2/3 cup (6 fl oz/160 ml) milk

1/4 cup (2 oz/60 g) sugar

1 tablespoon dark rum

1/8 teaspoon cinnamon

1 egg white

2 ripe bananas,
peeled and mashed

about 1/2 cup (4 fl oz/125 ml)
vegetable oil

confectioners' (icing) sugar

Combine flour, salt, butter, and whole egg in mixing bowl. Gradually beat in milk. Blend in sugar, rum, and cinnamon. Let batter rest 1 hour.

Beat egg white until it forms soft peaks. Fold into batter. Fold in bananas.

Heat oil in deep saucepan over medium high heat. Drop in tablespoonfuls of batter and fry until golden brown, 5 to 8 minutes. Drain on paper towels. Sprinkle with sugar and serve warm.

BANANES FLAMBÉES

SERVES 4 TO 6

Serve plain or with cream or ice cream.

1/4 cup (2 oz/60 g) unsalted butter

4 ripe but firm bananas, peeled and halved lengthwise

1/4 teaspoon cinnamon

1/3 cup (3 oz/80 g) sugar

2 teaspoons lime juice

1/3 cup (3 fl oz/80 ml) dark rum

Melt butter in frying pan over medium low heat. Gently add banana slices, being careful not to break them. Sprinkle with cinnamon and cook until lightly browned on both sides. Gently lift out bananas and keep warm. Add sugar and lime juice to pan and cook over low heat until sugar melts and a caramel sauce forms. Return bananas to pan. Just before serving, warm the rum, pour over bananas, and set alight at the table. Serve immediately.

TROPICAL FRUIT SALAD

SERVES 4

1/2 red papaya (pawpaw), peeled, seeded, and cubed

2 ripe mangoes, peeled, seeded, and cubed

1/2 watermelon, peeled, seeded, and cut into 1-inch (2.5 cm) cubes

2 bananas, peeled and sliced diagonally

1/2 fresh pineapple, peeled and cubed

10 cherries, preferably West Indian

2 teaspoons lime juice

1 tablespoon sugar

1/4 cup (2 fl oz/60 ml) water

juice of 1 orange

Combine all fruit in salad bowl and sprinkle with lime juice. Dissolve sugar in water in small saucepan. Add orange juice and cook 2 minutes over low heat. Cool and pour over fruit. Toss gently and serve chilled.

LIME PIE

MAKES ONE 9-INCH (23 CM) PIE

Pre-prepared or commercial shortcrust pastry can be used in this recipe.

Pastry:

2 cups (8 oz/250 g) all-purpose (plain) flour, sifted

1 tablespoon superfine (caster) sugar

1/2 cup (4 oz/125 g) margarine

about 1/4 cup (2 fl oz/60 ml) cold water

Filling:

2 1/2 cups (20 fl oz/625 ml) water

4 tablespoons cornstarch

1 tablespoon all-purpose (plain) flour

3/4 cup (6 oz/190 g) sugar

3 egg yolks, lightly beaten

1/4 cup (2 fl oz/60 ml) lime juice

2 1/2 teaspoons grated lime peel

1/2 teaspoon salt

Meringue:

3 egg whites

3 tablespoons superfine (caster) sugar

1 teaspoon lime juice

For pastry: Combine flour and sugar in bowl. Cut in margarine until mixture resembles coarse breadcrumbs. Using fork or fingertips, blend in just enough water to hold dough together.

Roll out pastry on floured surface into circle about 11 inches (27.5 cm) in diameter. Fit into 9-inch (23 cm) pie plate. Prick bottom and sides. Refrigerate 20 minutes.

Preheat oven to 425°F (220°C/Gas 7). Bake until crisp and golden, about 20 minutes. Let cool.

For filling: Adjust oven temperature to 400°F (200°C/Gas 6). Bring 2 cups (16 fl oz/500 ml) water to boil.

Mix cornstarch, flour, and sugar. Blend in remaining 1/2 cup (4 fl oz/125 ml) water. Blend in egg yolks. Gradually stir into boiling water and simmer 5 minutes, stirring constantly. Remove from heat and add lime juice, lime peel, and salt. Pour into baked crust.

For meringue: Beat egg whites until soft peaks begin to form. Beat in sugar 1 tablespoon at a time. Add lime juice. Spread over pie filling. Bake until top is lightly browned, 10 to 15 minutes. Cool before serving.

Lime Pie

TARTE AU COCO

SERVES 4 TO 6

Coconut cakes, pies, buns, tarts, and turnovers can be found throughout the Caribbean, with each country adding its own touch. This tart is found in the French-speaking islands and is indicative of the French influence on Caribbean desserts.

Pastry:

½ cup (4 oz/125 g) butter

2 cups (8 oz/250 g) all-purpose (plain) flour, sifted

1 egg

2 to 3 tablespoons cold water

Filling:

2 cups (8 oz/250 g) grated coconut

1½ cups (12 fl oz/375 ml) water

5 oz (155 g) sugar

¼ teaspoon almond extract, optional

¼ teaspoon cinnamon

2 egg whites

For pastry: Cut butter into flour until mixture resembles breadcrumbs. Blend in egg and just enough water to form a dough. Roll out pastry on floured surface into 10-inch (25 cm) circle. Transfer to buttered 8-inch (20 cm) pie plate, gently pressing into bottom and sides.

For filling: Combine coconut, water, and sugar in medium saucepan and bring to boil. Reduce heat and simmer 5 minutes. Drain coconut, discarding liquid, and cool. Stir in almond extract and cinnamon.

Preheat oven to 400°F (200°C/Gas 6).

Beat egg whites in clean bowl until they form soft peaks. Fold into coconut mixture. Pour into pastry and bake until golden brown, 25 to 30 minutes. Let cool before serving.

COCONUT PIE

SERVES 4 TO 6

Pastry:

2 cups (8 oz/250 g) all-purpose (plain) flour, sifted

pinch of salt

1/2 cup (4 oz/125 g) shortening or margarine

about 4 tablespoons ice water

Filling:

2 cups (16 fl oz/500 ml) milk

1/3 cup (2 oz/60 g) cornstarch

pinch of salt

3 egg yolks

3/4 cup (6 oz/185 g) sugar

3/4 teaspoon vanilla extract

1/2 teaspoon finely grated lemon peel

1 1/4 cups (5 oz/150 g) finely grated or flaked coconut

almond flakes for garnish, optional

For pastry: Sift flour and salt together. Cut in shortening until mixture resembles breadcrumbs. Blend in just enough water to form a dough. Roll out pastry on floured surface into 10-inch (25 cm) circle. Transfer to buttered 8-inch (20 cm) pie dish, gently pressing into bottom and sides. Prick bottom of pastry with fork to prevent bubbles from forming. Refrigerate 20 minutes.

Preheat oven to 400°F (200°C/Gas 6). Bake pastry until lightly golden, 20 to 25 minutes. Let cool.

For filling: Combine 1/3 cup (3 fl oz/80 ml) milk, cornstarch, and salt in saucepan. Add remaining milk and cook, stirring, until smooth. Beat yolks with sugar until light and fluffy in top of double boiler over low heat. Gradually add milk mixture and stir until smooth. Stir in vanilla and lemon peel and cook until a smooth custard forms, about 8 minutes. Remove from heat and stir in 1 cup coconut. Pour into bowl, cover, and refrigerate at least 2 hours.

Pour filling into baked pie shell. Garnish with almond flakes and remaining coconut.

TEMBLEQUE

SERVES 8 TO 10

A very popular Puerto Rican coconut custard.

1 teaspoon cinnamon
4 cups (1 l) coconut milk
(see page 289)
2/3 cup (5 oz/150 g) sugar
1/2 teaspoon salt
1/2 cup (3 oz/90 g) cornstarch

Wet a 10-inch (25 cm) round dish, 3 inches (8 cm) deep. Sprinkle half the cinnamon on the bottom. Combine 3 1/2 cups (28 fl oz/875 ml) coconut milk with sugar and salt in medium saucepan. Dissolve cornstarch in remaining coconut milk and add gradually to saucepan, stirring constantly. Cook over medium high heat, stirring constantly with a wooden spoon, until mixture begins to thicken, then reduce heat to medium and cook, stirring, until mixture reaches consistency of thick custard. Pour into prepared dish and sprinkle with remaining cinnamon. Refrigerate about 2 hours before serving.

Tembleque

FLOATING ISLAND

SERVES 6

Eaten throughout the Caribbean, this dish is known as Isla Flotante in the Spanish-speaking islands. The guava jelly in this recipe can be replaced with a fruit jam of your choice (e.g blackcurrant, raspberry) or left out completely. But try guava jelly—it really is worth it.

6 egg yolks

2/3 cup (5 oz/155 g) sugar

1/8 teaspoon salt

3 tablespoons cornstarch

1 teaspoon vanilla extract

4 cups (32 fl oz/1.5 l) hot milk

1 to 2 tablespoons golden rum, optional

4 egg whites

2 tablespoons (2 oz/60 g) superfine (caster) sugar

2 tablespoons guava jelly (see page 218), optional

In a double boiler or over low heat, beat yolks with sugar, salt, cornstarch, and vanilla. Slowly blend in milk and cook, stirring constantly, until mixture thickens. Add rum and cook 3 more minutes until custard is very thick. Remove from heat and pour custard into dessert dishes.

Beat egg whites until they form soft peaks. Add sugar and guava jelly and continue to beat until stiff peaks form. Drop by the teaspoonful over custard to form islands. Chill before serving.

PINE TART

MAKES 12 TO 15

One of Guyana's national dishes, and very popular, this recipe was shared with me by my Aunty Golin. These little triangular parcels of pineapple are easy to prepare.

Pastry:

2 cups (8 oz/250 g) all-purpose (plain) flour

pinch of salt

1 tablespoon superfine (caster) sugar

$1/2$ cup (4 oz/125 g) margarine or shortening

about 4 tablespoons ice water

Filling:

8 oz (250 g) fresh pineapple chunks

$1/2$ cup (4 fl oz/125 ml) water

$1/2$ cup (4 oz/125 g) sugar

1-inch (2.5 cm) cinnamon stick

1 teaspoon lime juice

For pastry: Combine flour, salt, and sugar in mixing bowl. Cut in margarine until mixture resembles fine breadcrumbs, lifting the flour as you do to trap air in the mixture. Add cold water by the tablespoon just until dough holds together, using a blunt knife to stir. Let pastry rest in refrigerator while preparing filling.

For filling: Puree pineapple in food processor or blender. Transfer to saucepan with water, sugar, cinnamon stick, and lime juice and bring to boil. Reduce heat to medium low and cook, stirring frequently, until mixture thickens to jamlike consistency. Let cool thoroughly. Remove cinnamon stick.

Preheat oven to 400°F (200°C/Gas 6). Roll out pastry on floured surface to $1/8$- to $1/4$-inch (3 to 5 mm) thickness. Cut into 4-inch (10 cm) squares and place 2 to 3 teaspoons pineapple mixture in middle of each. Wet edges with a few drops of water and fold pastry over to make a triangle; press edges together to seal. Prick each once with fork. Arrange on greased baking sheet and bake until golden, 15 to 20 minutes. Let cool before serving.

TOCINO DEL CIELO

SERVES 6 TO 8

This Spanish Caribbean dessert is a rich custard with caramel sauce. Serve it lightly chilled.

3/4 cup (6 oz/175 g) sugar
(for syrup)

3/4 cup (6 fl oz/175 ml) water

1/2-inch (1 cm) cinnamon stick

1 teaspoon lemon or lime juice

1 1/2 cups (12 oz/375 g) sugar
(for caramel)

3 whole eggs

1/2 cup (4 fl oz/125 ml) egg yolks

1/4 teaspoon salt

1 teaspoon finely grated
lime peel

1/4 teaspoon cinnamon

Combine sugar (for syrup), water, and cinnamon stick in saucepan and bring to boil. Reduce heat, add juice, and simmer until a syrup forms, 15 to 20 minutes. Let cool and remove cinnamon stick.

Lightly grease shallow dish, 6 to 8 inches (15 to 20 cm) in diameter. Place sugar (for caramel) in clean heavy medium saucepan and stir regularly with wooden spoon over medium heat until melted; be careful not to burn. Reduce heat to very low and immediately pour caramel into prepared dish to coat bottom and sides. Set aside.

Preheat oven to 350°F (180°C/Gas 4).

Combine eggs and yolks in saucepan and mix just to blend (don't beat). Add salt, peel, and cinnamon. Stir in 1 cup (8 fl oz/250 ml) of prepared syrup. Strain into caramel-lined dish. Place dish in roasting pan and pour enough hot water into pan to come 2 inches (5 cm) up side of custard dish. Cover custard dish with foil. Bake until a skewer inserted in middle of custard comes out clean, 1 1/2 to 2 hours. Uncover and leave custard in turned-off oven 5 minutes, then invert onto a platter. Cool, then refrigerate before serving.

Tocino del Cielo

CARROT PUDDING

SERVES 6

1/2 cup (4 oz/125 g) butter

1/2 cup (4 oz/125 g) raw sugar

2 eggs, beaten

1 cup (4 oz/125 g) grated carrot

3/4 cup (4 oz/125 g) seedless raisins

11/2 cups (6 oz/185 g) all-purpose (plain) flour

2 teaspoons baking powder

1/2 teaspoon salt

1/2 teaspoon cinnamon

1/2 teaspoon ground or freshly grated nutmeg

4 tablespoons dark rum, optional

1 tablespoon chopped nuts

Preheat oven to 350°F (180°C/Gas 4). Grease 6 x 4-inch (15 x 10 cm) loaf pan. Cream butter and sugar. Beat in eggs. Stir in carrot and raisins. Sift flour, baking powder, salt, cinnamon, and nutmeg. Stir into carrot mixture, adding rum and nuts. Pour into prepared pan and bake until skewer inserted in middle comes out clean, about 45 minutes. Turn out on a rack to cool.

KESIO

From Curaçao, a custard dripping with caramel sauce.

1 cup (8 oz/250 g) sugar

5 eggs

pinch of salt

2 teaspoons vanilla extract

2 cups (16 fl oz/500 ml)
warmed milk

1/3 cup (3 fl oz/80 ml) water

4 maraschino cherries
to garnish

golden rum, optional

Preheat oven to 350°F (180°C/Gas 4). Butter a 6-inch (15 cm) baking dish. Place half the sugar in saucepan and melt slowly over low heat, stirring constantly so that a smooth caramel forms. Spoon immediately into prepared dish and swirl dish to coat sides and bottom with caramel.

Beat eggs in large bowl until light. Add remaining sugar, salt, and vanilla. Slowly stir in milk. Pour mixture into caramel-lined dish. Set dish in roasting pan holding 1 inch (2.5 cm) hot water. Bake until custard is firm, about 1 hour. Remove from water bath; let cool.

Turn custard out onto shallow serving platter. Garnish with cherries. To serve, pour 1 tablespoon rum over each slice and set alight. Allow to burn for 5 to 10 seconds, then blow out.

BEVERAGES

Rum. It's literally everywhere in the Caribbean, and there's only one thing you can say about it—it's the best in the world! Grab a bottle and try a few of these recipes to create a taste of the Caribbean in your home. Of course, hand in hand with rum goes fresh fruit, so you can even tell yourself you're being healthy!

Curaçao's liqueur comes in so many wonderful flavors that the potential for cocktails is endless. However, the most common variety available outside of the Caribbean is the orange-flavored version. The liqueur has its origins in a crop of Valencia orange trees taken to the island by the Spanish. The arid soil and climate turned the orange into an inedible fruit, but one whose sun-dried peels contain an oil with an extraordinarily pleasing fragrance. This oil is what gives the liqueur its flavor.

With the vast array of fruit available in the West Indies, many beautiful and exotic punches can be found. Although other countries may not be blessed with such abundance, most fruit can be purchased in one form or another. Check the availability of canned and bottled ingredients and keep an eye out for fruits in season.

When it comes to non-alcoholic drinks, the snow cone is a fantastic, thirst-quenching refreshment that is very simple to make and perfect for those hot and sticky days in summer. If you are in the Caribbean, it's a treat to watch the vendors scraping and scooping the ice before covering it in luscious syrup.

Daiquiri, page 257

Nonalcoholic

SNOWCONES & SKY JUICE

SERVES 1

In the West Indies these snowcones, particularly popular with children, are available from many a street vendor. The vendor grates a huge slab of ice and piles the shavings into a cup until almost double the cup's height; then you can choose one of the many tempting fruit syrups on display.

The snowcone (or snowball as it is sometimes known) is eaten by sucking on the ice, drawing out the sweet syrup at the same time. In Jamaica, street vendors sell a similar refreshment known as sky juice; the crushed ice is served in a plastic bag and a straw is provided, as the ice melts quickly in the heat.

shaved or grated ice
fruit syrup of your choice

Shave or grate enough ice to fill a cup. Pile it up into a mound. Pour the syrup around the rim of the cup, then work your way up to the top.

TAMARIND DRINK

MAKES 4 CUPS (32 FL OZ/1 L)

This recipe comes from Tobago, although tamarinds are used to make drinks all over the region.

1 lb (500 g) tamarind, shelled
4 cups (32 fl oz/1 l) hot water
sugar

Cover tamarind with hot water and let stand overnight. Strain, discarding fruit. Stir in sugar to taste until dissolved. Bottle and serve chilled. Store in refrigerator for up to 2 days.

BARATARIA GRAPEFRUITADE

SERVES 4

In the Caribbean, ripe grapefruit is sweet while still retaining a hint of sharpness. In other parts of the world, yellow grapefruit is far too bitter to use, so I have substituted ripe oranges.

3 ripe oranges
1 grapefruit
4 cups (32 fl oz/1 l) water
1 cup (8 oz/250 g) sugar
1/4 teaspoon Angostura bitters

Squeeze juice from oranges and grapefruit. Place in pitcher. Add water and sugar, stirring constantly until sugar has completely dissolved. Stir in bitters and serve chilled with ice in tumblers or long glasses.

CARROT JUICE

MAKES ABOUT 4 CUPS (32 FL OZ/1 L)

I particularly like this drink. My mother used to serve it with a Sunday lunch of rice and peas and marinated beef stew (see pages 145 and 85). It's very refreshing on a hot day and always reminds my brothers' father of his home town in the West Indies.

4 cups (32 fl oz/1 l) canned or fresh carrot juice
14-oz (400 ml) can sweetened condensed milk
ground or freshly grated nutmeg
1/4 cup (2 fl oz/60 ml) rum, optional
1/4 teaspoon vanilla extract
raw sugar, optional

Pour carrot juice into a large pitcher. Add condensed milk and stir well. Add nutmeg to taste, rum (if desired), and vanilla and stir well. If desired, sweeten to taste with raw sugar. Serve well chilled over ice cubes.

PAPAYA AND MANGO DRINK

SERVES 4

This is a delicious and refreshing drink, and very healthy too! You need not use as much sugar as I have indicated—it is really to taste—but I think it's just right like this when served with ice.

2 ripe papayas (pawpaws), about 10 oz (300 g) each, peeled and seeded

1 ripe mango, about 8 to 10 oz (250 to 300 g), peeled and pitted

4 cups (32 fl oz/1 l) water

2 tablespoons lime juice

1/4 cup (2 oz/60 g) sugar or to taste

1/4 teaspoon ground or freshly grated nutmeg

Combine papaya and mango pulp in small bowl and mash into puree using back of fork, or puree in blender. Stir in water and lime juice. Strain, gently pressing pulp through sieve. Add sugar and stir until dissolved. Add nutmeg and chill. Serve over ice.

MANGO SHAKE

SERVES 2

This mango milkshake from Montego Bay, Jamaica, can be livened up with 1/4 cup (2 fl oz/60 ml) rum if you so wish!

about 2 cups (16 oz/500 g) mango flesh

1 1/2 cups (12 fl oz/375 ml) milk

1/3 cup (3 fl oz/80 ml) sweetened condensed milk

1/4 teaspoon vanilla extract

crushed ice

sprinkle of freshly grated nutmeg

Puree mango, milk, condensed milk, and vanilla in blender until smooth. Pour into tall glasses filled a third full with crushed ice and stir vigorously. Sprinkle a little nutmeg on top and serve.

Papaya and Mango Drink

GINGER BEER

MAKES ABOUT 10 CUPS (2.5 L)

Once fermented, the bottled ginger beer can be stored for weeks.

1 oz (30 g) fresh ginger, peeled and finely grated

3¼ to 3½ cups (26 to 28 oz/ 790 to 850 g) sugar

2 teaspoons lime juice

peel of ½ lime

12 cups (3 l) boiling water

3 whole cloves

1 teaspoon dry yeast

2 to 3 tablespoons warm water

Add ginger, sugar, lime juice, and peel to boiling water in large pot or crock and stir until sugar is dissolved. Add cloves and let cool until tepid.

In a cup, dissolve yeast in the warm water. Add to ginger mixture, cover, and let stand 48 hours. Strain and pour into sterilized bottles. Store in a cool dark place for 3 to 4 days before serving.

QUICK GINGER BEER

MAKES ABOUT 6 CUPS (1.5 L)

This flat-style ginger beer is a quicker version to make and is very refreshing served over ice.

1 oz (30 g) fresh ginger, peeled and finely grated

2-inch (5 cm) piece lime peel

5 cups (1.25 l) hot water

5 tablespoons sugar

¼ teaspoon Angostura bitters

Add ginger and lime peel to the water in a large pitcher. Cover and let stand overnight.

Strain liquid and add sugar, stirring until it dissolves. Add bitters and chill before serving. Can be stored in the refrigerator in sterilized bottles or a covered jar for about 2 to 3 days.

SORREL

MAKES ABOUT 16 CUPS (4 L)

Also known as roselle, rosella, Jamaica flower, or Jamaica sorrel, the botanical name of this plant is *Hibiscus sabdariffa*. It flowers around Christmastime in the Caribbean and so shows up on every dinner table during the Christmas season. The petals eventually wither and drop off, leaving behind the sepals that protect the seed. They continue to grow, becoming larger and more succulent. The sepals are used to produce a deep red, aromatic drink with a slightly tart taste. Add sugar to your taste, but I have given a quantity that seems just right!

8 cups (2 l) sorrel sepals

6 whole cloves

3 2-inch (5 cm) pieces orange peel

1/2-inch (1 cm) piece fresh ginger, grated, optional

12 cups (3 l) boiling water

1 1/2 cups (12 oz/350 g) sugar or to taste

1/2 cup (4 fl oz/125 ml) rum, optional

Place sorrel in large jar with cloves, orange peel, and ginger. Pour boiling water over (sorrel and peel should be covered). Let steep 24 hours.

Strain liquid and add sugar, stirring constantly until dissolved. Add rum. Pour into sterilized bottles and serve chilled. Can be stored for 3 to 4 months.

SOURSOP DRINK

MAKES ABOUT 4 CUPS (32 FL OZ/1 L)

Soursop fruit is both sweet and tart; the flesh has the consistency of a very thick custard. It is rich in minerals and vitamins.

1 ripe soursop (about 2 lb/1 kg)

4 cups (32 fl oz/1 l) water

1/4 cup (2 oz/60 g) sugar

1/2 teaspoon vanilla extract or a dash of Angostura bitters

Cut open the soursop and scoop out flesh. Place in bowl with 3 cups water and stir until the flesh loosens and the liquid becomes thick, about 3 minutes. Let stand 10 minutes, then stir again.

Strain the liquid, squeezing out as much liquid from the pulp as possible. Discard soursop flesh.

Stir sugar into 1 cup water until dissolved. Add to soursop mixture with vanilla and stir, adding another 1/2 cup (4 fl oz/125 ml) water if too thick. Serve chilled with ice.

DOMINICAN FRUIT COCKTAIL

SERVES 4

This cocktail uses very typical West Indian fruits; even the cherries grown in the Caribbean are different from the darker red variety grown in more temperate countries. (You can use either variety for this punch.) The golden apple has no real substitute, but I think pineapple makes a good stand-in.

2 star fruit, peeled

8 oz (250 g) cherries, pitted

1 guava, peeled, seeded, and quartered

2 golden apples or 1/4 pineapple

3 cups (24 fl oz/750 ml) water

sugar

Puree star fruit, cherries, guava, and pineapple separately. Strain each juice individually through a fine sieve and combine juices in pitcher. Add water, then sugar to taste, stirring constantly to dissolve. Serve chilled over ice cubes in long glasses.

JAMAICAN FRUIT PUNCH

SERVES 4

1 6-oz (185 g) papaya (pawpaw) or 1 cup (8 fl oz/250 ml) papaya (pawpaw) juice

1 8-oz (250 g) mango or 1 cup (8 fl oz/250 ml) mango juice

1 banana, peeled and chopped

1 1/2 cups pineapple chunks, fresh or canned, or 1 cup (8 fl oz/ 250 ml) pineapple juice

2 cups (16 fl oz/500 ml) water

1/3 cup (3 fl oz/80 ml) lime juice

1 tablespoon grenadine

If using whole fruit, peel, seed and cube papaya and mango. Puree each fruit separately in a blender or by passing through a sieve. Transfer to a large jug.

If using fruit juices, place in a large jug. Puree banana and add to juices.

Add remaining ingredients to jug and combine well. Chill. Serve in a glass filled with crushed ice.

Jamaican Fruit Punch

254

PEANUT PUNCH

SERVES 2

This is a very popular punch from Trinidad, often enjoyed at lunchtime. Very thick and filling, it is not recommended for those who wish to stay awake after lunch! Although the other islands have their own variations on peanut punch, the Trinidadian one is truly wonderful if you have a sweet tooth.

3/4 cup (6 oz/175 g) peanut butter

3/4 cup (6 oz/175 ml) evaporated milk

1 cup (8 oz/250 ml) sweetened condensed milk

2 cups (16 fl oz/500 ml) water

1/2 teaspoon vanilla extract

1 egg

3/4 cup (6 fl oz/175 ml) rum, optional

freshly grated nutmeg

Combine all ingredients except nutmeg in blender and process until smooth. Serve with a sprinkle of nutmeg.

MAUBY

MAKES ABOUT 8 CUPS (2 L)

Made from tree bark, this refreshingly bittersweet beverage is drunk in many of the islands. It can also be made with mauby syrup, bought already bottled in Caribbean supermarkets; dilute it to taste with water and sweeten to your liking.

1 tablespoon ground mauby bark

1/2-inch (1 cm) cinnamon stick

small piece of dried orange peel

2 whole cloves

8 cups (2 l) water

2 cups (1 lb/500 g) sugar

Boil mauby bark, cinnamon stick, orange peel, and cloves in 1 cup (8 fl oz/250 ml) water for 10 minutes. Cool and strain. Add sugar and remaining water, stirring until sugar dissolves. Pour into clean bottles and cover; do not fill to the top, as froth will develop during fermentation. Let stand at room temperature 2 days, then refrigerate. Serve chilled.

Alcoholic

DAIQUIRI

SERVES 1

The best daiquiries can be had in Havana, the home of this famous drink. The original version did not include fruit.

1 tablespoon superfine (caster) sugar

2 tablespoons lemon juice

1/4 cup (2 fl oz/60 ml) white or light rum

crushed ice

maraschino cherry for garnish

Dissolve sugar in lemon juice. In a shaker blend lemon juice mixture, rum, and 1½ glasses of ice until light and fluffy. Pour into a small wineglass or cocktail glass, piling up a small mound in the glass. Top with cherry and serve with a straw.

COQUITO

SERVES 6 TO 8

A popular Christmas drink in Puerto Rico. Although it takes a little while to prepare, it's worth it.

1 cup (8 fl oz/250 ml) white rum

3 cups (12 oz/375 g) freshly grated coconut, or 3 cups (12 oz/375 g) dried

2 egg yolks

1/8 teaspoon salt

6 fl oz (135 ml) sweetened condensed milk

cinnamon or freshly grated nutmeg

Pour half of rum into blender. Add 1/4 of coconut and blend until coconut is finely grated. Strain mixture into pitcher through a piece of cheesecloth (muslin), then squeeze cloth to extract as much coconut milk as possible. Discard coconut remaining in cloth.

Pour squeezed-out liquid back into blender, add another 1/4 of the coconut (but no rum), and repeat process until all coconut is used.

Return coconut milk mixture to blender. Add egg yolks, salt, and condensed milk and blend until smooth. Pour into large pitcher. Add remaining rum and stir. Refrigerate; remove from refrigerator 30 minutes before serving. Stir well and serve in small glasses, sprinkled liberally with cinnamon or nutmeg.

Piña Colada

SERVES 2

Some believe this drink originated in Puerto Rico; others think it came from Mexico. You can use canned coconut milk or follow the recipe on page 289 for fresh coconut milk.

2 cups (8 to 10 oz/250 to 315 g)
fresh or canned
pineapple chunks

2/3 cup (5 fl oz/160 ml)
coconut milk

1/3 cup (3 fl oz/80 ml) white rum

crushed ice

pineapple slice and
maraschino cherry to garnish

Combine all ingredients except garnish in blender. Serve with pineapple slice and maraschino cherry garnish.

Sorrel Liqueur

YIELDS ABOUT 3 CUPS (24 FL OZ / 750 ML)

Also known as roselle, rosella, Jamaica flower, or Jamaica sorrel, the seed pods of this plant are used to make a refreshing drink (see page 253). Sealed bottles can be stored for months.

2 lb (1 kg) sorrel with seed pods

3 cups (24 fl oz/750 ml)
golden rum

2 cups (16 fl oz/500 ml) water

1 1/2 cups (12 oz/350 g) sugar

2 teaspoons lime juice

Remove sepals from sorrel seed pods and discard seeds. Submerge sepals in rum in a heavy jar, cover, and let stand 10 days.

Boil water, sugar, and lime juice in small saucepan until a thin syrup is formed, about 10 minutes. Let cool. Add to sorrel mixture. Strain and pour into sterilized bottles. Seal bottles and store in a cool place for at least 2 weeks before serving.

Piña Colada

PASSIONFRUIT PUNCH

SERVES 2

This drink is from Dominica, where passionfruit is so abundant that it can be picked by the roadside, growing wild with many wondrous fruits and even coffee beans.

4 passionfruit, halved, or
1 1/2 oz (50 g) concentrated
passionfruit pulp

2/3 cup (5 fl oz/150 ml) cold water

4 teaspoons sugar

1/4 cup (2 fl oz/60 ml) water

4 teaspoons lime juice

6 tablespoons rum

2 dashes Angostura bitters

freshly grated nutmeg

pineapple slices and maraschino
cherries to garnish

Scoop flesh of passionfruit into a pitcher with 2/3 cup water and stir well. Let stand 5 minutes. Strain into cocktail shaker.

Combine sugar and 1/4 cup water and stir until sugar is dissolved. Add to shaker along with lime juice, rum, and bitters and shake well. Pour into 2 glasses filled with ice cubes. Grate a little nutmeg over each glass. Garnish with a slice of pineapple and a maraschino cherry.

TI-PUNCH

SERVES 1

"Ti" means small, which is exactly what this punch is. In Guadeloupe and Martinique, where it origi-nates, it is often served as a before-dinner drink. The cane sugar syrup gives the mix its distinctive taste, but if unavailable you can use 1 teaspoon superfine (caster) sugar dissolved in 1 tablespoon of water. A dash of Angostura bitters can also be added if you wish.

small wedge of lime

1 teaspoon cane sugar syrup, or
dissolved superfine (caster) sugar

1/2 teaspoon lime juice

3 tablespoons (1 1/2 fl oz/45 ml)
white rum

1 ice cube

Place lime wedge in a short tumbler. Add sugar syrup and lime juice and stir well. Add rum and stir again. Add ice cube and serve.

PLANTERS PUNCH

SERVES 2

This is another traditional Jamaican punch. One variation is to pour the drink into a dessert glass or wide-rimmed glass with sliced banana, diced apple pieces, and diced orange, and serve with a long spoon.

ice cubes

1/4 cup (2 oz/60 g) superfine (caster) sugar

6 tablespoons water

1/2 cup (4 fl oz/125 ml) light rum

1 tablespoon lime juice

2 dashes Angostura bitters

lime, pineapple, and/or orange slices to garnish

maraschino cherry to garnish

Place a few ice cubes into each of two tall glasses. Combine sugar and water to make a syrup, stirring until sugar dissolves. Combine rum, lime juice, and bitters with sugar syrup in a cocktail shaker and shake for 1 minute, or combine all ingredients in a pitcher and stir vigorously. Pour over the ice cubes. Garnish each glass with a slice of fruit and a cherry.

MANGO PUNCH

SERVES 2

3/4 cup (6 oz/175 ml) dark rum

1 tablespoon lime juice

4 teaspoons superfine (caster) sugar

1/2 cup (4 oz/125 g) mango pulp

1 teaspoon grenadine

crushed ice

pineapple slices and maraschino cherries to garnish

Combine all ingredients except garnish in blender and blend at high speed for 5 seconds. Pour into wine glasses, garnish, and serve.

COCONUT PUNCH

SERVES 2

½ cup (4 fl oz/125 ml) coconut milk (see page 289)

⅓ cup (3 fl oz/80 ml) sweetened condensed milk

¼ cup (2 fl oz/60 ml) light rum

¼ cup (2 fl oz/60 ml) coconut cream (see page 289)

¼ teaspoon Angostura bitters

crushed ice

freshly grated nutmeg

pineapple wedge and maraschino cherry to garnish

In a cocktail shaker or pitcher combine coconut milk, condensed milk, rum, coconut cream, and bitters and blend well. Fill two dessert glasses with crushed ice and pour coconut mixture over. Sprinkle with nutmeg and garnish with fruit

MUZIK DI ZUMBI

SERVES 1

In Papiamento (the local language spoken in Curaçao, Bonaire, and Aruba), "muzik di zumbi" means "spirit music." It is a mixture of African rhythms, reggae, and South American music. Like the music, this cocktail is a mixture of contrasting elements.

4 oz (125 g) mango flesh, cubed

¾ cup (6 fl oz/175 ml) water

3 tablespoons white rum

3 tablespoons (1½ fl oz/45 ml) blue Curaçao

1 tablespoon lime juice

1½ teaspoons superfine (caster) sugar

3 tablespoons grenadine

3 tablespoons superfine (caster) sugar

crushed ice

Blend mango with ½ cup (4 fl oz/125 ml) water until smooth. Stir in remaining water. Strain juice into cocktail shaker, blender, or pitcher. Add rum, Curaçao, lime juice, and 1½ teaspoons sugar and blend vigorously until sugar has dissolved.

Place grenadine in one small saucer, and 3 tablespoons sugar in another. Dip the rim of a glass into the grenadine, then into the sugar to make an even red edge. Fill glass with crushed ice, pour in drink mixture, and serve.

Muzik di Zumbi

MOJITO

SERVES 1

A very popular Cuban drink with a hint of mint. In Cuba they use a variety known as herbabuena, but any mint is a good substitute. Add a couple of drops of Angostura bitters for extra flavor.

1 stalk mint, washed

juice of 1/2 lemon

1 tablespoon superfine (caster) sugar

4 ice cubes

3 tablespoons (1 1/2 fl oz/45 ml) white rum

chilled club soda or carbonated mineral water

Place stalk of mint in tall glass. Combine lemon juice and sugar, stirring until sugar is dissolved. Place ice cubes in glass and add lemon mixture, then rum. Top up with club soda.

CUBANITO

SERVES 1

4 ice cubes

salt to taste

2 teaspoons lemon juice

1/2 cup (4 fl oz/125 ml) tomato juice

1/4 cup (2 fl oz/60 ml) white rum

1/2 teaspoon Worcestershire sauce

Angostura bitters

Tabasco sauce

Place ice cubes in a tall glass. Combine all remaining ingredients in a blender, then pour over ice.

Rum and Coconut Water

SERVES 1

I'm sure there is no water better than coconut water, not even Curaçao's distilled seawater or Barbados's limestone-filtered water (although both are very good). What's more, coconut water is said to have countless medicinal properties. This recipe calls for fresh coconut water, for which there is no substitute. If you can get a fresh green coconut, give it a try.

3 tablespoons (1¹/₂ fl oz/45 ml) light rum

1¹/₄ cups (10 fl oz/300 ml) coconut water, chilled

3 or 4 ice cubes

Pour rum into a tall glass and add coconut water. Drop in ice cubes and serve.

Brown Cow

SERVES 1

From Jamaica, an extraordinarily popular drink with an amusing name.

4 ice cubes

¹/₄ cup (2 fl oz/60 ml) coffee liqueur (e.g. Tía María)

1 cup (8 fl oz/250 ml) milk

freshly grated nutmeg

Place ice cubes in a tall glass, add coffee liqueur, and top with milk. Sprinkle with nutmeg.

Jamaican Coffee

SERVES 1

Jamaica's Blue Mountain region produces some of the best coffee in the world.

1 tablespoon dark rum

¹/₄ cup (2 fl oz/60 ml) coffee liqueur (e.g. Tía María)

1 cup (8 fl oz/250 ml) hot black coffee, preferably made with freshly ground coffee beans

1 teaspoon sugar or to taste

freshly grated nutmeg

Warm rum a little and place in coffee mug with liqueur. Pour in coffee. Stir in sugar and finish with a sprinkle of nutmeg.

SAUCES, SEASONINGS, AND CONDIMENTS

I t's in this section that you'll find the famous Caribbean hot pepper sauce. No dinner table is complete without it. For that matter, I don't think the table would be complete without mango chutney or table pickle either, so you'll also find recipes here for a variety of such condiments.

Limes are widely used in the preparation of Caribbean dishes, from marinating meat and fish to flavoring sauces and condiments. However, in mojo criollo and other Spanish Caribbean dishes, the Spanish-speaking islands sometimes use Seville oranges instead because they have the bitterness of citrus fruits yet impart a distinct orange flavor.

The Caribbean offers a vast array of herbs, hot, sweet, or seasoning peppers of all varieties, and many kinds of onions. We are lucky that today we can obtain virtually all of these ingredients—or good substitutes at least—in many countries of the world so that we can recapture the flavors and aromas of the traditional recipes.

The hot pepper is native to the region and was used by the indigenous population to season and preserve meats. Today it is used as the basis for many seasonings and marinades such as sofrito, a base seasoning used for many dishes in the Spanish-speaking countries which represents a mingling of native American elements with Spanish imports.

Because food is an important part of West Indian life, much care is taken to produce the right blend of flavors. With these recipes, you can prepare ingredients that will transform your meals by adding the authentic taste of the Caribbean. If you allow yourself the extra time, I promise you it will be well worth it.

Coconut Cream, page 289

PICKLED HOT PEPPERS

MAKES ABOUT 2^1/$_2$ CUPS (20 OZ/600 G)

The different hot chili peppers make this not only visually appealing but extra tasty, as they are at different stages of ripeness.

24 whole hot green, red, and yellow peppers, quartered and seeded

8 dried allspice berries or ^{1}/$_2$ teaspoon ground allspice

1 clove garlic, bruised

^{1}/$_2$ teaspoon salt or to taste

2 cups (16 fl oz/500 ml) white distilled vinegar

Combine peppers, allspice berries, garlic, and salt in nonaluminum bowl. Bring vinegar to boil and pour onto other ingredients. Stir and let cool thoroughly. Pour into sterilized jar.

MANGO KUCHILLA

MAKES 14 OZ/400 G

This mango pickle comes from Trinidad and Guyana, where most of the Caribbean's East Indian population is concentrated and where you will find lots of Indo-Caribbean dishes. This can be served as an accompaniment to snacks such as aloo pie (see page 21), phulourie (see page 24), aloo roti (see page 157), or doubles (see page 156).

8 underripe green mangoes, peeled and finely grated

1/4 cup (2 fl oz/60 ml) vegetable oil

2 teaspoons ground cumin

2 tablespoons masala (see page 284)

1 tablespoon packed brown sugar

12 cloves garlic

2 1/2 tablespoons white vinegar

2 hot red peppers, seeded

salt

3 tablespoons mustard oil

Wrap mango in cheesecloth (muslin) in batches and squeeze out all liquid. Discard liquid. Spread out the mango on a clean cloth and let dry 3 to 4 hours (preferably in the sun).

Heat vegetable oil in saucepan over medium heat. Add remaining ingredients except mustard oil and mix well. Simmer 5 minutes. Remove from heat and stir in mangoes and 2 tablespoons mustard oil. Bottle in sterilized jars and top with remaining mustard oil. The pickle will keep for months.

MANGO CHUTNEY

MAKES ABOUT 21 OZ/600 G

This is my favorite chutney of all time—and it's my grandma's! It's great eaten with phulourie (see page 24) or as an accompaniment to a curry. It is essential that you use green, unripe mangoes.

12 green, unripe mangoes, peeled

10 cloves garlic, peeled

4 large or 8 small hot red peppers

2 tablespoons vegetable oil

2 tablespoons garam masala

4 teaspoons cumin

1 tablespoon masala
(see page 284)

salt

2 to 3 tablespoons mustard oil

Grate mangoes into large mixing bowl. Mince garlic and peppers in blender or food processor. Add to mangoes.

Heat vegetable oil in saucepan. Add all ingredients except mustard oil and simmer 5 minutes. Let cool. Pour into sterilized jars, add just enough mustard oil to cover, and seal. Over time, as the jar is opened and the chutney is eaten, pour a little mustard oil over, just to cover, to preserve the chutney. This chutney will keep for months.

Mango Chutney

TAMARIND CHUTNEY

MAKES ABOUT 1½ CUPS (12 OZ/350 G)

Tamarind is a fruit that looks like a brown pod and can grow up to 5 inches (12 cm) long. Inside the pod is an acidic pulp that can be used in chutneys, drinks, and other recipes. You can also buy packaged tamarinds. Either is suitable for this recipe. This chutney can be eaten with aloo pie (see page 21), phoulourie (see page 24), doubles (see page 156), and bakes (see page 193).

8 oz (250 g) tamarind pods, shelled

¾ cup (6 fl oz/175 ml) water

¼ teaspoon cumin seeds

1 tablespoon white vinegar

3 cloves garlic, minced

1 teaspoon freshly grated ginger

2 tablespoons raw sugar

2 hot red or green peppers, seeded and minced

½ teaspoon ground cumin

¼ teaspoon freshly ground black pepper

salt

Wash tamarind and place in bowl with ½ cup (4 fl oz/125 ml) water. Let stand 15 minutes, then mash pulp with fork until it separates from seeds. Discard seeds.

Combine remaining water, cumin seeds, vinegar, garlic, ginger, and sugar in saucepan and simmer 3 minutes. Remove from heat and add tamarind, hot peppers, ground cumin, pepper, and salt. Mix well. Pour into sterilized jar.

PUERTO RICAN TABLE PICKLE

MAKES ABOUT 3 CUPS (24 OZ/750 G)

Serve with salads and any meal.

2 medium onions, sliced

6 cloves garlic

6 whole mixed hot red and green peppers

3 stalks cilantro (fresh coriander)

2 teaspoons peppercorns

3 cups (24 fl oz/750 ml) white distilled vinegar

salt

Combine all ingredients except vinegar and salt in sterilized large bottle or jar.

Bring vinegar and salt to boil in medium saucepan. Remove from heat and add to bottle or jar, stirring once to blend. Let cool, then cover.

HOT PEPPER SAUCE

MAKES ABOUT 3 CUPS (24 FL OZ/750 ML)

24 small hot red peppers, seeded
and sliced lengthwise

2 medium onions, chopped

2 cloves garlic, halved

1 tablespoon dry mustard

2 teaspoons salt

2 whole cloves

1 1/2 cups (12 fl oz/375 ml)
white distilled vinegar

Combine hot peppers, onions, and garlic in food processor or blender and puree. Add dry mustard, salt, cloves, and vinegar. Transfer to small nonaluminum saucepan and simmer over medium low heat, 3 to 4 minutes. Pour into a warm sterilized jar and seal.

HOT PEPPER SAUCE II

MAKES ABOUT 2 CUPS (16 FL OZ/500 ML)

From St Kitts to Haiti to Tobago you will find some variation of this pepper sauce.

1/4 cup (1 oz/30 g) grated
green underripe papaya (pawpaw)

about 1/3 cup (3 fl oz/80 ml) water

8 oz (250 g) hot red, yellow, or
orange peppers, seeded and
minced

1 medium onion, minced

3 cloves garlic

2 teaspoons salt or to taste

1 cup (8 fl oz/250 ml) white
distilled vinegar

1 tablespoon dry mustard

3 tablespoons olive or
vegetable oil

Cover papaya with water in nonaluminum saucepan and boil until tender, about 2 minutes. Add all remaining ingredients and process in blender or food processor until very finely minced. Return to saucepan and simmer uncovered 5 minutes. Let cool, pour into sterilized bottles and seal. Allow to stand for 2 to 3 days before serving. The bottled sauce will keep for several months.

Hot Pepper Sauce

SOFRITO

MAKES ABOUT 3 CUPS (24 FL OZ/750 ML)

Sofrito is an excellent seasoning used in many Puerto Rican and Cuban dishes. You can make it in large quantities and freeze some for future use. Here are two recipes; the first is more basic, but both can be added to many dishes of Spanish origin. An herb known as culantrillo is usually used in making sofrito but, as it is difficult to obtain, parsley is a good substitute. I have also used common hot peppers in this dish, whereas sweet hot peppers known as ajíes dulce are often used locally.

1/4 cup (2 fl oz/60 ml) olive oil

2 tablespoons annatto oil
(see page 285), optional

1 lb (2 kg) tomatoes, peeled,
seeded, and chopped

2 medium onions, chopped

1 green bell pepper (capsicum),
seeded and chopped

8 large hot peppers,
seeded and chopped

4 teaspoons finely chopped
cilantro (fresh coriander leaves)

1 teaspoon dried oregano

1 sprig parsley, finely chopped

Combine olive oil, annatto oil, and tomatoes in blender or food processor and puree. Stir in remaining ingredients.

SOFRITO II

MAKES ABOUT 3 CUPS (24 FL OZ/750 ML)

1 tablespoon vegetable oil

2 oz (60 g) ham, finely chopped

1 oz (30 g) bacon, finely chopped

1 onion, finely chopped

2 cloves garlic, crushed

2 tomatoes,
peeled, seeded,
and chopped

1 teaspoon finely chopped
cilantro (fresh coriander leaves)

1 teaspoon finely chopped parsley
or 1/2 teaspoon dried

1 teaspoon finely chopped
oregano or 1/4 teaspoon dried

1/2 green bell pepper (capsicum),
seeded and finely chopped

1 large hot pepper or 2 sweet hot
peppers, seeded and chopped

2 tablespoons annatto oil
(see page 285), optional

Heat oil in a saucepan over medium high heat and brown ham and bacon. Add onion and garlic. Reduce heat to low and add remaining ingredients except annatto oil. Simmer 10 minutes. Add annatto oil, increase heat to moderate, and cook for 1 more minute.

Mojo Criollo

MAKES ABOUT ¾ CUP(6 FL OZ/175 ML)

A Cuban sauce served cold over boiled or fried vegetables such as yams, sweet potato, or cassava. It is best prepared the same day, but it can be made the day before.

½ cup (4 fl oz/125 ml) vegetable or corn oil

1 clove garlic, crushed

¼ cup (2 fl oz/60 ml) white vinegar, lime juice, or juice of unripe orange

Combine all ingredients. Serve 1 to 2 teaspoons of sauce over each hot piece of vegetable.

Mojo Criollo II

MAKES ABOUT ½ CUP (4 FL OZ/125 ML)

A variation of mojo criollo is poured over roast or deep-fried pork or fried fish.

1 small onion, sliced

¼ cup (2 fl oz/60 ml) vegetable or corn oil

2 tablespoons white vinegar or juice of unripe orange

Lightly sauté onion in hot oil. Add vinegar or juice and stir well. Pour hot sauce over hot meat or fish.

MONTSERRAT MARMALADE

MAKES ABOUT 2 LBS/900 G

1/2 grapefruit, seeded and sliced

2 sweet oranges,
seeded and sliced

1/2 pineapple, peeled and sliced

about 8 cups (2 l) water

5 cups (2 1/2 lb/1.2 kg) sugar

juice of 1 lime

1/2 teaspoon ground or
freshly grated nutmeg

Layer grapefruit slices, then oranges, then pineapple in a medium saucepan and cover with water. Bring to boil, then reduce heat to medium and cook until peels are soft, about 25 minutes. Let cool. Remove pith and let stand overnight.

Drain fruit, reserving liquid. Chop peel into small pieces. Add sugar, lime juice, nutmeg, and 1 1/4 cups (10 fl oz/300 ml) of fruit liquid. Cook uncovered over medium heat until mixture thickens to almost a marmalade consistency, about 50 to 60 minutes, stirring regularly to avoid sticking. Pour into warm sterilized jars.

GUAVA JAM

MAKES ABOUT 4 CUPS (32 OZ/1 L)

I think pink guavas are best for this, and they look great, but white ones are equally as sweet in this jam.

4 lb (2 kg) ripe guavas,
peeled and halved

2 cups (16 fl oz/500 ml) water

6 cups (3 lb/1.5 kg) sugar

2-inch (5 cm) cinnamon stick

Place guavas and water in saucepan, making sure guavas are immersed. Boil until guavas are very soft, about 5 to 8 minutes. Drain and press through sieve to remove seeds.

Return guava puree to saucepan. Add sugar and cook over high heat, stirring constantly, until sugar is dissolved. Add cinnamon stick. Reduce heat slightly and simmer, stirring occasionally, until mixture thickens, about 30 to 40 minutes. Remove cinnamon stick. Pour into warm sterilized jars and seal.

Montserrat Marmalade

PINEAPPLE JAM

MAKES 1¹/₂ CUPS (12 OZ/350 G)

8 oz (250 g) fresh pineapple chunks
¹/₂ cup (4 oz/125 g) sugar
2 teaspoons lime juice
¹/₄ teaspoon freshly grated nutmeg

Chop pineapple in blender or food processor until nearly pureed. Transfer to saucepan with sugar and lime juice and bring to boil, then reduce heat to medium low and cook, stirring frequently, until thickened to jam consistency. Stir in nutmeg. Pour into warm sterilized jar and seal.

VANILLA SYRUP

MAKES ABOUT 1¹/₄ CUPS (10 FL OZ/300 ML)

Serve with buñuelos de viento (see page 209), or ice cream, or snowcones (see page 248).

³/₄ cup (6 oz/185 g) sugar
1¹/₂ cups (12 fl oz/375 ml) water
¹/₂ teaspoon lemon juice
2 teaspoons vanilla extract

Combine sugar, water, and lemon juice in saucepan and bring to boil. Boil 4 minutes, then reduce heat and simmer 20 minutes. Add vanilla and let cool.

CHOCOLATE SYRUP

MAKES ABOUT 1 CUP (8 FL OZ/250 ML)

A variation of vanilla syrup. You can use it in snowcones (see page 248) or serve with ice cream.

3/4 cup (6 oz/185 g) sugar
1 cup (8 fl oz/250 ml) water
1/4 teaspoon salt
8 oz (250 g) dark unsweetened chocolate, melted

Combine sugar, water, and salt in saucepan and boil 4 minutes. Add chocolate and simmer, stirring constantly in a zigzag motion, until mixture forms a syrup, about 5 to 6 minutes. Store in a sterilized jar.

PINEAPPLE SYRUP

MAKES ABOUT 1³/4 CUPS (14 FL OZ/400 ML)

Serve with buñuelos de viento (see page 209) or with desserts such as ice cream or snowcones (see page 248).

2 cups (16 fl oz/500 ml) fresh or canned pineapple juice
1¹/4 cups (10 oz/300 g) sugar
1/4 teaspoon lemon juice

Combine all ingredients in saucepan and bring to boil. Simmer until mixture is syrupy, about 10 to 15 minutes. Pour into warm sterilized bottle.

RUM SAUCE

MAKES ABOUT 2 CUPS (16 FL OZ/500 ML)

Serve with desserts such as Christmas cake (see page 205) and carrot pudding (see page 244) or ice cream.

3/4 cup (6 oz/180 g) butter

2 1/4 cups (18 oz/525 g) dark brown sugar

1 cup (8 fl oz/250 ml) water

1/2 cup (4 fl oz/125 ml) rum

3 tablespoons lime juice

Heat butter and sugar in medium saucepan over low heat until butter is melted. Add water and stir until sugar is dissolved. Add rum and lime juice and cook until sauce is thick and smooth, about 5 minutes. Serve warm.

CASSAREEP

MAKES ABOUT 1 CUP (8 FL OZ/250 G)

Cassareep is of Amerindian origin. It is a cassava syrup used for seasoning and preserving food, particularly Guyana's pepperpot (see page 42). It can be added to soups and stews to give extra flavor. See glossary for more information. To give an even richer color, gravy browning sauce can be added. The cassava flesh from this recipe can be used in cassava pudding (see page 232).

4 lb (2 kg) sweet cassava, peeled

1 cup (8 fl oz/250 ml) cold water

1 tablespoon packed dark brown sugar

3/4 teaspoon cinnamon

1/2 teaspoon ground cloves

Finely grate or chop cassava. Place in blender or food processor with water; grind finely. Let stand 5 minutes.

Squeeze cassava through dampened cheesecloth (muslin), twisting cloth to extract as much liquid as possible. Pour liquid into saucepan; discard flesh. Add remaining ingredients and bring to boil. Reduce heat and simmer, stirring occasionally, until thick and syrupy. Pour into sterilized bottle; store in refrigerator.

Cassareep

MASALA

MAKES ABOUT 6 TABLESPOONS

This is my grandma's masala; I call it her "magic potion" because it tastes sensational. It can be added to curries, dhal puri filling, chutneys, and a myriad of other recipes.

2 tablespoons black cumin seeds

2 tablespoons mustard seeds

2 tablespoons fenugreek seeds

2 whole cloves

1/2 teaspoon mixed spice, pumpkin pie spice, or cinnamon

Toast cumin, mustard, and fenugreek seeds separately by placing a thin layer of each spice in a small dry frying pan over medium high heat, stirring so that it is even, until they darken, about 3 to 4 minutes.

Grind seeds to a powder in grinder or with mortar and pestle, grinding cloves with the seeds. Stir in spice or cinnamon. Store in airtight container; keeps indefinitely.

ADOBO

MAKES 2 TABLESPOONS

Adobo means "seasoning" in the Spanish-speaking Caribbean. It is used on nearly all meats before cooking. This quantity of adobo suits about 4 lb (2 kg) chicken or other white meat. For pork and red meat, increase the garlic to 6 cloves and reduce the olive oil to 1 1/2 teaspoons.

4 cloves garlic, crushed

1 1/2 teaspoon dried oregano

3 1/2 teaspoons salt

1/4 teaspoon paprika

2 1/2 teaspoons olive oil

1 teaspoon white vinegar or lime juice

1/2 teaspoon freshly ground black pepper

1 small hot pepper, seeded and finely chopped, optional

Combine all ingredients to form a paste. Store in a clean jar in refrigerator.

ANNATTO OIL

MAKES 1 CUP (8 FL OZ/250 ML)

This oil is used mostly in Spanish- and French-speaking Caribbean countries. (It is known as roucou in French and achiote in Spanish.) It is also used in some dishes in Trinidad and Curaçao. The oil adds an orange-red hue to a dish, and some claim that it adds a very subtle taste as well. Paprika, alone or mixed with a bit of olive oil or saffron powder, makes a good substitute if annatto seeds are not available. Be careful not to burn the seeds or the oil will be bitter.

1 cup (8 fl oz/250 ml)
vegetable oil or lard

$^1/_2$ cup (2 oz/60 g) annatto seeds

Heat oil in small saucepan over medium heat. Add annatto seeds, reduce heat to low and cook, stirring occasionally, until oil is tinted a rich red, about 4 to 5 minutes. Let cool completely, then strain into clean container. Store in refrigerator.

BASIC CHICKEN STOCK

MAKES ABOUT 3 CUPS (24 FL OZ/750 ML)

This is a basic stock to which many seasonings can be added. The best stocks are made with the giblets, necks, skin, bones, feet, etc, but you can use any part of the chicken. If the stock is for use in dishes from the Spanish-speaking Caribbean, then follow the recipe below but add 1 sprig of cilantro (coriander leaves).

4 cups (32 fl oz/1 l) water
1 lb (500 g) chicken parts
1 stalk celery
1 bay leaf, optional
1 small onion
a few peppercorns
salt to taste

Place all ingredients in a large saucepan and bring to a boil. Reduce heat to moderate and simmer 5 minutes. Reduce heat to low and simmer 30 minutes, skiming off any scum that develops. Strain. Add salt to taste. Store in airtight containers in refrigerator or freezer.

FRESH SEASONING

MAKES ABOUT 1 CUP (4 OZ/125 G)

This can be used for seasoning chicken pieces, or even pork or fish, before shallow frying, barbecuing, or roasting in oven. You can vary this recipe by adding a sprig of marjoram and/or 1/4 teaspoon ground allspice.

3 small onions, minced

4 green onions, minced

3 cloves garlic, minced

2 sprigs parsley, finely chopped

3 sprigs thyme, finely chopped

8 celery leaves, minced

1 hot pepper, seeded and minced, optional

Combine all ingredients and store in a clean jar in the refrigerator for up to 4 days.

FISH SEASONING

MAKES ABOUT 1/4 CUP (2 OZ/60 ML)

This is a basic seasoning for frying fish. You can multiply the quantities if you wish, although you may not want to add salt in addition to the garlic and onion salt.

3/4 teaspoon garlic salt (see page 288)

1/2 teaspoon dried thyme

1 teaspoon dried parsley

1/2 teaspoon ground ginger

3/4 teaspoon onion salt

salt

1/2 teaspoon freshly ground black pepper

Combine all ingredients and store in airtight jar; keeps indefinitely.

Fresh Seasoning

CELERY SALT

MAKES 3 TO 4 TABLESPOONS

Celery salt is used a lot in Caribbean cookery for seasoning meat and fish. It is a good substitute for celery leaves, but make sure to reduce the amount of salt you use in the recipe.

3 stalks celery, cut into strips of equal size

fine salt

Preheat oven to 250°F (130°C/Gas ½). Place celery strips on a baking sheet in middle of oven and bake until completely dried out and almost crisp, about 1½ to 2 hours depending on the size and water content of the celery, turn the celery strips occasionally so that they dry out evenly. Cut strips into smaller pieces and grind to powder in spice grinder. Sift salt to taste into celery powder and blend. Store in airtight container; keeps indefinitely.

GARLIC SALT

MAKES ABOUT 3 TABLESPOONS

1 head garlic, peeled and cut into thin slices

salt to taste

Preheat oven to 225°F (110°C/Gas ¼).

Wash, then dry cloves of garlic. Place on baking sheet in middle of oven until they have completely dried, about 1½ hours, turning after 45 minutes. (Do not allow the garlic to turn brown or it will taste bitter.) In a grinder blend garlic with salt to taste until garlic resembles small granules. Store in an airtight container; keeps indefinitely.

SAUCES, SEASONINGS, AND CONDIMENTS

COCONUT MILK

MAKES ABOUT 2 CUPS (16 FL OZ/500 ML)

This recipe can be used for any dish requiring thin coconut milk. Canned coconut milk is not usually used in Caribbean cooking. You can, however, use creamed coconut for a good, quick-to-make alternative. This ingredient is purchased in blocks that will keep in the refrigerator for months. Dissolve 2 oz (60 g) creamed coconut in 1 cup (8 fl oz/250 ml) hot water for each cup of coconut milk required. For a richer milk, use a larger portion of creamed coconut.

You can substitute desiccated coconut for fresh coconut in the recipe below. To make 1½ cups (12 fl oz/375 ml) coconut milk, use 8 oz/250 g desiccated coconut and 2½ cups (20 fl oz/625 ml) hot water, and either let stand for 20 to 30 minutes or puree in blender for 1 minute and let stand for 5 minutes before squeezing out the milk.

For further information on coconut milk, see glossary.

1 medium coconut, about 1½ lb (750 g)

2 cups (16 fl oz/500 ml) water

Using a clean skewer or pointed utensil, bore two holes in eyes of coconut. Pour coconut water out into a bowl, then crack coconut open with hammer. (If working indoors, I suggest you do this over newspaper on the floor.)

Pry the flesh out of the shell. This is easier if you first bake the coconut pieces at 250°F (130°C/Gas ½) for 15 minutes.

Grate flesh into a bowl, or cut into very small pieces and grate in food processor. You can cut off the brown skin if you prefer, but it may be left on for making coconut milk.

Pour water over grated coconut in a deep bowl, making sure to cover it all. Let stand 20 minutes. Stir.

Squeeze out the milk: either press on the coconut in a sieve, or wrap it in a cloth and twist to extract as much of the milk as possible, or take handfuls of flesh and squeeze.

You can use the same grated coconut to repeat the soaking process, but the milk will be thinner and less concentrated each time.

Fresh coconut milk will keep only overnight in a refrigerator.

COCONUT CREAM

MAKES ABOUT ¾ CUP (6 FL OZ/180 ML)

This recipe can be used for any dish requiring thick coconut milk or coconut cream. It can also be served as an accompaniment to desserts such as fresh fruit salad. Prepare coconut milk as in previous recipe. Allow the milk to stand. A thicker white cream will rise to the top. Scoop off and retain the milk for another recipe.

289

GLOSSARY

Ackee (*blighia sapida*). Also known as akee, vegetable brain. Ackee was brought to the Caribbean from West Africa during the slave trade. It is said that Captain Bligh took it over on his ship, *The HMS Bounty* in 1778. The tree is a beautiful evergreen of medium size with small glossy leaves and small green/white flowers. The fruit, the ackee, adorns the tree, making it quite beautiful when in season. The ackee has a thick red-orange skin that usually contains three large shiny black seeds. Each seed is surrounded from its base by yellow colored flesh, called the aril. This is the part you eat. When the ackee is ripe it splits opens to reveal the seeds and flesh. *Caution:* the ackee is only safe to eat when it ripens and splits open. When still closed, it contains a large quantity of the poisonous substance, hypoglycine. When it is ripe, the amount of this substance is reduced. Ackees are always boiled before any preparation. The ackee is mostly seen in Jamaica and isn't as popular in other Caribbean countries. It's usually eaten with salted fish (see ackee and salt cod, page 124). It can be bought canned and is widely available.

Annatto (*bixa orellana*). Also known as achiote, roucou, woucou. Annatto are the red seeds found inside the seed pods of this native shrub. Growing up to 15 feet (4.5 m) long, they produce rust-colored, hairy seed pods containing many seeds. The seeds were used by the Caribs before Columbus' arrival. They are rich in vitamin A and are used to color food; for example, in the sofrito of the Spanish-speaking islands and the court bouillon of the French-speaking islands. The seeds are gently heated in oil to produce annatto seed oil, a very rich-colored oil which is added to food for coloring (see page 285). Liquid annatto is sometimes available. Paprika (or saffron) mixed with a little oil makes a good substitute.

Arrowroot (*maranta arundinacea*). Also known as St Vincent arrowroot. This white starch is derived from the rhizome of the herbaceous *maranta arundinacea* plant in the form of very fine grains. It is native to South America. Today, the island of St Vincent supplies most of the Caribbean countries with arrowroot. It can be used for many purposes in Caribbean cooking, including cakes and cookies (see page 212), and as a thickening agent for soups and stews. Because it is very easily digested, it is often used for those with special diets such as children and invalids. It is widely available.

Avocado (*persea americana*). Also known as alligator pear, aguacate in the Spanish-speaking islands, avocat in the French-speaking islands. This delectable fruit comes from an evergreen tree which grows up to 30 to 40 feet (9 to 12 m) high, producing small, light green leaves. They are native to Central America, although at the time of Spanish colonization they were also cultivated on the South American continent. The fruit varies in size, and can weigh up to 3 to 4 lbs (1.5 to 2 kg). They are usually pear-shaped and are covered in a thick green or dark purple skin. When ripe, the flesh is soft and cream colored for the most part with a pale green outer color. They are rich in protein, minerals, and vitamins, particularly A, E, and the B-complex vitamins. They can be eaten when still firm, and are best used in salads at this stage of maturity (see page 161). They are used in soups (see page 54), as accompaniments to meals, or just eaten on their own. Ripen at room temperature then store in the refrigerator.

Bajan. Meaning "of or from Barbados", the words Barbadian and Bajan can be used interchangeably.

Bois d'inde. Also known as baies d'inde. It is unclear whether bois d'inde is actually bay rum berries (*pimenta acris*) or if it is simply a spice very closely related to allspice. When I first came across it, I was convinced from its aroma that it was allspice. The spice is characteristic of Caribbean food. Allspice berries or bay rum berries make good substitutes. Allspice berries, dried or ground, are readily available.

Bora (*vigna sesquipedalis*). Also known as bodi beans, yard long beans, snake beans, Chinese beans. Native to tropical Asia these beans can grow up to 20 inches (50 cm) long. They look and taste similar to runner beans, which make a good substitute. When buying bora look for a good green color and make sure they are crisp. Rich in potassium, vitamins A and C, and fiber. They are usually sautéed (see page 172) or just boiled in salted water, and are often added to fried rice, chow mein, soups, and stews. Store in the refrigerator for up to 2 weeks.

Breadfruit (*artocarpus altilis*). Also known as breadnut, fruit à pain in French-speaking islands, pana de pepita in Spanish-speaking islands. Introduced to the Caribbean in 1793 by Captain Bligh, breadfruit was brought from Tahiti to feed the slaves. The tree grows to a height of 60 feet (18 m), with dark, deeply lobed leaves of around 2 feet (60 cm), and bears fruit of varying size. The fruit can weigh up to 10 lb (5 kg) and is round with a bumpy skin. When the breadfruit is ripe, the skin is yellow-green. The flesh is pale yellow-brown, starchy, and soft, and rich in carbohydrates. Breadfruit is quite bland so it is usually roasted in an oven or over coals, fried, or stuffed with meat and baked (see pages 180 and 181). Breadfruit usually accompanies a main meal along with, or in place of, other starch vegetables. Although first introduced to Jamaica and St Vincent, it is fairly widespread throughout the region. The seeds of the breadfruit are edible, resembling chesnuts; they taste good when boiled then salted. Choose firm fruit, with no soft spots and with a yellowish green skin. The best variety for roasting is yellow heart which has a moist texture. Sometimes available fresh in West Indian or Asian markets, sometimes canned.

Callaloo. Also known calaloo, calalou, callalou. Callaloo usually refers to the well-known West Indian soup (see page 40) which uses greens of the same name as one of its main ingredients. The name callaloo also refers to two different types of greens. The first is a plant with spear-shaped leaves, the roots of which form the many and varied ground provisions used in West Indian cuisine, such as dasheen and eddo (also known as taro). The young leaves of these root vegetables are used. The other type of greens it refers to are known as either Chinese pak choi (*brassica campestris*) or Indian kale (*xanthosoma sagittisolium*) or bhaji (as it is known in Guyana, Trinidad, and Jamaica). Among other leaves used

for callaloo are alligator weed and parsley. Callaloo can be found in West Indian or Chinese markets. Good substitutes are English spinach and silverbeet (Swiss chard). Store in a sealed, plastic bag in the refrigerator for up to 5 days.

Carailla (*momordica charantia*). Also known as caraillee, carailli, bitter cucumber, bitter melon, bitter gourd, foo gwa. This pale green pod-shaped vegetable is very bitter even when ripe. It grows up to 6 inches (16 cm) long and is pointed at one end. The skin is rough with many crevices. When cut open it contains seeds and a yellow flesh which is scooped out and discarded. To reduce the bitterness, salt is sprinkled onto the washed and sliced carailla and then it is squeezed to extract the bitter juices. It is usually sautéed, or used in stir frys or curries (see page 170). Carailla is high in vitamin C. Ripen at room temperature then refrigerate. There is no substitute.

Cassava (bitter cassava—*manihot esculenta*; sweet casssava—*manihot dulcis*). Also known as manioc, tapioca, yuca, Brazilian arrowroot. Cassava originated in tropical Brazil and was used by the Arawaks long before the Spanish arrived. The cassava shrub grows to about 6½ to 10 feet (2 to 3 m) in height. The tuberous roots form the very starchy vegetable we know as cassava—large, elongated, oval shapes with dark brown skin. Cassava was used by the Arawaks to produce the preservative, cassareep. The Arawaks and Caribs used the grated cassava, squeezed of its poisonous juice, to make cassava bread which we still enjoy today. Both the bitter and sweet varieties of cassava are widely used throughout the Caribbean. The bitter cassava contains a poisonous substance, prussic acid, which is expelled when cooked. The Amerindians use the juice to produce powerful drinks! See page 185. Cassava is high in vitamin C and contains small amounts of B1. Store the roots in a cool, dark place. Available fresh or packaged and frozen. Good substitutes for cassava in soups, stews or as an accompaniment are potato, yam, or eddo. Tapioca comes from cassava and is usually found in grains. It is used in Caribbean cookery for many dishes. It can be bought in packets in Asian or West Indian supermarkets.

Cassava flour. Also known as farine de manioc or just farine in the French-speaking islands. The flour is made from the root of the cassava plant which is squeezed of its poisonous juice and ground. It is used to make dishes such as feroce d'avocat (see page 33) or desserts, including pone (see page 228).

Cassareep. A traditional preservative first made by the indigenous population of Guyana. It is made from squeezing the poisonous juice from the grated cassava root and boiling the juice to neutralize the poison. It is boiled with cloves, cinnamon, and little dark brown sugar until it is thick (see page 282). It is now used not only as a preservative but to add a very distinctive flavor to stews and soups. It is used in Guyana's pepperpot (see page 42) and can be found in other Caribbean countries. There is no substitute for its unique taste.

Choka. The term choka comes from East Indian cooking. It refers to the method of roasting vegetables until they are soft and mashing them with spices. Garlic is usually placed on top with very hot vegetable oil poured over to bring out the flavor before mixing it into the vegetables. See pages 162 and 164.

Christophene (*sechium edule*). Also known as chayote squash, cho-cho, choko. This pale green, pear-shaped fruit with a single seed originates in Mexico and is used throughout the Caribbean. It is a member of the squash family and, when cooked, is very similar in texture, appearance, and taste to squash. It contains small quantities of vitamin C and can be cooked (the French-speaking islands produce an excellent gratin, see page 34) or eaten raw in salads. Purchased fresh, christophenes will keep in the refrigerator for up to 2 weeks.

Coconut (*cocos nucifera*). The coconut tree is a tall palm (up to 98 feet/30 m) that has no branches; instead the leaves grow out of the top of the trunk. As the trees grow well in sandy soil, they line many beaches in the West Indies. The coconut itself is extremely versatile. When young and green it contains a large quantity of coconut water and the kernel is actually a deliciously edible jelly. When young, the coconut has a thick outer husk which is so tough that a machete is needed to get inside. When maturing (drying out), the coconut develops a hard, brown, hairy shell which is also relatively tough.

It is in this dried or mature state that many of us are used to seeing coconuts. Coconut water is the clear liquid found in abundance inside green coconuts, and in lesser quantity in mature ones. This is sometimes referred to as the "milk" but is different from the coconut milk or cream made for use in cooking (see page 289). As well as using coconut in a huge array of dishes, the dried coconut also produces coconut oil, often used in West Indian cooking and in the making of soap. Mature coconuts are a good source of phosphorous and iron and will keep for weeks. Canned and packaged coconut is available in various forms and is easily obtainable in supermarkets or in West Indian or Asian stores.

Conch (*strombus gigas*). Also known as conk, lambi in the French-speaking islands. This large mollusc from the gastropod class is eaten throughout the Caribbean in soups, chowders, stews, salads, and fritters (see pages 137 and 169). The pinkish meat found inside the pink (fading to grey) shell is very tough and has to be pounded and marinated before cooking. The shell is fashioned into ornate objects as well as serving as a horn. Conch tastes rather sweet. Abalone or the meat of any large mollusc can be used as satisfactory (but not exact) substitutes.

Custard apple (*annona reticula*). See Soursop.

Cumin (*cuminum cyminum*). Also known by the Indian word jeera. This distinctive spice is used in many East Indian recipes and in the recipes of the Spanish-speaking islands. Its strong taste means it should be used with discretion. Cumin seeds and powdered cumin are readily available. Black cumin (*nigella sativa*) has a similar aroma and taste but is not used as much. Both are used to make curry powder and black cumin features in masala.

Dasheen (*colocasia esculenta* var. *esculenta*). Also known as eddo, taro, coco. There is much confusion and disagreement about the botanical and popular names of dasheen and other tubers. One of the many root vegetables found in the West Indies, dasheen is a herbaceous perennial, native to West Africa, that can grow to 5 feet (1.5 m) high. The young leaves of the plant are known as callaloo and are used in making callaloo soup (see Callaloo). The roots can grow up to 8 or 9 lbs (4 to 5 kg) and are covered in a dark brown skin. This starchy vegetable tastes similar to potatoes, is a good source of dietary fiber, and contains fair amounts of potassium. Dasheen can be boiled, roasted, fried, or mashed then served as an accompaniment to a meal or they can be added to soups or stews (see page 185). They should be cooked properly or they can cause indigestion. When buying dasheen make sure the root, when cut, has no blemishes. Store in a cool dark place, but do not refrigerate. Yam, tannia, and potato make good substitutes.

Dried shrimp. These shrimp (prawns) have been dried or sun-dried then packaged. They have a strong shrimp flavor so fewer are needed than fresh shrimp. Before using, you can steep them in hot water for 10 minutes to soften, but it is not necessary. Add to fried rice, chow mein, fried bhaji (see page 185), and soups. They keep for months in an airtight container or sealed bag.

Eddo (*colocasia esculenta* var. *antiquorum*). Also known as taro. Very similar to dasheen, both these vegetables are made up of a central bulb (or corm) with side tubers. Dasheen has a larger central bulb with fewer, smaller side tubers whereas eddo has a small central bulb but has more and larger side tubers. See Dasheen for other details, and page 185.

Eggplant (*solanum melongena*). Also known as aubergine, melongene, chinese eggplant, bélangere in the French-speaking islands, baigan, garden egg, berenjena in the Spanish-speaking islands. Very popular throughout the Caribbean, either fried, stuffed, or used in making fritters, salads, stews, and choka. The glossy, deep purple skin is edible, although the flesh itself has a slightly bitter taste and is often sprinkled with salt to extract some of the bitter juices then rinsed before cooking, but this is not necessary. Best bought when firm to touch; avoid any whose skin show signs of shrivelling. They have a very high water content and have small quantities of most minerals. Keeps for about 1 week in a sealed plastic bag in the refrigerator.

Garam masala. A mixture of spices that can vary in combination and quantity. The mix is usually based on cloves, cinnamon, and cardamom seeds. Nutmeg, black peppercorns, corriander seeds, or mace may be added. It is used in many dishes of East Indian origin, such as curries, dhal, and phulourie. Buy ready-made or make it yourself.

Genip (*melicocca bijuga*). Also known as ginip, akee (in Barbados). The genip tree is a medium-sized evergreen, native to the Caribbean, with dense foliage. It bears small, round green fruit about 1 inch (2.5 cm) in diameter that resemble large grapes. Unlike grapes, the skin is thin but hard and needs to be cracked open. This is best done by gently biting the fruit between your teeth. You can then peel off the skin to reveal a sweet, thick, creamy-peach flesh that surrounds a large seed. The fruit is eaten raw.

Ghee. Also known as clarified butter. Ghee is butter fat that has had all the milk solids extracted from it by boiling. The product that remains can sustain very high temperatures without burning. Ghee also has a distinctive flavor. A mix of half oil and half ghee is a good combination that is not as rich as ghee alone. Ghee has come to the Caribbean through Indian cooking and is used in many East Indian breads such as roti, and dhal puri (see pages 196 and 197). It can be bought in cans and is solid when cool but liquifies at warm temperatures. It will keep for months. My aunt in Trinidad tells me that the best ghee is Australian ghee.

Giambo. Also known as gumbo. This is a term for okra but in the Dutch-speaking islands also refers to a thick and tasty okra soup made with fish. See okra.

Ginger (*zingiber officinale*). This perennial herbaceous plant produces a tuberous rhizome from which we get ginger. Although the plant is native to South East Asia, Jamaica is well known in the region for cultivating ginger in large quantities for export and domestic consumption. The spice can be used in many savory and sweet dishes as well as in ginger beer (see page 252) and candies.

Golden apple. Also known as pomme cythère. This pear-shaped citrus fruit has a thick yellow-green skin. When the inedible skin is peeled, it reveals a fragrant orange-colored flesh with a large stone that can be eaten raw or used to make preserves, jams, and drinks. A substitute is difficult to suggest but an orange, shaddock (see Grapefruit), or tangerine would suffice.

Grapefruit (*citrus paradisi*). Also known as pomelo. This fruit is a relatively new addition to the Caribbean. It was actually created in the 18th century in either Barbados or Jamaica when Captain Shaddock carried a pink-fleshed citrus fruit (known as a shaddock) from the Pacific Islands to the Caribbean. The shaddock (*citrus grandis*)—also known as pummelo or pommelo—is a large, round fruit with a yellow-pink juicy flesh and a thick light green-yellow rind. It is fragrant but rather bitter. Either by hybridization or natural selection the grapefruit evolved from the shaddock and the sweet orange. In the West Indies, ripe grapefruits are about 6 inches (15 cm) in diameter, have a green-yellow rind and a sweet flesh with a slightly bitter taste. However, because they are picked unripe for export they never actually ripen fully in more temperate countries resulting in a bitter fruit.

Guava (*psidium guajava*). Also known as yellow guava. A native fruit to tropical America and the Caribbean, the guava tree can grow to 20 to 30 feet (6 to 9 m) and produces small, white flowers. The guavas are small and roundish and about 2 inches (5 cm) in diameter with a green-yellow skin. The skin turns yellow when ripe. The guava flesh can be white, pink, or sometimes a very deep pink. Guavas are sweet and aromatic and best picked ripe from the tree. When cut open, many seeds can be seen embedded in the flesh. They can be removed by passing the flesh through a sieve. Guavas can be eaten stewed (see page 218) or raw and are used to make guava jelly (see page 278), guava cheese (see page 228), liqueurs, and fruit punches. They are extremely rich in vitamin C and a good source of vitamin A. Ripen at room temperature away from direct sunlight. Best eaten immediately although they can be refrigerated for 2 days. Available fresh and canned, particularly in West Indian supermarkets. Canned guava paste and guava jelly are also available.

Guinea corn (*sorghum vulgare*). A type of sorghum grown in Asia, Africa, and the USA. It is a tropical cereal that is used in the making of the Bajan Christmas dish jug-jug (see page 142). Good substitutes are first, ground rolled oats, and second, millet.

Hot peppers. Also known as chili peppers, pimiento in the Spanish-speaking islands, piment in the French-speaking islands. Hot peppers in their numerous varieties were grown by the indigenous population of present day Mexico some 9000 years ago. This large spice group falls into two botanical categories: *capsicum annum* and *capsicum frutescens* belonging to the *Solanaceae* family. Both hot and mild peppers fall into both categories. The Arawaks and Caribs were using hot peppers to season meat by the time Colombus arrived (see the hot pepper sauce recipe on page 274). The Spanish took peppers back to Spain with them and eventually the hot pepper spread around the world. Today the hottest peppers are said to be found in either Uganda or Japan. Red, yellow, orange, or green, hot, mild, or sweet, there are many different peppers used in the Caribbean, from Guyana's wiri wiri peppers to Jamaica's Scotch bonnet. In Guyana there is a super hot pepper that is the size of a little blueberry but it is so powerful you would only need one for the whole dish! Hot peppers are not always used, sometimes a milder one will add just enough heat and flavor. The different colored peppers are at different stages of ripeness. Scotch bonnets are available in good supermarkets and at West Indian markets. Any hot pepper will substitute.

Jackfruit (*artocarpus heterophyllus*). Also known as jak fruit. Native to Malaysia and Sri Lanka, the jackfruit is very closely related to the breadfruit, and the two are often confused. Unlike breadfruit, jackfruit grows on short stalks closely attached to the bark. The fruit itself is green and can grow to a massive size, up to 40 lb (20 kg). When ripe, it will give off a rather pungent odor. The flesh is white and gelatinous with many seeds. These chestnut-like seeds are edible if boiled or roasted. Jackfruit is not as widely used in the Caribbean as breadfruit. It is usually curried. A good source of vitamin A and B-complex. Store at room temperature away from direct sunlight; when ripe, it will keep in the refrigerator for a couple of days.

Mango (*mangifera indica*). From a beautiful evergreen, native to South East Asia, the mango has been described as the fruit of paradise. (And I have to say, I do agree!) Mangoes reached the Caribbean via Brazil where they had been introduced in the late 17th century. The tree can grow up 50 to 60 feet (15 to 18 m) and the dense leaves form a crown that provides good shade (much needed in the hot Caribbean climate). The leaves themselves are thick and range from reddish to dark, dull green. The mango fruit hangs off stalks and varies in color and shape. Usually yellow, orange, pink, or a mixture of shades, they will sometimes have small black or brown spots. The juicy yellow-orange flesh surrounds a large stone with many fibers, and tastes both sweet and spicy. When eating a mango allow yourself plenty of time to enjoy the experience and to clean up afterwards! They are fairly messy but well worth it. Mangoes can also be used green (see page 37) as a vegetable in curries (particularly with fish) or in salads, chutneys, and pickles. Ripe mangoes are used in an endless variety of drinks and desserts. They are rich in vitamin A and a fair source of vitamins C and B1 and minerals. They are best bought fresh, but are also available canned.

Mauby (*colubrina elliptica* or *colubrina arborescens*). Also known as mawby or mabí in the Spanish-speaking islands. Mauby is the bark of some small trees native to the Caribbean. It is boiled with spices and orange or lime peel and sweetened with sugar. The resulting drink has a distinctive bitter-sweet taste and is very refreshing when served with ice (see page 256). It can be bought as a bottled cordial which is a very good substitute; just dilute and add sugar. It is widely available in West Indian supermarkets.

Mustard seed oil. This is made from the oil of yellow mustard seeds and is used in small quantities to cover chutneys and pickles as a means of preserving them while adding extra flavor. It is available bottled from Indian supermarkets. If unavailable, you could use a little olive oil, but this is not essential when making a chutney or pickle.

Okra (*hibiscus esculentus*). Also known as ochroes, gumbo in the Dutch-speaking islands, gombo in the French-speaking islands, lady's fingers, bamie, bindi, quingombós in the Spanish-speaking islands. Native to Africa and brought to the Caribbean during the slave trade in the 17th century, the plant produces pretty, yellow flowers from which the okras develop. Okras are green, pod-like in shape and contain many edible, glutinous seeds. There are two varieties of okra: those about 4 to 5 inches (10 to 13 cm) long and a smaller variety only 2 to 3 inches (5 to 8 cm)

long, both with a diameter of around 1/2 to 3/4 inch (1 to 2 cm). Okras are very popular in the Caribbean for their distinctive taste and texture. They are very slimy when cut open and are often added to soups and stews for thickening, particulary the islands' callaloo soup (see page 40) and pepperpot dishes (see page 42). They are eaten in a variety of ways—sautéed, in cou-cou (see page 152), or just boiled. The contain small quantaties of vitamin B and C and minerals and are low in calories (kilojoules). When buying okras look for unblemished ones; the smaller are better because they are tastier and less fibrous. Okras can be bought fresh in many supermarkets or in West Indian markets and are also available canned, although fresh is better.

Papaya (*carica papaya*). Also known as paw paw, pawpaw, fruta bomba in Spanish-speaking countries. The fast-growing, unusually-branched papaya tree has deeply-lobed leaves and a soft hollow stem that can hold papayas up to 10 lbs (5 kg) in weight. Meat can be wrapped in papaya leaves (which contain the enzyme, papain) and boiled to tenderize it. The papaya fruit is yellow-orange when ripe, green when unripe. It can be eaten fresh with a squeeze of lime juice or used in drinks, jams, ice creams, and fruit salads. Green papaya is said to to be good for high blood pressure and is often cooked as a vegetable in curries or salads or used for chutneys or pickles. The fruit is a good source of vitamin C and dietary fiber and contains some iron. Choose fruit that is firm to touch and unbruised, with a slight aroma. Ripen at room temperature then refrigerate.

Passionfruit (*passiflora edulis*). Passionfruit comes from a woody vine that can grow up to 50 feet (15 m) long and is native to tropical America. The flowers, known as passion flowers, are white tinged with purple. The Spanish so named the fruit because of the unique shape and arrangement of the flowers' parts—they are said to look like Christ's crucifixion. The purple corona resembles the crown of thorns, the stamens represent Christ's wounds and the three styles take the image of Christ on the cross. Passionfruit have a thick wrinkled skin that is dark brown to dark purple. They are about the size of a golf ball. Inside, there is an aromatic, bright yellow pulp with many small black seeds that can be extracted by passing the pulp through a sieve. The fruit is grown throughout the region and is very popular in Dominica. An excellent source of vitamin C, they contain some vitamin A. They are often used in drinks, desserts, and fruit salads rather than being eaten on their own. Passionfruit are available fresh from good supermarkets or can be substituted with canned pulp. Best stored in a plastic bag in the refrigerator.

Pigeon peas (*cajanus cajan*). Also known as gungo peas, congo peas, gunga peas, gandules in the Spanish-speaking islands. The peas come from a perennial bush that grows up to 9 feet (3 m) and produces dark green-brown pods about 2 inches (5 cm) long. Inside the pods, three or four green or off-green peas can be found. They are said to be native to Africa, where they grow wild, or India, but it is not known for certain. Today they are cultivated throughout the tropics. They are usually eaten fresh or dried and are a good source of dietary fiber, iron, and potassium. The fresh peas only take about 25 minutes to cook when boiled, the dried take longer, about 1 hour, and are best soaked before using. Pigeon peas are predominantly used in making the West Indian rice and peas (see page 145), Barbados' jug-jug (see page 142) and in soup from the Dutch Windward Islands. Pigeon peas are widely available and are also sold canned. There is no real substitute.

Plantain (*musa sapientum*). Also known as green banana or, when ripe, as yellow plantain. Plantains are very closely related to bananas. There are two main groups of bananas: the ones you can eat straight off the tree, which originated in the Malay archipelago, and the ones that have to be cooked before they are consumed, which originated in India. Neither are native to the Caribbean, yet bananas historically and today are an important part of the West Indian economies, and in some cases it is the main export. Bananas were brought from the Canary Islands and introduced to Hispanola in 1512. Plantains are usually longer and more angular than bananas, with a sweeter taste. They are green, turning yellow when ripe. Plantains are a staple food and are eaten throughout the region as well as in Africa, India, and tropical America. Green plantains can be boiled or mashed as in the dish foo foo (see page 158) or made into chips (see page 29), added to soups and stews or

served as an accompaniment to a main meal. The yellow plantain can used in the same way, or just peeled, sliced, and fried, or cooked and pounded to make mofongo (see page 158). They are a good source of protein, potassium, and vitamin B1 with some iron and calcium. Plantain chips can be bought in packets from many West Indian supermarkets. Store plantains at room temperature away from direct sunlight.

Pineapple (*ananas comosus*). Also known as pine, piña in the Spanish-speaking islands, ananas in French-speaking islands. Native to the Caribbean and South America, the pineapple is a perennial, herbaceous plant. Its flowers grow in the center of its leaves. Once the plant flowers, the pineapple is ready for picking about 8 months later. They are in abundance on most of the islands as they grow well, even in dry conditions. Antigua has a very sweet and delicious variety known as "black" pineapple which is well worth trying. When selecting a pineapple, choose those with deep green leaves, slightly yellow areas on the skin, and no soft spots. They are readily available fresh but canned fruit or juice make good substitutes. Keep in a cool place or refrigerate. They are a good source of vitamin C and dietary fiber with some vitamins A and B1.

Roti. This is a general term used to describe any of the various breads brought to the Caribbean by the East Indian community. There are several different types of roti some of which I have included in this book such as sada roti (see page 192) and dhal puri (see page 197); others include dosti roti and cassava roti. You can often buy roti filled with choka or a vegetable curry at roadside vendors in Trinidad and Guyana. Rotis are cooked on a special griddle known as a tawa but a flat or large frying pan will do.

Paratha roti. Often just referred to as roti (see page 196), paratha roti is perhaps the most commonly eaten. It is known as "buss-up-shut" in Trinidad because of the way it bursts up while cooking. Traditionally this roti is clapped between the hands when cooking to break up the roti into small pieces. A version of this roti is popular in Trinidad, Guyana, and St Lucia, where historically there have been large settlements of East Indians. However, it has become so well liked that it can be found all over the region from the fast food roti joints of Barbados to the Bahamas.

Sada roti. Not as popular as paratha roti but quicker to make and containing less oil and/or ghee. It is often eaten for breakfast or to accompany tomato choka or eggplant choka (see pages 162 and 164).

Aloo roti. Made exactly the same way as sada roti except a seasoned potato filling is placed on the dough. It is rolled up and rolled out again before cooking.

Dhal puri. Made in a similar way to paratha roti except this roti has a seasoned, split pea filling and takes much longer to prepare. It is filled, then rolled out, and cooked in the same way, but not "clapped". It is the tastiest of the rotis and is usually served with a curry on a special occasion (see page 197).

Salt cod. Also known as salt fish, bacalao in the Spanish-speaking islands, morue in the French-speaking islands. Salt fish, as it is commonly called, usually refers to salted cod fish, but it can sometimes be salted haddock or mackerel. Salt fish was originally imported to feed the slaves. Salting was used to preserve the fish in the days when refrigeration was not an option. The Portuguese also used salted fish to feed their crews on the long voyages made in centuries gone by. Today, salt fish dishes not unlike those prepared in the Caribbean can be found in Portugal. Over time salt fish has become central to countless Caribbean recipes throughout the region with some excellent dishes evolving.

The best way to prepare salt fish is to soak it overnight or for several hours in cold water. Change the water and boil the fish for about 10 minutes. If you do not have the time to soak the fish overnight you can boil it in several changes of water to extract some of the excess salt, although I think this method reduces the flavor of the fish. The salt fish has a very distinctive flavor and is perhaps an acquired taste, but when you acquire it you will really enjoy it! It is very rich is protein. Until recently it had been very cheap to obtain in the West Indies, however due to shortages it has become expensive. When buying salt fish, look for white rather than yellowish flesh. The whiter, the fresher. Cooking time will be longer if the fish is old and tough. Salt fish can be bought packaged, dried or sometimes fresh, in good delicatessens or West Indian markets.

Salted meat. As was the case with salt cod, salting or pickling meat, particularly beef, pork, and pigs tail, was a form of preservation in a hot climate that quickly ruined fresh meat. Nowadays, salted meats are still used to obtain what has become a distinctively Caribbean flavor. People have been using them for so long that they have become very much part of everyday food. Because people are becoming more conscious of the high salt content, some are reducing the amount of salted meat they use but it is still an integral ingredient in many dishes. If you have difficulty in obtaining salted meat, you can use corned beef, stewing beef, smoked ham hocks, smoked ham, or bacon as substitutes (without soaking them, of course).

Sapodilla (*manilkara zapota*). Also known as naseberry, níspero in the Spanish-speaking countries, sapotille in the French-speaking countries, marmalade plum, chiku. Native to the Caribbean and tropical America, the sapodilla comes from a slow-growing evergreen which grows up to 50 feet (15 m) high. The fruit is round or slightly oval shaped, about 3 inches (7 cm) in diameter, with a thick, dark reddish or brown skin. The sweet, fragrant pulp is transparent with a few black seeds and is eaten raw or used to make sapodilla custard, ice cream, and sorbets. From the tree trunk a sap is extracted which produces latex (called "chicle"), used for the manufacturing of chewing gum, an important industry in Belize. The timber is good and hardy and is sold commercially. Sapodillas are a source of vitamin A and dietary fiber with some calcium. Choose fruit without any marks. They are soft when ripe and are best eaten immediately but can be stored in the refrigerator for 2 days.

Soursop (*annona muricata*). Also known as guanabana. The small tree with long, oval shiny leaves is native to the Caribbean and tropical America. The fruit can grow up to 6 lb (3 kg) in weight and 8 inches (20 cm) in diameter. It is usually heart shaped with a slightly prickly, green skin. The flesh is whitish and thick with several large, black, shiny seeds. They are a good source of protein, B1, B3, and iron, and are high in carbohydrates. A popular fruit, it is fragrant and slightly tart and is delicious served as a cream or made into ice cream. It also makes a beautiful drink blended with water, sugar, and a few drops of bitters. The **sweetsop** (*annona*

GLOSSARY

squamosa), also known as sugar apple, is a very close relative and comes from a similar tree. The delightfully sweet flesh can also be eaten raw. It contains a hard black seed. The **custard apple** (*annona reticulata*), also known as bullocks heart, is also very closely related to both these fruits. The tree grows up to 20 feet (6 m) high and produces heart-shaped fruit with darkish yellow-green, granular skin. At about 4 inches (10 cm) in diameter, it is smaller than the soursop. Its flesh too is deliciously sweet with a white, creamy custard appearance and contains several black, shiny seeds. Rich in vitamin B, C, and minerals. All these fruit should be ripened at room temperature and eaten as soon as possible.

Souse. This word refers to both a dish and a technique for seasoning and pickling meat, usually pig parts such as trotters (feet) or head. Lean pork can be used (see page 26). A version of souse is found in many countries in the Caribbean.

Star apple (*chrysophyllum cainito*). Also known as caimito. This evergreen tree grows up to 50 feet (15 m) and is native to tropical America and the Caribbean. It produces small, white-purple flowers. The glossy, purple fruit has a smooth, thick skin and grows to 3 to 4 inches (7 to 10 cm) in diameter. When cut, the purple pigment forms around 10 cells (the calyx) situated in the middle of the apple in a star shape. The inner pulp is translucent. Another variety of star apple has a green skin. The gelatinous flesh is sweet and mild and is usually eaten raw or in fruit salads. It is a good source of vitamin B3 and is high in carbohydrates. Ripen at room temperature away from direct sunlight then store in the refrigerator. Available in West Indian markets.

Sweet potato (*ipomoea batatas*). Also known as yam, batatas in the Spanish-speaking islands, patates douces in the French-speaking islands. Native to South America, this root vegetable is a sweet, elongated tuber and forms part of the staple diet in the Caribbean. The sweet potato is the swollen root of the leafy vine and comes in red (or orange) and white varieties. Both are sweet and are used as a vegetable, as an accompaniment to a meal, and for making desserts such as conkies (see page 208) or nísperos (see page 209). Rich in carbohydrates and vitamin C and a good source of fiber. Choose firm sweet

potatoes with no cracks or blemishes. Store in a cool, well ventilated place. The red or orange variety is often more readily available.

Tamarind (*tamarindus indica*). Also known as tamarin. The tamarind tree grows to 50 to 60 feet (15 to 18 m) and has dark green dense foliage with feathery leaves. The wood is hard and is good for furniture making. The tree produces brown pods 2 to 5 inches (5 to 12 cm) long. When ripe, tamarind flesh is tart and spicy and is used in making preserves, candies (see page 216), and drinks (see page 248). When still unripe, it can be used for chutneys and curries. Tamarinds are used in the secret recipe of Angostura Bitters and for Worcestershire sauce. Tamarinds can sometimes be found fresh in markets but are readily available in packets from Indian or West Indian supermarkets.

Tannia (*xanthosoma sagittifolium*). Native to the Caribbean, this tuber is very similar to eddo and taro. All three are said to be among the oldest crops cultivated in the world. Tannia is more hardy and disease resistant than eddo and taro but is used in similar dishes (see page 185). Particularly good in soups, tannia is also used for making desserts in Dominica.

Taro. See Dasheen and Eddo.

Tawa. A flat, cast iron griddle used in the making of rotis. It is usually about 9 inches (22 cm) in diameter.

Yam (*dioscorea* sp.). Also known as igname (see also Sweet Potato). A native of tropical America, this vine-like plant can reach a height of 8 feet (2.5 m) producing yams up to 20 lb (10 kg). The swollen tubers form the yams and have a thick, brown hairy skin. When cut, the flesh is white and should not be discolored. Yams are rich in carbohydrates and form part of the staple diet in the entire Caribbean region (see page 185). Store in a cool, well ventilated place. Widely available.

INDEX

accras de Morue 25
ackee and salt cod 124
adobo 284
aloo curry 176
aloo pie 21
aloo roti 157
Antigua
    ducana 30
    pelau rice 81
arrowroot drops 212
arroz con gandules 140
arroz con habichuelas 149
arroz con pollo 74
Aruba: sopitu 56
aubergine *see* eggplant
avocados
    féroce d'avocat 33
    salad 161

baigan choka 164
bajan brown stew 73
bajan fried chicken 72
baked chicken 65
bakes 193
bami 77
bammies 190
bananas
    beignets de bananes 232
    bread 202
    flambées 233
    green, salad 160
    tarte à la banane 230
Barataria grapefruitade 249
Barbados
    bajan brown stew 73
    bajan fried chicken 72
    bol jul 33
    cou-cou 152
    frizzle salt cod 110
    guava jelly 218
    jug-jug 142
    macaroni pie 182
beans
    see also red kidney beans
    frijoles negros 142
    moros y cristianos 144
    salad 165
    sautéed bora 172
bébélé 101
beef
    bajan brown stew 73
    empaná 17
    Jamaican patties 16
    marinated stew 85
    pastelles 20
    picadillo 88
    ragoût de boeuf 89
    sopa de amendoim 48
beignets de bananes 232
bhaji *see* callaloo

black bean moros y cristianos 144
black kidney bean frijoles negros 142
blaff 120
boiled white rice 174
bojo 232
bol jul 33
boniatillo con mango 229
bora, sautéed 172
bread
    aloo roti 157
    bakes 193
    bammies 190
    banana 202
    coconut 202
    doubles 156
    johnny cakes 193
    sada roti 192
    salara buns 188
    West Indian bun 190
breadfruit
    cou-cou 152
    roast 180
    soup 53
    stuffed 181
brown cow 265
buns
    bammies 190
    salara 188
buñuelos de viento 209

cabbage coleslaw 160
cake
    Guyana Christmas 205
    hojaldre 189
    pineapple upside-down 204
cakes
    grater 213
    West Indian rock 189
callaloo
    bhaji 150
    aux crabes 41
    shrimp and rice 133
    soup 40
camarones a la vinagreta 133
candied papaya 217
carailla, fried 170
carrot
    juice 249
    pudding 244
cassareep 282
cassava
    bojo 232
    bread 190
    cassareep 282
    fried 172
    pone 228
channa 24
chicharrones
    de pollo 28
    pork 28

chicken
    arroz con pollo 74
    Bajan fried 72
    baked 65
    chicharrones de pollo 28
    chop suey 78
    chow mein 76
    colombo de poulet 66
    Creole 102
    curry 64
    Essequibo 69
    fricassée de poulet 65
    fricasseed 73
    jerk 68
    and peanut sopa de amondoim 48
    poulet au lait de coco 66
    sopa de pollo 50
    Trinidad pilau 80
chicken livers
    curry 104
    marinated 104
chickpeas
    channa 24
    doubles 156
    garbanzo soup 52
chili bean Jamaica red pea soup 48
chilis *see* hot peppers
chocolate syrup 281
choka
    smoked herring 134
    tomato 162
chop suey 78
chow mein, chicken 76
Christmas cake, Guyana 205
christophenes
    gratin 34
    salad 180
chutney
    mango 270
    tamarind 272
coconut
    bread 202
    chips 25
    cream 289
    drops 212
    grater cakes 213
    ice cream 222
    ices 220
    milk 289
    pie 237
    punch 262
    rice and peas 145
    tablettes de coco 220
    tarte au coco 236
    tembleque 238
coconut water and rum 265
cod, salt *see* salt cod
coffee, Jamaican 265
coffee liqueur brown cow 265
coleslaw 160

colombo de porc 96
colombo de poulet 66
conch
    chowder 53
    salad 169
    stewed 137
conkies 208
coquito 257
corn
    soup 56
    tamales 18
cornmeal funchi 150
cou-cou 152
    breadfruit 152
court bouillon de poisson 118
crab
    calalou aux crabes 41
    matété 137
    stuffed 37
crapaud, mountain chicken 105
cream of garbanzo soup 52
Creole chicken 102
Creole sauce 126, 128
Cuba
    arroz con pollo 74
    boniatillo con mango 229
    coconut ice cream 222
    daiquiri 257
    enchilada de camarones 129
    frijoles negros 142
    mojito 264
    mojo criollo 277
    moros y cristianos 144
    pasteles 210
    picadillo 88
    pork fillets 96
    sopa de pollo 50
    tamales 18
    tostones de plátano verde 29
cubanito 264
Curaçao
    cream of garbanzo soup 52
    funchi 150
    giambo soup 58
    keshi yena 36
    kesio 245
    mondongo soup 57
    muzik di zumbi 262
    sopa de amendoim 48
    sopitu 56
    stobá di cabrito 92
curry
    aloo 176
    baked sprats 116
    chicken 64
    chicken liver 104
    colombo de poulet 66
    fish with green mangoes 122
    goat 90
    hassar 124
    jackfruit 177
    lamb 93
    lobster 125
    pumpkin 173
    shrimp 125

custard
    kesio 245
    tocino del cielo 242

daiquiri 257
dhal 153
Dominica
    callaloo soup 40
    chicharrones de pollo 28
    fruit cocktail 254
    mountain chicken 105
    passionfruit punch 260
    seafood in "gros" sauce 136
    shrimp with Creole sauce 128
    stuffed crab backs 37
    tuna in brown stew 126
doubles 156
ducana 30
dumplings 154
    spinners 154
Dutch Antilles
    empaná 17
    karni kabritu stobá 94

eggplant
    baigan choka 164
    salade d'aubergines 164
empaná 17
enchilada de camarones 129
ensalada mixta 184
Essequibo chicken 69

féroce d'avocat 33
fish seasoning 286
fish "tea" 120
flan de piña 210
floating island 240
fresh seasoning 286
fricassée de langouste 134
fricassée de poulet 65
fricasseed chicken 73
fried carailla 170
fried cassava 172
fried fish 108, 110
fried okra 178
fried plantains 170
fried rice 174
    with shrimp 132
frijoles negros 142
fritters
    accras de Morue 25
    beignets de bananes 232
    phulourie 24
    stamp-and-go 32
    yam 182
frizzle salt cod 110
frog, mountain chicken 105
fruit cocktail, Dominican 254
fruit punch, Jamaican 254
fruit salad, tropical 233
fudge, rum and raisin 221
funchi 150

garbanzos see chickpeas
garlic pork 94

giambo soup 58
ginger beer 252
giraumon soup 49
goat
    curry 90
    karni kabritu stobá 94
    mannish water 61
    water 105
grapefruitade, Barataria 249
grater cakes 213
gratin de christophène 34
green banana salad 168
green salad 160
Grenada: oil down 102
griot 78
gros sauce 136
Guadeloupe
    calalou aux crabes 41
    colombo de poulet 66
    court bouillon de poisson 118
    féroce d'avocat 33
    poulet au lait de coco 66
    stuffed crab backs 37
    tarte à la banane 230
    ti-punch 260
guavas
    cheese 228
    floating island 240
    jam 278
    jelly 218
    pasteles 210
    sorbet 225
    stewed 218
Guyana
    aloo pie 21
    bakes 193
    Christmas cake 205
    dumplings 154
    Essequibo chicken 69
    garlic pork 94
    hassar curry 124
    jalebi 213
    johnny cakes 193
    mango kuchilla 269
    metagee 44
    pepperpot 42
    phulourie 24
    pine tart 241
    salara buns 188
    smoked herring choka 134
    tomato choka 162

habichuelas rojas 148
Haiti
    giraumon soup 49
    griot 78
    poulet au lait de coco 66
haricots rouges 141
hassar curry 124
herring, smoked see smoked
    herring
hojaldre 189
hot peppers
    pickled 268
    sauce 274

ice cream
    coconut 222
    mango 226
    papaya 224
    soursop 224

jackfruit curry 177
jalebi 213
jam
    guava 278
    Montserrat marmalade 278
    pineapple 280
Jamaica
    ackee and salt cod 124
    beef patties 16
    brown cow 265
    chop suey 78
    coconut drops 212
    coffee 265
    curry lobster 125
    curry shrimp 125
    fish "tea" 120
    fricasseed chicken 73
    fruit punch 254
    goat curry 90
    jerk chicken 68
    mango shake 250
    mannish water 61
    pepperpot soup 42
    pineapple upside-down cake 204
    planters punch 261
    red pea soup 48
    rice and peas in coconut 145
    roast fish 116
    run down 122
    spinners 154
    stamp-and-go 32
    stewed red peas 141
    sweet potato pudding 229
    West Indian bun 190
jelly, guava 218
jerk chicken 68
johnny cakes 193
jug-jug 142

karni kabritu stobá 94
keshi yena 36
kesio 245
kidney beans
    see also red kidney beans
    frijoles negros 142

lamb
    curry 93
    stobá di cabrito 92
lechón asado 98
lime pie 234
lobster
    curry 125
    fricassée de langouste 134
    grilled 132

macaroni pie 182
mangoes
    boniatillo con mango 229

chutney 270
ice cream 226
kuchilla 269
mousse 226
muzik di zumbi 262
    and papaya drink 250
preserved 217
punch 261
shake 250
souskaï de mangues vertes 37
mannish water 61
marinated beef stew 85
marinated chicken livers 104
marinated roast pork 98
marmalade, Montserrat 278
Martinique
    colombo de porc 96
    colombo de poulet 66
    court bouillon de poisson 118
    féroce d'avocat 33
    fish in Creole sauce 126
    pâté en pot 60
    poisson au four 121
    poisson frit 108
    poisson grillé 117
    poulet au lait de coco 66
    ragoût de boeuf 89
    salade de tomates 162
    stuffed crab backs 37
    ti-punch 260
masala 284
matété crab 137
mauby 256
metagee 44
mixed bean salad 165
mojito 264
mojo criollo 277
moksie alesie 100
mondongo soup 57
Montserrat
    goat water 105
    marmalade 278
    mountain chicken 105
moros y cristianos 144
mountain chicken 105
mousse, mango 226
muzik di zumbi 262

Nevis: conch chowder 53
nísperos de batata 209
noodles
    bami 77
    chicken chow mein 76

oil down 102
okra
    fried 178
    sautéed, with shrimp 178
    sopa de quingombos 58
orange
    Barataria grapefruitade 249
    Montserrat marmalade 278

papaya
    candied 217

ice cream 224
    and mango drink 250
passionfruit punch 260
pasteles 210
pastelles 20
pâté en pot 60
pawpaw *see* papaya
peanut
    brittle 221
    and chicken sopa de amendoim 48
    punch 256
    soup 52
peas
    see also chickpeas
    arroz con gandules 140
    dhal 153
    stewed red peas 141
pelau rice 81
pepperpot 42
peppers, hot *see* hot peppers
phulourie 24
picadillo 88
pickle
    see also chutney
    hot peppers 268
    mango kuchilla 269
    Puerto Rican table 273
pie
    aloo 21
    coconut 237
    lime 234
    macaroni 182
pigeon peas, arroz con gandules 140
pilau, Trinidad 80
piña colada 258
pine tart 241
pineapple
    flan de piña 210
    jam 280
    pine tart 241
    syrup 281
    upside-down cake 204
plantains
    chips 29
    fried 170
    tostones de plátano verde 29
planters punch 261
poisson au four 121
poisson frit 108
poisson grillé 117
pork
    colombo de porc 96
    Cuban fillets 96
    garlic 94
    griot 78
    lechón asado 98
    marinated roast 98
    souse 26
    sweet and sour 97
pork crackling chicharrones 28
potato
    aloo curry 176
    aloo pie 21
    aloo roti 157
    salad 161

INDEX

poulet au lait de coco 66
prawns *see* shrimp
preserved mangoes 217
Puerto Rico
    arroz con gandules 140
    chicharrones 28
    coquito 257
    flan de piña 210
    guava cheese 228
    lechón asado 98
    serenata 169
    sopa de quingombos 58
    table pickle 273
    tembleque 238
    tostones de plátano verde 29
pumpkin
    curry 173
    soup 49

ragoût de boeuf 89
red kidney beans
    arroz con habichuelas 149
    habichuelas rojas 148
    haricots rouges 141
    Jamaica red pea soup 48
    and rice in coconut 145
red peas, stewed 141
rice
    arroz con gandules 140
    arroz con habichuelas 149
    boiled 174
    with chicken 74
    fried 174
    fried, with shrimp 132
    moksie alesie 100
    and peas in coconut 145
    pelau 81
    Trinidad pilau 80
roast breadfruit 180
rock cakes, West Indian 189
ropa vieja 89
roselle *see* sorrel
rum
    see also white rum
    coconut punch 262
    and coconut water 265
    daiquiri 257
    Jamaican coffee 265
    mango punch 261
    passionfruit punch 260
    planters punch 261
    and raisin fudge 221
    sauce 282
    sorrel liqueur 258
run down 122

sada roti 192
salad
    d'aubergines 164
    avocado 161
    christophène 180
    coleslaw 160
    conch 169
    ensalada mixta 184
    green 160

green banana 168
mixed bean 165
potato 161
serenata 169
smoked herring 136
de tomates 162
salara buns 188
salt cod
    and ackee 124
    bol jul 33
    féroce d'avocat 33
    frizzle 110
    sauce 30
    serenata 169
    stamp-and-go 32
salt fish cakes 32
sancoche 45
sancocho 84
sautéed bora 172
sautéed okra with shrimp 178
serenata 169
shrimp
    camarones a la vinagreta 133
    with Creole sauce 128
    curry 125
    enchilada de camarones 129
    with fried rice 132
    rice and callaloo 133
    with sautéed okra 178
sky juice 248
smoked herring
    choka 134
    salad 136
snake beans, sautéed bora 172
snowcones 248
sofrito 276
sopa de amendoim 48
sopa de pollo 50
sopa de quingombos 58
sopitu 56
sorbet, guava 225
sorrel
    drink 253
    liqueur 258
soursop
    drink 253
    ice cream 224
souse 26
souskaï de mangues vertes 37
spinach bhaji 150
spinners 154
split pea dhal 153
sprats, curried baked 116
St. Kitts: conch chowder 53
St. Martin: sopitu 56
St. Vincent: arrowroot drops 212
stamp-and-go 32
stewed guavas 218
stobá di cabrito 92
stuffed breadfruit 181
stuffed crab backs 37
Suriname
    bami 77
    bojo 232
    moksie alesie 100

sweet and sour pork 97
sweet potato
    boniatillo con mango 229
    nisperos de batata 209
    pudding 229

tablettes de coco 220
tamales 18
tamarind
    balls 216
    chutney 272
    drink 248
tannia soup 61
tarts
    à la banane 230
    au coco 236
    pasteles 210
    pine 241
tembleque 238
ti-punch 260
Tobago: tamarind drink 248
tocino del cielo 242
tomato
    choka 162
    salade de tomates 162
tooloom 216
tostones de plátano verde 29
Trinidad
    aloo pie 21
    breadfruit soup 53
    doubles 156
    mango kuchilla 269
    pastelles 20
    phulourie 24
    pilau 80
    sancoche 45
    smoked herring choka 134
tripe
    bébélé 101
    mondongo soup 57
tropical fruit salad 233
tuna in brown stew 126

upside-down cake, pineapple 204

vanilla syrup 280
vinaigrette 160

West Indian bun 190
West Indian rock cakes 189
white rum
    coquito 257
    cubanito 264
    daiquiri 257
    mojito 264
    muzik di zumbi 262
    piña colada 258
    ti-punch 260

yam fritters 182
yard-long beans, sautéed bora 172
yellow split pea dhal 153

ACKNOWLEDGMENTS

A special thank you to Phillip Sandberg. Without his continuous support, expertise, and love this book would not have been possible. His help with completing this book has been priceless.

I would like to thank my family for their help and support throughout the duration of this book and my life: Jim (Peoby) Singh; Michael Singh; Jenny Singh; Jennifer Singh; Aunty Golin; Kenny Gosling (thanks for showing me so much about Jamaican cookery); Sankar and Sita Mohabir; Sharmala Baal; Krishna Baal; Anita; Suneeta; Sandra; Lily; Uncle Bodia; and Aunty Eso.

In Australia: To all the people who have helped in countless ways with my research and work for this book. I thank you for your support and friendship. Jeff Barcham; Dr John Brotherton; Robyn Crowley; Carmen Dearmas; Clare Gale; Caroline Hocking; Jenny Holdcroft; Steve Irons; Judi Kuepper; Angel Lumley; Ken McGuffin; Jo McIntyre; John Minns; Joan Mitchell; Ian Rintoul; Leanne Robinson; Lisa Milner; Jay Robinson; Lynne Spender; Kirsten Tilgals (thanks for your patience and tireless work), Joe Ungaro; and Virginia Walker.

A huge thanks to all the people and friends around the Caribbean that have helped me to put this book together which I once thought was too enormous to take on. *In Antigua:* Eugenie White; Doris Jacobs; Brothers B's Restaurant, St Johns; George E.A. Richards. *In Barbados:* Elaine Ford from Collin's Place, Bridgetown; Denisa Forte and Cheryl Archer from the Barbados Board of Tourism; Dawn Thomas and the boys (Michael, Brian and Tom) from Blue Wave Studios. *In Cuba:* Thanks to Angélica Suárez for her enthusiasm and inspiration; Livan Nuñes Aleman and Coral Charón

Querra; Julia Miláan Odelin from Havana Libre; Herminio. *In Curaçao:* Erwin Singodiojo and Richard Peters from the Caribana Restaurant, Willemstadt. *In Dominica:* Thanks to Yolande Cools-Lartigue for your advice and inspiration; Mary Lestredall. *In the Dominican Republic:* Danny Reybre from Restaurant Boga Boga. *In Guadeloupe:* Carmelia Bertojil, Point a Pitre; Mmes France-Lise and Huguette Rilcy from La Restaurant Fougére—thank you for the demonstrations, excellent food, and all the help you've given. *In Jamaica:* Thanks to Rosewell Robb from Hot Pot Restaurant, Kingston, for teaching me many traditional dishes in one fun afternoon; Devon Singleton from Three Little Bears Restaurant, Kingston—I am deeply touched and grateful for the help you have given me; thanks to Trevor L.A. Burt from Montego Bay—an excellent chef, much in demand, and a dear friend; Charles Crossfield, the best taxi driver in Jamaica; Hyacinth Forde and the Jamaica Tourist Board, Montego Bay. *In Martinique:* Mme Josette Paruta from Le Renoveau Restaurant; Jocelyne and Fortuné from the Grand Marché—thanks for your warmth and willingness to help; the Tourist Office in Saint Pierre. *In Miami:* El Viajante Restaurant, Miami Beach. *In Montserrat:* Florence Perkins from the Hangout Bar & Restaurant Downtown, Plymouth. *In Puerto Rico:* Tallulah Rodriguez; Olga Perez, a special thank you for your warmth and hospitality; Edgardo Nieves Oltiz and the rest of the staff at Cafe de Armas; Fernando Fernandez. *In St Vincent:* Julia Richardson, Vee Jays Rooftop Diner & Pub. *In Trinidad & Tobago:* Terry and the National Carnival Commission of Trinidad and Tobago—thanks for the insights on Trinidadian history and food; Trinidad and Tobago Tourism Development Authority.